SURVIVAL OF THE QUICKEST

Across Africa. In a Porsche.

Ben Coombs

For my Grandparents

CONTENTS

PREFACE

The weak Mongolian sunshine had been trickling through the window for half a day before it coaxed me from an empty sleep. Consciousness came slowly, my heavy inertia gradually giving way to a rasping thirst. I rubbed my eyes, sat up and glanced around. Yet another dingy hotel room swam into focus, and I remembered little of it from our arrival the night before – two sagging beds, a worn carpet, beige walls and some throwaway wooden furniture. The usual fare. I noticed some money resting on the television; a few dollars and a couple of thousand togrog which Anthony must have left when he hurried to catch his flight at five that morning. I quietly thanked him, imagining how tough it must have been to embark on the long journey back to Britain after only three hours' sleep; especially given what we'd just been through.

My battered old rucksack was resting in the corner of the room. It had been thrown down in many such corners over the previous month. I retrieved a toothbrush and set about removing the coarse, unpleasant taste of dehydration from my mouth, then washed my face for the first time in five days. The cold water cut through my mind's sluggishness as the sink ran black with oil, petrol, sweat and grease.

It was over.

I'd actually done it.

A smile crept across my unkempt face, as pangs of disbelief ricocheted through my mind.

Have I really just driven halfway around the world, from England to Mongolia, in that pensionable little Mini?

Of course I had. The previous four weeks and ten thousand miles had been no dream. Despite this, I indulgently let the disbelieving questions continue to race through my mind. They generated a warm sense of pride and increased the heady sense of achievement.

Did we really just drive for forty hours non-stop across Siberia, with almost no headlights, to get Anthony to his flight?

Memories of the journey started surging through my mind, vivid snapshots of places and people, laden with emotions. They revitalised me like smelling salts. The smile on my face grew as our accomplishment slowly sank in. I continued to wash. The cold water, white porcelain and clinical lighting seemed luxurious after what felt like a grimy lifetime on the road.

Once clean, I fumbled together a coffee and turned on the television. An old British film flickered onto the screen. It was 1940 and the brave few were flying their Spitfires over the home counties, chattering away enthusiastically in Chinese as they did so. On the surface, I chuckled at the primitive dubbing but inside me a wave of homesickness was triggered. Brummy – as Anthony was universally known – would be at Moscow Airport by now, already halfway back to England. I envied him.

After finishing the coffee, I wandered outside. Daisy, my cute white Mini, sat patiently in front of the hotel. She looked battered, yet ever defiant and ready for more. Her electrics had failed two thousand miles ago and her suspension had collapsed in the Kazakh wilderness but she had done it. Over the previous month she had fought across fourteen countries, through deserts and steppes, over mountains and rivers. She had been our home, our team-mate and our friend. She had spoken to us and we'd responded. We had learnt to tell when she was fine and when she was struggling. We felt bad when we treated her roughly, and pride when she performed well. I was sure that back home, nobody would understand this bond – *with a car?* But I didn't care. It had been real. I knew then that I would miss her.

After stealing a last glance at Daisy, I drifted off into town. I didn't want to linger. Maybe a part of me felt guilty for what I'd put her through. Maybe I knew that without the electrics being fixed her engine wouldn't start and it saddened me. I left her to rest, to have a day off. She had earned it.

As I neared the city centre, Ulaanbataar bustled exotically around me to a gradually increasing tempo. Introverted by my fatigue, I was sadly numb to its charms. Another Soviet influenced city, a vision of decaying communist ideals stamped upon an unenthused, individualistic society. We had passed through many such places during our journey and here at the finish, tiredness and the heady feeling of accomplishment outweighed any pleasures to be gained from exploring. I felt strangely detached from my surroundings, as if experiencing them from within a vacuum.

Among the unloved buildings, an eclectic mix of people went about their days. Monks in flowing saffron robes chatted eagerly in small, busy groups. Self-conscious businessmen hurried about, their clothing and mannerisms mirroring the Western professional. Crumbling taxis and primitive buses jostled all around, pumping fumes into the laden air which mixed with the dust to soften the sun's focus. Floating on the temporary feeling of invincibility that comes from achieving a difficult, long-cherished dream, I drifted on through the city's turbulent heart.

As I wandered, I sought out a bank that would accept my cash card. It was futile. Through the tiredness, it dawned on me that I was stuck thousands of miles from home, with almost no money and no easy means to get any. I wasn't worried though. I'd overcome worse problems in the previous four weeks. I'd be able to sort it out. *It would be fine.*

Confidently, I dropped into a particularly homely looking Irish bar, spent the last of my cash on an ice cold beer and relaxed. Everything in Mongolia seemed to carry the 'Genghis' moniker, but his beer at least was unexpectedly good. I sat contentedly, watching the world go by as the previous month continued to race through my mind.

9

* * *

We had just completed the 2006 Mongol Rally, an anarchic yearly event in which entrants attempt to drive from Europe to Mongolia in as inappropriate a vehicle as possible.

I had heard about the rally a year previously and thought it looked like a tremendous challenge. Fortuitously, I'd mentioned it in passing to a friend named Lee over a beer. Two days later I glanced out of my flat window, only to see him parking a quirky red Mini outside, with a huge grin on his face.

'Looks like we're going to Mongolia then,' I said excitedly in greeting.

'Marvellous!' he replied, still bearing his trademark grin.

I soon splashed out the grand total of four hundred pounds on a white Mini and talked my friend Tiffany into co-driving with me. Meanwhile, Brummy had joined forces with Lee in his little car.

The following summer, armed with little more than our two ancient Minis, an intimidating pile of maps and several rolls of gaffa tape, we set off into the unknown.

Despite the maps, within minutes of crossing the start line in London a wrong turn led to us getting thoroughly lost and we were an hour late for our ferry to France – a fairly inauspicious start by anyone's standards. Undeterred, we were soon surging off the ferry onto the continent, full of the unshakable confidence of the naïve. Striking out east, Western Europe was crossed rapidly, as we savoured the smooth tarmac and reached Prague within twenty-four hours of our departure.

From Prague, we nursed hangovers north into Poland, then curved through the Baltic states of Lithuania and Latvia to the Russian border, where a curtain of indecipherable bureaucracy hung in our path. For hours, we tried to force a way through the seemingly impenetrable red tape of immigration and customs. The paperwork was all penned in Cyrillic script and the language barrier often seemed like a brick wall. Then, worryingly, a tear was found on the photo page of my passport and I was led away by a gun-toting 'Babushka' to explain myself.

'If you hear a gunshot, run,' Tiffany suggested to the others as I disappeared for my interrogation. Fortunately there was an English-speaking guard at the border and I was able to talk myself out of the predicament, with a vague promise to go to the British Embassy in Moscow to resolve the issue.

Eventually, we were allowed through the austere barriers into Russia, the setting sun casting our Minis' shadows far into the surrounding plain. A bossy policeman pulled us over as the sky darkened and insisted we follow him to a certain hotel. My paranoid mind swam heavy with outdated thoughts of bugged rooms and informers.

Heading up to St Petersburg, we marvelled at the beautiful neo-classical architecture as we gradually adjusted to the change in culture. A terrifying night drive then took us along the fractured tarmac to Moscow, dodging blinding trucks and aggressive locals all the way. We recovered from the ordeal by wandering around Red Square for a day, a surreal experience given the mutual suspicions which had distanced this nation from the West for most of the previous century. Back on the road, the unfamiliar landscape phased through dense forests and relaxing farmlands, before morphing into a featureless steppe at the Kazakh border. Northern Kazakhstan passed in a blur of roadworks and semi-desert and before we knew it we were arcing south towards the Aral Sea, on one of the more notorious roads this planet has to offer.

For two hundred miles, the rough tarmac had fractured in a manner one would think to be achievable only through bombardment. It seemed impossible that our little Minis could meet the challenge but nonetheless, we pushed on blindly through the forty degree heat. The few locals seemed to have the right idea, driving on the open desert to

11

either side of the tortured road. Joining them, we surfed our little Minis through the sand, savouring the adventure. Both of our cars lost their exhausts in the empty desert but we simply tied them back on using speaker cable and carried on. We camped out in the sands that night, with only stars and camels for company and reached the town of Aralsk the following day.

Once a busy fishing port on the shores of the Aral Sea, the town's fortunes had faded since the 1970s, when overbearing Soviet planners had diverted the sea's inlets in an attempt to irrigate cotton fields to the southeast. The scheme failed and the sea began to dry up, shrinking so much that the port of Aralsk was soon twenty miles from its shores. It made for a sad sight. The carcasses of abandoned fishing boats lay decomposing in the sand, while a mosaic of dead marine life crunched beneath our feet as we walked, a poignant reminder of the futility of humankind's attempts to dominate the natural world.

Morosely, we left the bleak dustbowl and continued to Shymkent, where one of the red Mini's wheel bearings chose to go no further. With little common language, broken down in a world where Minis don't exist, we found ourselves staring failure in the face. Nothing we tried seemed to work, until eventually, Lee found a solution. We got hold of the equivalent part from an old Russian Lada, which wouldn't quite fit, and it jammed into position using bits of a drinks can as crude spacers, enabling us to hit the road again.

That evening we crossed out of Kazakhstan but the Uzbek border had already closed for the day, leaving us trapped between the two countries. Nervously, we slept in no-man's-land, cooped up in the locked cars, while shifty soldiers with machine guns wandered around us, and took a worryingly deep interest in my blonde co-driver.

Once we finally made it into Uzbekistan, the glorious town of Samarqand inspired us all. Well, all except Brummy that is, whose delicate insides were too busy being

'Uzbek'ed', preventing him from going more than ten feet from the sanctuary of a bathroom. The red Mini's brakes had packed up the previous day, so Lee worked on them while Tiffany and I took in the sights. The Registan, a complex of Madrasahs completed in the sixteenth century, stood bold against the steel blue sky, the intricacy of its details lending it a gravitas unmatched by more modern structures. We visited Tamerlane's grandiose Bibi-khanym Mosque and marvelled at the iridescent skyline of blue domes floating above the city. It felt good to take a break from the endless cycle of roads, repairs, stress and sleep. We were able to turn off our minds and drift through our time there. For the first time on the trip, we relaxed.

The look on the hostel owner's face said it all. When he apologetically held up the remains of my passport I understood immediately.

How could I be so stupid as to have left it in my trouser pocket and then put the damn trousers through the washing machine?

I felt sick. I could tell Tiffany was angry. Lee couldn't stop giggling like a schoolgirl and as for Brummy, well, fortunately Brummy was still far too ill to even consider bringing his razor-sharp wit to bear. We picked through the remains. Evidently passports aren't machine washable. My visas were tattered, but at least vaguely legible, however the car ownership documents were also in my pocket. Gone.

The next morning we sheepishly headed up to the British Embassy in Tashkent, convinced our journey was over. Our visas expired that day, so we needed to find a solution fast as the corrupt police state of Uzbekistan is not a place to be on the wrong side of the authorities. Through the bulletproof glass and heavy security, I nervously explained the problem. The embassy staff could do nothing about the tattered visas, but were at least able to provide me with a temporary passport. As for the car's ownership documents, a computer printout, taken from a scan we had, would have to suffice. I didn't believe that this would get us to Mongolia, but had no choice but to try.

Lee and Brummy had already gone on ahead, through the Fergana Valley to Kyrgyzstan. It was too late to follow them, so instead we rushed north, back to Kazakhstan, where we were nervously able to explain our way across the border in the nick of time, only a few hours before our Uzbek visas expired.

A week later, the two Minis were reunited in a peaceful meadow just inside Russia. Daisy's rear suspension had collapsed but a temporary repair, using a climbing sling and some ratchet straps, had kept us moving. However Babs, as the red Mini was affectionately known, was suffering much more. Its brakes remained untrustworthy and a section of one of its axles had sheared, requiring the whole assembly to be drilled and then pinned together with a piece of car jack. Finally, the engine was sounding very ill and burning oil as though it were going out of fashion. It was still soldiering on though, so we limped across Siberia together, losing time every few hundred miles when yet another repair would inevitably be required. And so it was that Brummy found himself with fifty hours in which to get across the Mongolian border and catch his flight home. We still had almost two thousand miles to go. Action was needed, so Brummy joined me in 'reliable' Daisy while Tiffany reluctantly swapped over to join Lee in the seemingly terminal red Mini. Goodbyes were said and off we raced towards the Mongolian border.

Siberia is a vast, ominous place. We inched through its foreboding nothingness for two days straight; day and night, non-stop. Unfriendly skies taunted us with squally showers, while the isolating blackness of each night seemed to last a lifetime. The failing electrics on the car meant our lights were dim as glow-worms, our wipers sluggish beyond belief. We couldn't stop the engine as not enough charge was being accumulated to power the starter motor.

Inexorably, we crawled onwards through the grimy industrial towns dotting Russia's great wilderness of forest and taiga. Krasnayorask, Irktusk, and Ulan Ude crept bleakly past our windows before, exhausted, we reached the Mongolian border in the nick of time, only two hours before it closed for the weekend. We made it across with minutes to spare and were soon trying to navigate into Ulaanbaatar with what was left of our feeble headlights. Our ten thousand mile journey was over with only five hours in hand before Brummy's flight left. Somehow, we had done it.

* * *

My beer was empty but it was time. I phoned the bank in England to get some money wired to Mongolia and continued to watch Ulaanbaatar thrum by. I didn't expect the red Mini to arrive for another few days and was settling in for a relaxing wait. Already, life was different from a month before. The fatigue hadn't yet lifted but my thoughts were already racing away into the future. I had just completed the most audacious achievement of my life but knew with absolute certainty that I would surpass it in the future. I had no idea how, only that I would.

My mind fizzed with excitement at the prospect.

ONE

BEGINNINGS

March 2007
Wiltshire, England

It was a cold March night. The motorway slid gently past as my mind wandered lazily from thought to thought. The Porsche purred away around me, feeling solid and dependable, as it always did. Progress was effortless. It felt good.

I had owned my trusty Porsche 944 for five years and had come to respect it hugely. It was a good car, beautifully engineered and solidly built. It wouldn't let me down. I knew it was getting old and that it would soon be time for a change but somehow the thought seemed wrong. After the sterling service it had given, it didn't sit right with me to simply sell it to a stranger. We would have to part one day, but I had no idea how. Even Brummy's continuous jokes about yuppies and the inadequacies of sports car owners failed to dampen my enthusiasm for it.

My mind dwelled on the fate of the Porsche before becoming bored of such worthy thoughts and veered off on a tangent, reliving past glories. I thought of my trip to Mongolia. *Was that really half a year ago already?* So much had happened since then and it already felt a lifetime away. I chuckled nervously as I thought back to my more recent journey along Norway's Arctic Highway in a little Fiat. Deep inside the Arctic Circle, we had negotiated ice roads, blizzards and breakdowns, while the northern lights danced hauntingly against the heavens above. *Driving to the Arctic in winter, in a tiny old Fiat? That was such a stupid thing to do!*

The guidebook to the highway spoke of serious four-wheel-drives and treacherous conditions, advised against driving the road in winter, and suggested that such an adventure should definitely not be undertaken by anyone who doesn't already know the route in the daylight of summer.

Ignoring this, Brummy, a friend named Jim and I had crammed ourselves into a tiny Fiat 126 – not so much a car as a breadbin on wheels – strapped our bags to the roof and driven to the Arctic anyway. Already I had forgotten the cold, the tension and the danger we faced, and looked back on the trip as a thrilling adventure shared humorously between friends.

Two impressive road trips in the past eight months – I was clearly addicted. As with any addicted mind I was automatically looking for a bigger rush, a way of venturing deeper into the unknown and challenging myself further. But how could I surpass what had gone before?

Suddenly, my mind stopped drifting vaguely along its lethargic tangents and came to a pin-sharp focus. I had no idea why. Somewhere deep in my subconscious, a neuron had fired.

Africa.

I could drive the Porsche across Africa!

Why not? What an adventure that would be!

My heart beat a little faster as I imagined pointing the Porsche's angular nose south and setting off. *Would it actually be possible? What obstacles would we face? Could the Porsche survive such a trip?* I didn't really know. The idea was exciting and daunting at the same time. As soon as it struck me, I felt invigorated by suddenly having a goal to work towards and to dream about. I knew little of Africa at the time but through my ignorance I knew then with total conviction that I would do it. I just would.

It was the early hours of the morning when I arrived home and parked the Porsche. Its chunky white 1980s bodywork already looked different in my mind. Energised. It had a raison d'être – no longer just a car, it now encapsulated a dream to be fulfilled.

I went to bed but couldn't sleep. *Africa!* I knew so very little about the place. In my mind, its mountains, lakes, rivers and nations blurred into an amorphous whole within the familiar outline of the continent. I knew it was poor but I had no idea how poor. I knew of dictatorships and corruption, of war and famine; though only vaguely. But really, I knew nothing about Africa, as never before had I felt it drawing me to look closer.

Hungrily, I pulled out my atlas and started poring over inspiring maps of far-flung places, recalled from so many faint memories. As I traced my finger down potential routes, their names captivated me. Timbuktu, the Nile, Kilimanjaro. Rwanda, the Congo, the Sahara! Many of the names sprang from the page with a long-forgotten familiarity, as if they had been lurking deep within my mind for years, patiently waiting for this moment. With the new familiarity born from seeing them nestling together on the map, I felt a gravity inexorably calling me towards them. Already, Africa was ceasing to be a swathe of blankness in my mind and had started to be coloured in, with the most vivid, intriguing brushstrokes possible.

* * *

It was a quiet evening in the Seymour Arms. A few stoical locals sat at the bar furtively whiling away the hours while chatting to Brian, the barman. Dull thuds echoed over from the pool table. I sat catching up with Brummy; an activity which generally involves listening impotently as he unleashes a series of well-rehearsed, comical rants from behind a pint of Guinness. After a few drinks, the ranting petered out and I nervously told him of my idea.

'Why Africa?' he asked.

'Why not?' I fired back coolly.

'Because it's a shithole?'

'No it isn't…'

'Seriously, it's a hole.'

'Well, doesn't that make it the perfect place for one of our road trips? Don't we always go travelling in shitholes?' I countered, sensing the futility of a sensible discussion.

'Why can't we just fly to somewhere nice and clean and drink cheap beer on a beach?' Brummy asked. 'No breakdowns, no potholes, no filthy Uzbek toilets, an actual HOLIDAY!'

'Where would the fun in that be? And anyway, it's your round,' I said, holding up my empty glass suggestively.

'So it is. Pint of Kronenbourg then? I bet they don't have them in Africa.'

I knew Brummy was joking and that he would find a few days on a beach just as boring as I. However, evidently I still had some work to do convincing him of the merits of my idea. I had plenty of time to do so though. It was spring 2007. I decided I would aim to leave the UK in the autumn of 2008. This gave me about eighteen months to get a team together, complete my African education, prepare the Porsche and make the journey a reality.

Over the following weeks, the fifty-three individual countries which make up the African continent separated and slotted together like a jigsaw. Gradually my knowledge of these newly comprehended nations increased and my mind flooded with their tortured histories and current uncertainties. The more I researched, the more my understanding of the continent became mired in a depressing cycle of selfishness, suffering and oppression. I read of Zaire's President Mobutu embezzling a personal fortune of billions of dollars and chartering Concorde to fly pink champagne into his village, while his country-folk starved all around. I learnt how AIDS was ripping through the continent, decimating families and reducing life expectancies to less than thirty years in some areas. I found unimaginable genocide in Rwanda, war and starvation in Ethiopia and apartheid in South Africa. The more I researched, the more my initially colourful perception of Africa was darkened.

The continent seemed to have stagnated under colonial exploitation, before its decimation beneath the dictatorial fists of the 'big men' who had evicted their European masters in the name of liberty. The past, the present and the future all seemed to epitomise hopelessness. Whenever I learnt something positive, it would instantly be smothered by a negative, and new veneers of sadness seemed to build as my knowledge increased. No sooner had my mind recognised Botswana as a stable democracy, than the scourge of AIDS overwhelmed it. The inevitability of a politician being righteously overthrown for his corruption, only to be replaced by like, sickened me.

However, in spite of all the continent's problems, Africa also seemed to harbour an unexpected warmth and optimism. Occasionally a photograph of a beaming face would signal to me that life wasn't actually all that bad, or an insightful quote would bring rational hope of a better future. The extremes of human nature existing on the continent fascinated me and I felt drawn to see them for myself.

When told of my idea, most people were openly dismissive. 'You can't drive across Africa in a Porsche!' was something I tired of hearing from a very early stage of the project. 'You need a Land Rover, not some silly sports car. It's impossible!' Most people seemed to view Africa as an obstacle, an incomprehensible region of danger and uncertainty. It may be that many of the fears and opinions stemmed from naivety – but that same naivety seemed to fuel my confidence. Before the Mongol Rally, I had found that one of the hardest parts of planning the trip was ignoring the self-appointed experts who insisted it couldn't be done. As then, other people's negativity only hardened my resolve to complete the journey, *any journey*, across the continent in my trusty sports car. 'I've proved the doubters wrong before,' I kept telling myself. If people didn't understand my motivations, or my choice of transport, then so be it.

I could understand the reservations however. The Porsche was too small, too low slung, too fragile and too complicated. It was twenty-three years old and had already covered over two hundred thousand miles. We would barely have space for all the things we'd need to take. There would be no Porsche garages on route and no chance of obtaining any spare parts. The car would probably be shredded by the rough African roads or end up stranded in some muddy quagmire. I never admitted it at the time, but the doubters had a very real point. To me, however, this was all part of the appeal. I wanted the journey to be a challenge. I wanted it to be uncertain. A reliable 4x4 just wouldn't offer the same potential for problems. Without problems, there is no adventure. To attempt the journey in the Porsche was to venture into the unknown, to face up to a challenge which may or may not be possible. I savoured that challenge. Having just driven to Mongolia in a tiny Mini, and the Arctic in the breadbox Fiat, undertaking the African journey in a more suitable steed just wouldn't do. It had to be the Porsche.

But with whom?

For a start, I knew Brummy would be coming along. He'd been there on the Mongol Rally and the Arctic trip and seemed incapable of saying no. Fortunately, he was always an entertaining person to travel with and his ability to dredge up humour from even the worst of predicaments had become legendary; a quality which would almost certainly prove its worth in Africa.

Brummy wasn't the first member of the team to commit fully to the Africa expedition however. Tom was a friend of mine who shared my passion for the more adventurous forms of travel. Previously, we had been on several rock-climbing holidays to France together, as well as a more adventurous mountaineering trip to Morocco. He exuded an aura of dependability, and I was quietly reassured to have him on board. Other folk had talked enthusiastically about joining the trip but they were people who I knew I couldn't count on to come along. Tom's quiet, considered commitment was that of someone I could rely on not to go back on their word. Privately, I also felt that his more serious approach to things would provide a good counter to Brummy's carefree humour.

So that made three of us. Three people could never fit in the Porsche, so we'd need to take a second car. Two people per car would make sense, to share the driving, so we needed at least one more team member and our old Mongol Rally friends couldn't make it. Tiffany would be studying for an MSc, while Lee had become embroiled in a very different kind of adventure: fatherhood.

With the expedition less than a year away, a fourth team member remained unrecruited.

* * *

As 2007 drew to a close, our lack of plans for the forthcoming New Year celebrations became a pressing issue. I was at a loss as to what to do until one evening after work. Lazing contentedly on the sofa, I had poured a whisky and put on the classic British film 'The Italian Job'. Michael Caine was darting through the streets of Turin in a convoy of beautiful old Minis, outwitting the Mafia and almost getting away with the gold. Suddenly, it was all too obvious. I had a classic Mini parked outside, which I'd bought in a fit of nostalgia for my Mongolian escapades. Why not take it to Turin for New Year, in homage to the film? Predictably, Brummy was up for the idea within seconds of hearing the plan, but would be taking his shiny, practical Peugeot in lieu of a Mini. It didn't take long for us to recruit enough people to make the road trip worthwhile, so we left the UK in late December, bound for an appointment with Italy and 2008.

And so it was that I found myself sat next to Laura as I guided the already ailing Mini towards Dover. We'd met only a few times before, via mutual friends during balmy holidays rock-climbing on the sandstone boulders of Fontainebleau, near Paris. She was as I remembered her; petite, dark haired and immediately attractive, with a disarming smile and a vivacious glint in her eyes. Previously, Laura had struck me as a rather prim and proper girl, shy in a group and quick to blush; I quickly found out how wrong first impressions could be.

Laura had always been a keen traveller, and the climbing trips on which we had met were only the tip of an adventurous iceberg which had taken her as far afield as South America and New Zealand and seen her living and working in southern Africa on more than one occasion. Travel and adventure obviously ran thick in her blood.

So off we went on a hedonistic, wintery bimble around Europe. The Mini suffered at the hands of the cold, the rain and the speed bumps, while its occupants were pounded continuously by late nights and lock-ins in various bars around Europe. We lost count of the number of times the exhaust broke and had to be repaired. We lost count of the number of times we ran out of fuel due to the broken fuel gauge and the way the car's little engine could never quite decide whether to run on three or four cylinders. And we lost count of the number of jokes Brummy cracked about our unreliable, long-suffering steed.

Against the odds, New Year's Eve saw us barrelling out of the Italian Alps towards Turin. The evening was predictably hazy. A night out in a pizzeria, followed by copious amounts of free champagne and a lock-in, meant we found ourselves enthusiastically dancing on tables with the Italian clientele at two in the morning. None of them quite knew what to make of our heady claims that we had driven there in a thirty-four year old Mini but then none of them would have remembered the following morning anyway.

We headed over to Venice, then on to Slovenia. Two nights were spent in the Slovenian town of Bled, an idyllic place where a fairytale church nestles on an island in an alpine lake, surrounded by watchful snowy peaks and overlooked by a fine castle. We hit the road with forty hours in which to get back to Calais and catch our ferry. Plenty of time. Unfortunately, I looked at the map just before we left.

'Let's go to Croatia!' I said enthusiastically.

'What?' asked Brummy.

'Croatia. It's just over there,' I said, pointing optimistically south. 'We can come back through Hungary too. I think it's a marvellous idea.'

On most other holidays such a suggestion would seem irrational. Fortunately however, this wasn't a run-of-the-mill holiday, so we all agreed it was a splendid idea. The resultant forty hours Laura and I spent cooped up together in the Mini are somewhat of a blur.

In Croatia, we crossed a blank land in which the snow was mirrored by the overcast sky, forming a world of austere whiteness. Darkness had descended by the time we reached the potholes of Hungary, where the exhaust snapped. It was late at night and I was forced to repair it with only what I had with me. Fortunately it had split cleanly where two sections of pipe had been poorly welded. Using jubilee clips and tent pegs, I was able to splint it back together, saving our hearing from the horrendous din which was the only alternative.

We then pushed on through the night, stopping only to snatch an uncomfortable few hours' sleep in the cars while parked up in Austria. Awaking at sunrise, we found we had fifteen hours to coax the tired Mini across Germany and the Low Countries to the ferry. This mission was embarked on confidently but by nightfall the odds were lengthening. A breakdown in a tunnel in Luxembourg cost precious time, while in Belgium it began to rain, causing the poor Mini to misfire sickeningly, limiting it to sixty miles per hour.

25

We pushed on as best we could, refusing to accept defeat when we were so close. The rain kept coming and with forty-five minutes to go, we were still over fifty miles away. Drastic action was needed. Laura woke from her shallow sleep as we screeched to a halt on the side of the road.

'What's happening?'

'Quick two minute pit stop. Don't worry; no way are we missing the ferry!'

I jumped out and flung open the bonnet, revealing the soaked engine. The electrical contacts had been affected by the moisture and needed drying, so I sprayed liberal amounts of water repellent wherever it might make a difference. Ninety seconds later we were accelerating away with all our fingers crossed. The speed rose. Fifty, sixty, sixty-five miles per hour. We pushed on to an indicated speed of nearly eighty, the tired engine screaming blue murder. Brummy's Peugeot, bimbling along at sixty a few miles down the road, was dispatched quickly but then instantly accelerated into our slipstream, buoyed on by our sudden turn of speed.

Laura and I felt like we were riding some angry bucking bronco as our tired car was thrown around by the gusting wind and the pitted road surface, scrabbling desperately at the tarmac. Fuelled solely by adrenaline after forty hours without proper sleep, we flew into the ferry port surprised and exhilarated to have made it. The crossing was quiet, the nervous laughter of the deeply fatigued punctuating conversations about just how stupid the previous forty hours had been.

As we pulled off the ferry in Dover, the poor Mini ran out of fuel. Maybe it was trying to tell us something.

In those long hours together, frantically and comically struggling towards our common goal, Laura and I developed a definite bond. We had worked well together, overcoming a seemingly impossible task. Negotiating the darkness of northern Europe, we had got to know each other well, chatting continuously to make sure we both stayed awake. Exciting stories of Africa and Mongolia had hung in the night, fending off the infinite appeal of sleep. Laura had told me how much she had enjoyed this unusual take on travel, pitting an inappropriate car against the unknown, adding that she wished she'd known me better a few years earlier as she would have loved to come on the Mongol Rally. My response was predictable: 'Don't say that too often or I'll talk you into coming on the Africa trip.' At the time, she dismissed the idea due to her commitments as a medical student; however evidently, a seed was sown in her mind.

When we finally made it back home to Plymouth, I hadn't had an uninterrupted night's sleep for sixty hours. Running purely on adrenaline and buoyed up by an unhealthy measure of machismo, I agreed to meet a friend for a drink in the Seymour Arms. I fell asleep on the bar stool before I'd finished my pint.

Sometimes you can push things too far.

* * *

The fresh spring breeze played among the moored yachts, challenging them to cast off their winter slumber and strike out into the open seas beyond the breakwater. Above, seagulls whirled confidently on the invisible currents of air. The sun was unexpectedly warm for late March and vied with the cool wind for our attentions as we sipped our drinks on Plymouth's ancient waterfront.

For one fleeting day, an Indian summer had descended. An exuberant, bustling crowd packed the bars of the historic Barbican and spilled out to dine at the sun-dappled tables that covered the cobbled quay.

A few metres from where Laura, Brummy and I sat, the Mayflower Steps dropped to the sea, commemorating the spot where, in 1620, the Pilgrim Fathers had boarded their vessel and left Europe forever on their uncertain voyage to the New World, where they founded the first permanent settlement of Europeans in America. It was the perfect place for talk of epic journeys and adventures.

'So, you're coming to Africa then?' Brummy asked Laura pointedly, from behind his trademark pint of Guinness.

'No. I've already said I can't. Some of us have to finish medical school next year.'

'You could take a year out,' he suggested.

'Not really.'

'So nobody has ever taken a year out of medical school to pursue some other interest?' I said.

'Well yes, people have…'

'So why is it different for you then?' questioned Brummy, going in for the kill.

'Well it isn't, but I...'

'Why not?' I asked. 'You said before how much you'd love to come along and how much you'd regret it if you missed out on going to Africa because you were too afraid to say yes.'

'I've already been to Africa,' she replied, 'three times.'

'Not in a Porsche you haven't,' I pointed out.

'You won't either. The Porsche hasn't a *hope* of making it to Africa,' Brummy added.

'So what are you taking?' Laura asked Brummy.

'Something better than a Porsche. I'm not stupid!'

Brummy and I argued light-heartedly about the merits of various unlikely vehicles for a while and as we did so, Laura sat quietly, staring out across the marina. I could tell she was considering her options and I hoped she'd come along but she wasn't one to make such decisions lightly. Whereas many others would make their choice impulsively, Laura always analysed the pros and cons of such a decision exhaustively, until one side of the argument gained ascendancy in her mind. Eventually, the waves in favour of joining us began to gain the upper hand, and she spoke.

'I would love to come along. Last New Year was so much fun, and I'm not ready to walk away from adventures

28

just yet. If I miss this opportunity, I could be a doctor in a year and there'll be no chance of getting the time off to do something like this. I'm still not sure if I should though.'

'Why? What's stopping you?' I asked.

'I'd feel guilty. I really should be getting on with my career.'

'What difference is one year going to make, in the grand scheme of things?' I asked.

'I'll have to think about it. But I suppose I could have a word with the university, just to find out if it's a possibility.'

'Just don't tell them you want to take a Porsche across Africa. They'll never give you the time off to do something that stupid,' Brummy pointed out with a smirk.

Four months previously, I'd seen Laura weigh up the merits of spending New Year with a relative stranger in a tattered Mini. Over a week or so of rational consideration, her negative thoughts had been exorcised and she'd agreed to come along. I could see that the same process of drawn-out consideration was going on all over again and knew that soon, the weight of positive thought would become irresistibly strong. Sure enough, a few days later the doubts had been washed away and she agreed to join us.

Four people meant two cars. The Porsche plus one. Brummy and Tom agreed to buy a vehicle for the trip, while Laura joined me in the Porsche. With teams sorted, we turned our thoughts to which route to take across the continent. The momentum was finally building.

There were three main options. The first idea was to make a big loop across the Sahara, heading down to Dakar, then across to Cairo, before returning to the UK via the Middle East. The second option was similar to the route made famous by Ewan McGregor and Charlie Boorman in their *Long Way Down* extravaganza – following the East Coast of Africa down from Egypt, before detouring across to the gorgeous desert vistas of Namibia and on to journey's end in Cape Town. The third possible option also ended in Cape Town but instead exotically took the West Coast, through the likes of Nigeria and the Congo.

Brummy and Tom had only been able to wangle nine weeks off work for the trip, so we would have to move quickly. This counted against the unpredictable West Coast route. All it would take would be one closed road or border and our timings would become impossibly tight. The Sahara option appealed hugely to all parties and was favoured by both Brummy and I for a while; however security uncertainties around the critical Mali/Niger/Algeria border also made this option an uncertain thing to commit to. Because of this, we decided to go for the East Coast route.

We planned a route that would take us through Eastern Europe and the Middle East, before boarding the ferry to Egypt. From there, we would head south through the deserts and mountains of Sudan, Ethiopia and Kenya and into Uganda. Looping around Lake Victoria, we planned to take in Rwanda, nip across Tanzania and down to Malawi, before striking out west across Zambia and Botswana to Namibia then finally, South Africa. The route definitely looked audacious when traced on the map. All those countries; all that uncertainty. My knowledge of the places involved may have been limited, but it was sufficient to know that what we happily referred to as the 'easy' route over a few beers in the UK would turn out to be a whole lot tougher when we finally hit the road.

Pushing on with our planning, we found it would just be possible to complete our proposed route in nine weeks. Tight, but possible. Sudanese and Syrian visas were obtained, vaccinations administered and the intricacies of taking private vehicles through the various countries researched and understood. The RAC agreed to supply us with the vital 'Carnet du Passage' documents, which were essential for us to clear the vehicles through customs in many of the countries on our route.

As spring gradually dovetailed into summer, by necessity the trip planning moved up a gear. Brummy and Tom had set their hearts on taking along a chunky Mitsubishi Shogun four-wheel-drive, much to my mockery. I mean, why would you want to take a butch off-roader to Africa? After looking at a few, we found one on the Internet and bought it for £1,000. Its sheer bulk made it look incongruous when parked next to the Porsche, as if designed for a completely different world. Which, I suppose, it was.

* * *

Laura and I had been brought much closer together by our trip around Europe than we realised at the time. Despite living far apart and being embroiled in our own lives, rarely a day went by without some carefree conversation passing between us and by the time she agreed to join the trip, we could both sense a mutual attraction developing. Our conversations became more carefree and flirtatious as we tested the waters to see how each other felt, treading trepidatiously for fear of damaging our friendship after committing to cross Africa together. However, by early summer, the waves of suggestion had become overwhelmingly strong and we finally discussed our obvious mutual attraction. At that time, Laura was getting to grips with her stressful end of year medical exams and hence didn't want to launch straight into a relationship. I respected her situation and despite our similar feelings, we both agreed to put the subject of relationships on hold until after the exams were over. I left her to her studies and continued to slog away, getting everything ready for our departure date.

Predictably, these things are never as simple as they seem. A few weeks later Laura announced she had met someone at a party, but it was all dismissed fairly casually. After all, she wasn't interested in a relationship and anyway, we'd both agreed to discuss the subject after her exams. I trusted her to see our agreement through, but a niggling doubt remained. *Surely she wouldn't risk jeopardising Africa over someone she'd just met, would she?* I plodded on and tried to ignore the situation, blindly believing that I'd be rewarded for doing the right thing.

A week later, she told me that she'd decided to date the other guy.

I didn't realise how emotionally involved in the whole affair I'd become until that moment. I'd believed Laura would honour our previous conversations about relationships and it felt like she'd taken liberties with my trust.

I also felt irrationally angry; angry at the fact that I would still have to spend months sitting next to Laura, all the way across Africa, after what had happened. Angry that whenever I worked on the car, the route plan, or any other part of the trip, someone I felt hurt by was gaining equal benefit. It was a vicious circle. The more I worked towards Africa, the more the situation grated with me and the more my resentment was directed disproportionately at Laura. *Do I really have to spend months stuck in a car with her?* I was sure I couldn't enjoy the journey now but it was a Catch-22. Too much had been invested in the trip for me to just walk away.

For the rest of the summer we barely spoke. When we did, it was with the overtly cold, formal manner of two people who had a job to do but nothing more. The warm friendship forged at New Year seemed lost forever. Quite understandably, Laura felt misjudged and misunderstood and privately considered leaving the expedition. My once heady enthusiasm for the trip dried up, replaced by a resignation that it would be a painful few months.

We met in person only once that summer. It was horrible. Events had hurt us both and neither of us could look forward to the long months together in Africa. It was such a shame given how well we had worked as a team on the New Year's trip.

While the atmosphere in the Porsche's cramped cabin promised to be somewhat uncomfortable, in most other respects trip planning was going remarkably smoothly. A local garage, which had been looking after the Porsche for years, agreed to help prepare the car for the African roads by increasing its ground clearance. I bought a second Porsche identical to my own – though in much worse condition – to provide spare parts for the trip. One hot July day, my brother and I trailered the car from Lincoln to a compound near my parents' home in South Wales, where I could slowly dismantle it. It looked tatty and unloved and we knew nothing of the car's history, but the important parts all seemed to be in an acceptable condition. With a little persuasion the engine begrudgingly coughed into life and ran for a few minutes, before promptly becoming sick and cutting out. Following this brief interruption to its slumber, it refused to start again.

With a few months to go, spare parts were sourced for the Shogun and 'African Porsche Expedition' stickers applied to the vehicles. We even acquired two more team members.

A friend of Tom's named Louise decided to come along in the Shogun, making us a team of five. She was already very well travelled, having spent her childhood growing up in many far-flung places. She had spent the previous year roaming to the far corners of China and Mongolia, sleeping on strangers' sofas and accepting whatever trials the world threw at her. Like Laura, she didn't seem quite ready to give up the travelling bug and slot into a career just yet.

Libby was to be the final team member but only for a small part of the trip. As a newly qualified doctor, she could only get a couple of weeks off work and elected to join us for the Middle Eastern leg of our journey, flying into Istanbul to met us a few days after our departure and leaving the expedition at Cairo about ten days later. I had known Libby for years and her reputation for flirtatiousness, together with an unashamed love of attention, meant that time around her was always eventful. I had no idea how the more conservative areas of the Middle East would react to her but knew the result would be a source of amusement at the very least.

And so there were six of us. As the clock ticked down, everything was in hand, and the trip planning seemed to be going remarkably smoothly.

Almost too smoothly.

TWO

THE SHOW MUST GO ON

14th September 2008
Devon, England

It was a distinct clunk, a sharp metallic thud that signalled something had parted company with the car. I listened helplessly to further reports as the object ricocheted beneath me, striking tarmac and metal, until its echoes were lost in the night. Within a second the noises had ceased and the car continued to purr along but something was different. The steering was suddenly heavy and the warning lights for the car's electrics lit up the dashboard.

I stopped to investigate. Opening the bonnet, I could see the rubber belts on the front of the engine were twisted at strange angles, where the pulleys driving them had come adrift. The noises must have been the bolt holding the pulleys working loose and falling off. I took stock of the situation. I now had no power steering and the alternator would no longer charge the car's battery or power the lights. It was pitch black and I was half an hour from home. I decided to push on before the battery ran out, extinguishing the headlights and leaving me stranded in the darkness. Uneasily, I rejoined the highway and carried on towards Plymouth.

The Porsche ambled along as normal but I felt uneasy, as if stalked by something malevolent. My limited knowledge of how the engine worked said all should be fine, but I couldn't get the paranoid worry from my mind. I left the dual carriageway and slowed down to enter town. Suddenly, a multitude of warning lights lit up the dashboard and the engine lost power. I took in the information as fast as I could. The oil pressure was reading zero. As quickly as I could in my slightly confused state, I dipped the clutch, stopped the engine and pulled over, hoping to prevent any long-term damage but already expecting the worst. Oil is the lubricating lifeblood of an engine and without its softening influence metal grinds on metal in a most destructive manner. Nervously, I opened the bonnet. A thick cascade of the stuff was bleeding from the front of the engine where the bolt had worked loose. It dripped to the ground with a heavy finality. The smell of burning saturated the air around me. I knew then that the worst was probably the best I could expect.

Unknown to me at the time, the bolt which had worked loose didn't only hold the pulleys in place; it also locked the oil pump in position. Following the failure, the pump had continued to work for a while but eventually it worked free, ceasing to lubricate the engine and sealing its fate.

The recovery truck took an hour to arrive. I waited in the car, stewing over my options. If the engine was damaged, it might be possible to have it rebuilt, but that would cost a fortune and couldn't be done in time for Africa. Could we leave later? Not really, given the visas and Team Shogun's strict timeframe. We could just not go. As obstacles go, we'd hit a major one and there would be no shame in bowing out. It was also a good excuse not to spend months cooped up in a car with Laura. I knew that she too would welcome a reason to not to spend all that time in my company; but I didn't want to let my friends in the Shogun down. Could we take the engine out of the donor car and fit it in time? Possibly, but the only time I'd run it, it hadn't worked properly and we knew next to nothing about its condition or history. Also, all the paperwork was made out using the engine number from the broken engine. I shivered at the thought of setting off across Africa with a newly installed, untried second-hand engine in the Porsche – as if the odds weren't weighed against us enough already!

The recovery truck finally appeared in a crescendo of pulsating orange lights. I wandered over to the driver and introduced myself.

'This one's gonna make you laugh!' I said, trying to appear relaxed, to hide the nervous tension in my voice.

He surveyed the car with its roof rack and gaudy 'African Porsche Expedition' stickers.

'Has it been to Africa yet?'

'Nope. We're off in seventeen days.'

I showed him the still smouldering cascade of oil down the front of the engine and he agreed with my diagnosis – we were going nowhere in seventeen days! Without any further discussion as to whether it was fixable, we got the Porsche onto the recovery lorry and left.

Next morning, the car was already booked into the garage to have its suspension raised, to better cope with the African roads. Its arrival on the back of the recovery truck caused hearts to sink. The look of disbelief on the faces of the proprietors, who had only agreed to help with the expedition a week previously, was painful. They promised to find out whether the engine had been destroyed as soon as possible. I was pretty sure I knew the answer already.

I walked home from the garage in a tired daze. In the single act-of-god event of a bolt working loose, I felt my whole dream had been taken from me. I could no longer imagine driving among the Pyramids or cruising past game in the Serengeti. I felt sick. I had enough problems with Laura, why this on top of it all? Despite the still-present animosity between us, I felt like I'd let her down. She had trusted me to have the car ready for our leaving date and now even leaving at all was an improbable concept.

That day, the expedition appeared in the local newspaper, under the somewhat optimistic headline 'Epic Road Trip in a Classic Porsche.' Life has a strange sense of irony sometimes.

Once the car was in the garage's professional hands, all I could do was await their verdict on the damage to the engine. I passed the time by putting the finishing touches to our route plan and the paperwork, and trying unsuccessfully to be positive.

With less than two weeks to go, I spoke to the garage. They were unable to get the engine running as several metal pulleys on the front of the engine had been badly worn during its failure and would no longer fit properly. Previously frustrated by my inability to help, I sprang into action and, at the earliest opportunity, headed up to the donor car in Wales to source the parts. With ten days remaining, I found myself wrestling with the front of its engine, dismantling what had already fallen off the expedition car. It was well after dark on that chilly Tuesday night when I finally had the parts the garage had asked for, and following a few hours' sleep, I headed back to Plymouth to deliver them.

After dropping them off, I jumped straight back into my borrowed car and headed back up to Bristol, where my day job required me to survey a cargo ship. As I drove, I dwelled on whether the parts would enable the garage to fix the engine. I'd done all I could but despite my efforts, I didn't hold out much hope. The decisive few seconds when the engine was spinning without lubricating oil lingered in my mind.

That afternoon the garage phoned.

'Hello.'

'Hi Ben,' came a familiar Northern accent. 'Dan from Oakdens Garage here.'

'Oh, hello Dan,' I replied. 'What's the news?'

'Well, we got the pulleys fitted and turned the engine over.'

'But?'

'But there was a horrible grinding noise when we turned it over.'

'Bearings?'

'Well we won't know for sure without taking it apart, but it sounds like it, yes.'

I said nothing. The Porsche was dead.

'What do you want us to do?' Dan asked, as tactfully as he could.

'I don't know. I'll have a think and call you back in an hour or so.'

I felt dazed, but there was no time for me to dwell on what had just happened. I considered my options. We couldn't leave much later than planned due to the dates on our Syrian and Sudanese visas and the inflexibility of Team Shogun's leave dates. The engine couldn't be rebuilt in time. The only possible option we had was to remove the dubious, unknown engine from the donor car, install it in the broken Porsche, and hope it could be made to work.

I considered the timescale. We had nine days in total until the Friday evening on which we were due to leave. I was working for the first two of those available days. This meant I would have less than a week to go to South Wales, remove the engine from the donor car, get it to the garage in Plymouth, have it fitted and checked over, have the suspension raised and complete all the other last-minute preparations. Less than a week for all that. It seemed vaguely achievable but I doubted things would go smoothly enough to make it possible. In a manner which set a precedent for the whole trip, I had no choice but to apply myself to this solution in lieu of a more realistic option.

On the Saturday evening before our planned departure date, I got a lift to Bristol with Sam, an old university friend. We chatted away about my predicament with a resignation that deferred to the enormity of the task. I took the attitude that I would do what I could, give it my best shot and let what happens, happen. It was late when I finally arrived in South Wales but I was up at first light to get to grips with the donor car. If there was any chance of success, the engine had to be lifted out on Monday. I had one day to do the groundwork.

The morning's murky greyness slowly morphed into an overcast day as I drove towards the compound where the donor car and its precious engine lay in wait. Already tired from the cumulative efforts of organising the trip, I felt dwarfed by the task in hand. It felt like the adventure, with its obstacles and challenges, had started early. As I approached the compound, the laden grey clouds started spitting rain, as the car's speakers filled with the stirring sounds of the rock group Queen. *The show must go on*, pleaded the great Freddie Mercury, to an emotive crescendo of drums and guitar. The song worked its way under my prickling skin. Fissions of electricity pulsated up and down my spine and my temples pounded with the drama of the situation. The show must indeed go on and it was now or never for this particular show.

I parked next to the donor car. It looked tired and abused. Opening the bonnet exposed the dauntingly complex engine. Hemmed in tightly by the car's red bodywork, the inanimate lump of dirty metal on which our hopes rested lay hidden beneath a bewildering tangle of pipes and cables. This did nothing to relax me, as I'm certainly no mechanic. During past journeys I've often felt slightly fraudulent by appearing competent at such things, when in reality I've got by on a hefty dose of good luck aided by a small sprinkling of engineering common sense.

'Well,' I said to myself, 'life's full of small challenges, and now is as good a time as any to learn.'

I looked in the workshop manual I'd purchased years before but had barely opened since and started following the instructions. With a bit of guesswork, I unbolted various components from the dense mass of the engine block, gradually chipping away at its size and weight until it could be removed from the car. Wielding my socket set, I located and removed the starter motor, earthing cables, alternator and many other components whose identity I was only now becoming aware of. Cables, hoses and wiring were unplugged from the now impotent engine, its links to the car in which it had nestled for twenty-five years becoming ever more tenuous. But it was not all plain sailing. Many of the bolts seemed to have set solid in the quarter of a century since they were tightened in the factory. Some, like the exhaust bolts, were so tight that I couldn't release them;

others sheared in two when I attempted to turn them. Evidently my mechanical expertise was not going to be entirely sufficient to complete the task.

The sun seemed to have arced across the sky more quickly than usual and soon it was getting dark. I had achieved some small successes, although many aspects of the job had defeated me and progress had been much slower than I had hoped. Filthy with oil and grime, tired and morose, I completed the half-hour drive to my parents' house beneath the darkening gloom. The lack of progress depressed me. A day earlier, my ignorance had produced a naïve confidence. I thought I would be able to quickly unbolt everything from the engine and have it all ready for removal within the day. I was wrong. I had managed barely half the required tasks in the manual, and some of the remaining jobs had soundly defeated me. We were due to leave for Africa in five days and it had come to this. I was exhausted and felt depressed at the situation I found myself in.

Why? Why did the engine have to fail in such an act-of-god manner?

I knew the futility of such thoughts. I knew I had to remain positive and look to the future but the chances of being ready in time appeared impossibly slim. Reaching my parents' house, I was greeted enthusiastically but this merely grated with the hollowness I was feeling inside. I tried to put a brave face on things before retreating to bed, shattered by the trial through which I was struggling. Africa was still a million miles away.

The next morning arrived bright and clear, lifting my spirits slightly. The sun was hovering lazily just above the horizon as I set to work. A friend of my brother – who had access to a workshop – had agreed to help lift the engine out that evening. It was now or never. Relaxed by a night's sleep, I was more positive that morning as I set about some of the tasks which had defeated me the previous day, and managed to figure out ways of overcoming some of the trickier jobs. Still more continued to defeat me however, and it was a morning of mixed emotions – the satisfaction of success in one task generally being offset by a frustrating failure on another.

It was mid-afternoon when my brother arrived with a trailer, ready to take the donor car to the workshop. The car was still a long way from being ready to have its engine lifted out but I hoped his friend would have the expertise to nonchalantly overcome the tasks which had defeated me. And fortunately, so he did; because of work commitments, it was gone eight in the evening before we started the job, but his aura of relaxed confidence made me optimistic. Rapidly, his experienced hands overcame problems that had stopped me in my tracks and soon the vital lump of metal was attached to a pair of lifting strops, being willed to escape from the engine bay. By eleven that evening, we were manoeuvring it into the back of a van, ready to be taken to the garage.

Yet another inadequate night's sleep, followed by another early start, had me on the motorway towards Plymouth by six in the morning. I should have been happy, as the engine that could salvage the expedition rattled behind me in the van, but I just couldn't feel it. I was far too run down for such emotions.

At the garage, the engine was carefully hoisted out of the van and positioned on the floor next to the crippled white Porsche. Things were out of my hands now. It was up to the garage to fit it, and given how little we knew about the engine's condition, it was in the lap of the gods as to whether or not it could actually be made to work. My forced smiles faded as I left the garage, feeling tired and dazed by my efforts, yet relieved that a little of the pressure would be off me for a few days.

While the garage worked on the car, I morosely got to grips with the remaining jobs. I still didn't believe we would be going to Africa, but I had little choice other than to act like we would be. Half-heartedly, I got on with the last of the paperwork, completed the route plan and buried my living room floor under a large pile of tools, camping gear and bits of old Porsche. I also set about modifying the roof rack I'd sourced for the car to contain a storage box and a fold-out platform able to receive my tent, enabling us to camp on the vehicle's roof in the finest overland tradition.

I also phoned our friend Paul at the RAC carnet office.

'Paul, we're thinking of swapping the engine in the Porsche for a better one, which should be more reliable. How will that affect our paperwork?'

'It's not the one out of the old banger you bought off eBay is it?' he asked, knowingly.

'Erm, nope...' I lied, feeling cornered.

'Okay,' he replied sceptically. 'That should be fine. We can give you a letter to go with the carnet documents saying the engine was changed in the UK before you left. No problem.'

Importantly, I also went to the pub that evening to unwind, as for the first time in days the pressure wasn't squarely on my shoulders. Everyone was keen to know how the car was, whether we would be off to Africa in a few days and whether Laura and I were getting along any better. My responses were mostly negative. Feeling giddy from my recent efforts, I was ambling home tipsily after three beers.

Thursday.

The day before our planned departure.

I spoke to the garage in the morning, only to hear that they were yet to get the engine installed and running. With no choice but to keep going, I went back to the endless paperwork, the taxing woodwork of modifying the roof rack and the myriad of other last-minute tasks that were awaiting my attention before we left.

That afternoon, with thirty hours to go before our planned departure, the garage phoned. The engine was in and had run for a few minutes. They were hoping to have the suspension raised by the following afternoon. I breathed a sigh of relief but a nervous tension built inside me suddenly, as I thought about what faced us. A thirteen thousand mile journey across the Middle East and Africa in a flimsy sports car was stupid enough, without relying wholly on an unknown engine taken from a piece of scrap metal masquerading as a car. We must be mad to even consider it. But the timetable was set, even though inwardly the stresses of the previous few weeks had left me feeling destroyed. There was no way I would be able to face leaving for Africa the following day.

I phoned Laura that afternoon to tell her the news and felt my resolve crumble away further. The lack of understanding between us was still there and here we were planning on spending months together, teaming up to fight our way through thick and thin? I just couldn't face it and I knew she was equally unenthused by the prospect. Where had it all gone wrong? I was supposed to be leaving on the biggest adventure of my life, yet our vehicle was too untrustworthy even to drive to the shops and the mere thought of my co-driver made my heart sink and my blood boil!

I tried to put a brave face on things, to be the unfazed adventurer I wished I was, but inside I felt small and unequal to what I faced. The stress and exertions of the previous weeks had left me physically and emotionally weakened. I wished the trip would somehow just go away and leave me alone. But it wasn't about to. It had been part of my life for over a year now and our fortunes were too intertwined for separation. I even found myself wishing the replacement engine hadn't worked, giving me an easy excuse to walk away. But it had worked, if only for a few minutes. No more excuses.

That evening, the evening before our planned departure, I went to the pub and once again tried to forget about it all. I couldn't. My predicament had taken me over, dominating my thoughts and refusing to allow me to relax. I'd lost weight over the previous weeks and looked pale and gaunt. The well-meaning barrage of interrogation from concerned friends didn't help.

'How's the car?'

'Well the engine ran today for about two minutes, beyond that who knows?'

'Is Laura okay?'

'I don't really know. She's up in Barnstable with that bloke of hers. We haven't really spoken much lately. Don't really care to be honest.'

'Oh. So are you guys actually going through with this tomorrow?'

'I don't know. I just don't know.'

Friday dawned grey and oppressive. D-day. I didn't wake until after ten, then set about playing catch-up, indifferently buying food and getting a multitude of last-minute tasks done prior to our planned departure. Laura text messaged me; her boyfriend's car had been parked in and they couldn't move it. She'd be late getting to Plymouth. I wasn't too bothered; we didn't have a car yet anyway. Rarely an hour went by when my phone didn't ring with someone querying our progress. My answer was always the same: 'I don't know.' The garage would probably have the suspension raised that evening, in time for our departure but I couldn't face it. I found myself looking for an excuse not to go, not to commit to this shipwreck of a trip. My thoughts dwelled on our impending failure. After all, I'd been saying for many months that we were going to drive a Porsche across Africa. Many people had declared our goal unattainable and might even take pleasure in seeing us fail and having their opinions vindicated. The old, unloved engine on which our hopes rested was something I knew full well would break embarrassingly before we even left Europe. Despondently, I went about the day's tasks as these thoughts drifted through my mind. Without a watertight reason not to go ahead with the trip, the only thing I could do was keep going through the motions, as if it would happen. All too soon the day was gone.

It was seven in the evening when the garage had finally completed their work on the car. Seeing the Porsche with its suspension raised for the first time would have cheered me slightly, had I not been so completely destroyed by my efforts up to that point. It did look good though, its newly serious stance setting off the car's garish stickers perfectly. The professionals at the garage shared my worries about the engine and recommended driving it around locally for a week or two, ironing out any problems before cautiously venturing further afield. I assured them I wouldn't do anything rash, paid up for their hard work, threw in a few crates of beer in thanks and we said our goodbyes.

I nervously drove out of the garage. The engine seemed to work, though I remained distrustful of it. By working, it was clearly just lulling me into a false sense of security while it bided its time, waiting for the worst possible moment to leave me stranded. Driving home, the oil pressure gauge seemed permanently pinned to its maximum reading, while the oil warning light gave the smallest of glows, hinting at the same problem which destroyed the previous engine. I knew that given all which had gone before, things wouldn't go smoothly. Parking on my drive, my confidence in the vehicle remained zero.

Not only were we running an untried, unknown engine but also because of the time taken changing the motor, many other jobs to prepare the vehicle for Africa had remained undone. We hadn't got around to installing any protection for the Porsche's vulnerable, low-slung underside. One of the exhaust mountings remained broken, making it an easy target for a malicious African rock. The bonnet release remained broken, as did the cooling fan and many other important parts. Just as importantly, the friendship between my co-driver and I was still as barren as the Sahara.

46

It was dark when Laura finally arrived. Her boyfriend, evidently aware of the tension, dropped her off and left with the smallest of goodbyes and no introductions. We were due at our leaving party in an hour, yet I was still fitting the roof rack and wiring up the spotlights we'd optimistically fitted to it. Laura apologised for her lateness and we spoke face to face for only the second time in two months. Frustratingly, she looked as good as ever, in complete contrast to my run-down appearance. We both tried to appear as if it was business as usual, that nothing had changed but it was an empty and formal exchange which did nothing for my mood. As if out of necessity, we set about packing our things into the poor Porsche, finished the last-minute work on the roof rack and drove down to a local bar where relaxed friends were waiting to give us a Friday night send off.

Team Shogun had already arrived and couldn't hide their surprise as I parked outside. The adrenaline of the situation lifted me at first as I showed people around the altered familiarity of the Porsche, explained how the roof tent would work and discussed the hectic events of the previous few weeks. I took some satisfaction in the awed respect accorded to the fact the car was there at all. However despite this, I still felt a fraud. The Porsche wasn't ready, far from it. We'd got it back on the road and driven it a single mile, but that was a world away from being ready to tackle the harsh realities of Africa. As friends partied all around me, excited at what we were apparently about to do, I sat quietly; unable to get my mind to stop analysing the worrying oil pressure readings the new engine was giving.

My fatigue quickly caught up with me. Like a marathon runner collapsing across the line, I'd given it my all to get this far and could go no further. I'd been living in a state of continuous nervous tension, and hadn't slept properly in weeks. I was finished. I voiced my feelings to Laura first and she understood. She could see the cumulative results of my exertions in my gaunt face, my dull eyes and slurred composure. I was in no fit state to go anywhere. I made the excuse that I wanted to check a few things on the engine before we left, and set lunchtime the following day as our new departure time. Everyone agreed, relaxing me instantly. For a few hours, it was over. I'd got a respite from the continuous pressure in which to relax and try to recompose myself. Tomorrow was another day and I felt sure something on the car would prevent our departure, providing an excuse for me to get out of committing to our foolhardy venture.

By the early hours of the morning, our well-wishing friends had drifted away, leaving only the five condemned members of the African Porsche Expedition burning the midnight oil in Bar Cuba. The atmosphere was polar, the rowdy optimism of Brummy, Tom and Louise in the Shogun contrasting sharply with Laura and I, quietly awaiting our fate while trying to put a brave face on things. I slept well that night, though awoke just as terminally fatigued as ever. My thought processes had slowed to a crawl and forgetfulness plagued my attempts to complete any last-minute preparations. I was destroyed, in need of a holiday, not the most daunting undertaking of my life.

Over a morning coffee, Laura and I put aside our differences as best we could and pondered the big question – would the car make it to Cape Town? Almost certainly not but we'd never know for sure unless we tried. Discussing our situation, we agreed that it would be fifteen hundred miles until we were out of Western Europe, with its infrastructure of Porsche garages. We might as well just set off and see what happens, crossing our fingers that any problems manifest themselves in that first leg of the journey. Our tight schedule gave us little other option.

It took hours to complete the plethora of last-minute jobs, such was my inability to concentrate. Without being reminded, I would have forgotten to take many items, including much of my camping gear and a waterproof jacket. I felt like an exhausted old drunk, ambling along in only arbitrary control of his destiny. The sky was oppressively grey, which blended depressingly with the dull terraced houses on my street. Often, when I went outside to attend to the Porsche, a blustery shower would erupt and send me shuffling back inside. The atmosphere had a brooding animosity about it. Eventually, I could remember no more items to be packed and the minimum of last-minute preparations were done. The guys in the Shogun arrived full of enthusiasm and eager to get going. It was time.

While everyone else chatted outside, I stole a last, pained moment on my own before leaving my flat for the last time. I simply couldn't face the ridiculous challenge lying ahead of me. My mind felt heavy, numbed by fatigue and the enormity of it all. I just wanted to crawl away and sleep, to escape the pressures of the trip. But I had no more excuses. Closing the front door, I joined the others waiting by the cars, bright eyed and eager to leave. I collapsed into the driver's seat, finished. Laura was already inside, looking at me with a detached concern. She was the last person I wanted to see. Overwhelmed, I stifled back the tears as I selected reverse and backed the Porsche off my drive for the last time. I had done the same manoeuvre hundreds of times in the past. To go to work, to the shops, to see friends. This time, however, it was different. Half the world lay ahead.

THREE

THROUGH THE DARKNESS

4th October 2008
Plymouth, England

On a blustery autumn day, Plymouth has an air of the past about it. The blocky greyness of its buildings merges with the leaden clouds, creating the sensation of being within an austere old photograph. Seagulls swoop and cry out sharply, while the people below are intermittently raked by cold, harsh rain. The crisp air is infused with the maritime smell of salt water. It feels like the city is hunkering down against the onslaught, awaiting better times. Africa it is not. I could sympathise with the city's mood. I felt just the same.

Laura's mood matched mine, but was not so exaggerated by fatigue. We stuttered along through the traffic with barely a smile passing between us, trying to generate some normality through boringly polite conversation. The bad feeling between us was not entirely to blame; a hefty degree of nervousness was also stifling our ability to relax.

Only a small part of my attention was directed towards Laura, as the new engine worried me hugely. I focused intently on every noise and vibration it made, trying to learn its character and recognise any problems. It felt somehow different to the previous engine but I couldn't quite put my finger on why or whether it should worry me so much. It seemed to run acceptably though, except for the oil pressure worries.

Evidently the engine wasn't going to give me an excuse to stop our ridiculous folly just yet so we drifted onwards, out of Plymouth's monotonous grey. Leaving town, we accelerated up to sixty miles per hour for the first time. Still the engine chugged away okay, though I couldn't escape the feeling that I was already on borrowed time, as it malevolently waited for the most inopportune moment to fail.

Painfully slowly, we crawled across southern England behind the chunky Shogun, bound for Dover and a ferry across the English Channel; fifty-eight miles per hour all the way. *Sports cars and 4x4s were never designed to travel together in convoy!* The first hour saw us nervously stopping on two occasions to check the engine over. Nothing looked obviously wrong, so each time we pushed on towards our destiny.

After a few hours, Laura took control of the Porsche for the first time. A fish out of water, it took her a while to adjust to its sports-car-sharp responses, heavy gears and poor visibility. I could tell she felt bad about treating the car roughly but my attempts to reassure her came out awkwardly, blunted by the cold atmosphere between us. Fortunately, she quickly adapted and was soon cruising down the sodden motorway like a natural. My first spell in the passenger seat was spent in silence, gradually remembering all the spare parts I'd forgotten to bring along. We had no spare alternator, fuel filter, head gasket or injectors, and all were important, fragile components which could potentially end the expedition for us.

Half of England was behind us as the overcast sky dulled to night. Darkness meant the oil warning light glowed brighter than ever, tormenting my paranoid subconscious. It also brought anonymity from the curious glances of other motorists, which was welcome given how fraudulent the 'African Porsche Expedition' stickers covering the car made me feel. There wasn't a hope in hell of us making it to Africa.

At ten o'clock that evening we reached Dover, where we went to the port and paid over the odds for some ferry tickets. We hadn't booked them in advance as we hadn't seriously believed the Porsche would make it even that far.

The weather had deteriorated, becoming even more blustery and autumnal, and the car's mood seemed to have worsened in sympathy. Negotiating the ferry port, the oil warning light intensified its protest every time the engine was allowed to run slowly, its red glow becoming etched in my mind. The engine also seemed to have acquired a rough, lumpy misfire at low speeds, coughing away and threatening to stall at any moment. It was not a happy car. It had more in common with a rusty old lawnmower than a Porsche.

The sea was not happy either. The worsening weather had built into a full-blown storm. White foam scudded across the distressed water while rain lashed our cars as we waited to board our ferry. In the distance, waves exploded skyward as they hit the breakwater, warning of worse conditions out in the Channel. It felt apocalyptic, like the end of the world. It was strangely fitting.

Our poor car rocked limply on its suspension as each gust of wind hit it, while Laura and I sheltered silently within its cramped cabin, feeling condemned. We didn't want to talk. The weather, the car, us; everything felt wrong. Still as exhausted as ever, I shut my eyes and dozed for a few valuable minutes before we had to leave. The engine spluttered into its rough, uneven patter and I followed the Shogun through the deluge into the tranquillity of the car deck.

The weather delayed our departure for France by an hour, giving the five of us time to get reacquainted. Laura and I were particularly glad to be in the company of other people. It had been a difficult first day for us and neither of us was remotely optimistic about spending the rest of the trip together. As the rest of the group chatted away, I opened the car's workshop manual in an attempt to get to the bottom of the oil pressure issues. Eventually I came to the conclusion that either the oil pressure sensor was giving an inaccurate reading, or the engine bearings were almost worn out, allowing the pressure to drop. I thought further about this. If it was the sensor, we had little to worry about and the engine might even be capable of going the distance. If the bearings were worn out, the engine would already be shot and there was nothing at all we could do about it, short of a full overhaul. But without access to a garage, we had no way to prove whether the bearings were at fault and I had no previous experience of this problem to fall back on. Therefore, for the second time that day we had no choice but to just cross our fingers, push onwards and see what happened. Without any solid proof that the car was terminally ill, there was no way I could justify holding up the expedition at such an early stage, however much I wanted to.

While I was reading up on our ailing steed's symptoms, I passively listened to the rest of the team chatting away. Laura appeared overjoyed at having company other than me, revelling in the chance to laugh and joke with the Shogun crew. Her seemingly carefree banter did nothing for my mood. Brummy was his usual self, all smiles and humour, firing off jokes at a heady rate, playing off Laura and Louise while Tom interjected wearily from time to time. They all seemed pleased to finally be getting on with the expedition after all the months of talk and planning. We had a good group of people, the majority of whom were in good spirits. At least that was something we had going for us. I only hoped Laura and I could put our differences behind us and prevent our journey being a living hell. On that bitter October night, such a mellowing of our relationship seemed a world away.

It was gone midnight when the ferry, aided by a tugboat, slowly eased out of the harbour into the stormy Channel. A rough couple of hours saw us in Calais, where we pushed onwards into the darkness. We'd decided to drive through the night on this first leg of the journey, hoping to get all the way to Slovenia in one push. Time was of the essence as we were due to meet Libby in Istanbul two days hence and had a ferry booked in southern Egypt two weeks after our departure. While I wasn't remotely confident we would get as far as Egypt, I still had no choice but to act as if we would. We had to keep pushing on through the uncertainty, however pointless it felt.

Laura and I took turns to negotiate the efficient sameness of Europe's highways. Exhausted as ever, while Laura drove I succumbed to a few uncomfortable hours' sleep, memorable only for tormenting dreams of oil warning lights and failure. Sometimes when I was driving I could tell Laura was feigning sleep, to make our silence feel less unnatural.

The tarmac of France and Belgium was blandly behind us when a stormy dawn began to break over northern Germany. We passed signs for the Nurburgring, a legendary racetrack synonymous with the Porsche marque, celebrated as much for its extreme danger as for its sinuous corners. The Porsche had come this way once before in more carefree circumstances. Years earlier, on the way back from a trip to France, a detour had resulted in it being flung amateurishly around the circuit; the only car there overloaded comically to the roof with rock climbing gear and duty free booze.

Such unbridled excitement felt a world away as we cruised onwards, silently following signs for Stuttgart. My fatigue was worse than ever after a cramped night in the car and, in place of enthusiasm, all I could muster was mild surprise at the fact we hadn't broken down yet. I didn't feel any emotion about this. I was resigned to the journey, where it took us, and where it finally chose to end. I felt too weak to have any influence on its outcome; I was merely along for the ride. The trip had already shown it was the boss of me.

Further south, the weather improved as we escaped the influence of the previous night's storms. A weak sun broke through the milky overcast while the wind propelled clouds of brown leaves into our path, which danced in our slipstream as we passed. Looping past Stuttgart, we felt like we'd driven the Porsche home. The legendary carmaker had been working its magic there for sixty years and the well-worn badge on our bonnet was modelled on the city's coat of arms. As if to remind us, one of the factory's Porsche 'Panamera' prototypes growled past us on the autobahn, all futuristic curves and cutting edge technology, contrasting starkly with our ailing 1980s steed.

The sun was creeping towards the horizon as we crossed Bavaria, where the landscape's gentle undulations increased their amplitude and frequency. The eastern ranges of the Alps lay ahead; these ripples were their first harbingers.

The mountains made their first appearance to our right, shimmering ethereally on the horizon. A narrow strip of jagged lightness, their clean limestone faces and snow-choked gullies were brought to life by the oblique rays of the setting sun. Around us, the more hospitable foothills were dotted with any number of quaint villages, each huddling around a pristine church spire.

The road climbed inexorably upwards as the ribbon of mountains drifted closer until suddenly, we were among them. Twisting through charmed passes, our necks craned to take in the thinly powdered sweeps of perfect rock and beautiful summits. Behind us, a mellifluous sunset was already thickening to dusk and a faint alpenglow lent a pink dusting to our charismatic surroundings. Daylight faded quickly as we descended into a deep valley where an inky lake appeared to our left, completing the Alpine cliché. The mountains retreated into the darkness, their ghostly white faces hanging high above as our headlights cut a pale tunnel of light through the night. It was beautiful, but I didn't care. I would rather have been anywhere else than there, sat in the Porsche, next to Laura.

We were tired and hungry when we reached the Austrian border after a gruelling thirty hours on the road, so a dinner stop was called. Team Shogun was in high spirits and Laura's mood lifted once she was out of the Porsche. The happiness wasn't contagious however and I remained defiantly downbeat, sitting quietly while the others chatted away.

Sometimes a country just lives up to its stereotypes. We had been across the border for a grand total of fifteen minutes when Austria chose to do just that. Louise spotted it first.

'That man's got a beaver on his head!'

'What?'

'Over there. Look, lots of them!'

Indeed there were. Filing in from the darkness was a whole clan of folk dressed un-ironically in leather shorts, braces, check shirts and a variety of jovial headpieces. The group was characterised as much by their happily swaying aura of inebriation as by their unusual dress sense. The air filled with the guttural harmonics of beer fuelled Germanic banter and the merry ring of bells. And sure enough, near the front of the ambling mass of leather and kitsch, a finely detailed miniature beaver perched improbably on the head of its unsteady owner.

Brummy's face lit up the moment he saw it.

'Wow, I've got to have one of those! Go and get it Laura…'

The glint in Laura's eyes hinted she was up for a spot of friendly international banter.

And so it was that one of the first group discussions of the African Porsche Expedition evaluated the possibility of 'acquiring' the fake beaver from our Austrian friend's head and making a clean getaway. I stayed out of what felt like an inappropriately upbeat conversation and fortunately, everyone's sobriety quickly led to the conclusion that we were outnumbered about ten to one by this merry gathering of lederhosen and to end the expedition in an Austrian hospital probably wouldn't impress the folks back home too much. Begrudgingly, international relations were left untarnished and we settled for photographs, finishing our meals in a disappointingly beaver-less state.

It was completely dark when we resumed the drive. We'd decided to push on to the picturesque Slovenian town of Bled that evening, meaning that Austria would pass in a blur of tunnels and darkness – and so it did.

Setting off on the final one hundred and fifty miles of our marathon drive across Western Europe crushed my fragile spirits immediately. The engine thudded unenthusiastically to life, spluttering away on the verge of stalling, while the oil warning light appeared to be burning through the darkness brighter than ever. My paranoid mind could only assume the worst. *The light is obviously brighter because the bearings are slowly wearing out and maybe the rough running is because the battered old engine's head gasket is failing too?* Laura pretended to sleep as we slid through the unseen Alps, my mind dwelling on the car's problems and my spirits plummeting accordingly. With the darkness came the return of my smothering tiredness, worse than ever after a day and a half on the road.

It was nearly midnight when we arrived in Bled, but the pubs were still open. We headed straight for 'Bar 2000', a favourite haunt from our visit to the area the previous New Year. I remained detached, unable to stop thinking about the condition of the engine. While everyone else went for a hard earned beer, I dug out my torch and opened the bonnet to investigate. With the engine puttering away anaemically, I could hear a hiss of air escaping under pressure. It had to be a vacuum leak and the probable cause of the rough running. This was good news, as it was unlikely to get any worse and should prove fairly straightforward to fix. Unfortunately however, the oil issues remained unresolved and there would be no getting to the bottom of them that evening.

I felt guilty when I finally ventured into Bar 2000. I had more important things to do than relax. Louise bought me a beer as the rest of the group laughed and joked the evening away around a familiar table. I joined them and struggled through my drink barely saying a word, lost in my own fatalistic thoughts. I was overwhelmingly tired and fed up and didn't want to believe the crushing predicament I found myself in. Soon, the bar closed and we headed around the lake to the youth hostel for a cheap night's sleep.

The following day dawned crisp and promising, as only days in the mountains truly can. I went for breakfast, trying to put my unsettled night's sleep behind me and forget the predictable dreams of failure which had plagued it. Several young couples were already occupying the buffet area. I listened as self-consciously whispered discussions regarding the day's activities passed between each couple. Hiking, cycling, sightseeing. They sounded excited. I felt inordinately jealous of them with their seemingly resolved lives and apparently easily fulfilled holiday aspirations.

Why did I want to drive to Cape Town in such a stupid car, with someone I irrationally despise? Why couldn't I be happy just being normal? What was I trying to prove? What was I even doing here?

Of course deep down I knew that I would always gravitate towards the preposterous and the unknown, that I could never be happy just living, but at that moment the relaxed lives of those around me looked positively blissful.

Finishing my toast and orange juice, I resolved to get the car to a garage that day to have the oil pressure checked before we carried on to less forgiving surroundings. It was decided that Brummy and I would take the cars to the garage, while Tom, Louise and Laura would pass the day sightseeing around Bled.

Negotiating Bled's narrow streets, our eyes were permanently drawn to the stunning vista in which we found ourselves. Snuggling up to the tranquil shores of an Alpine lake and surrounded on all sides by the snow-capped spires of the Julian Alps, Bled couldn't fail to stir the soul. As we drove, gaps between the unpretentious dwellings gifted us views of the lake, complete with its elegant church, rising from an island in its centre. A castle stood sentry from a rocky bluff above the scene. In the crisp, clear air, I felt as if I could reach out and touch it.

The garage in Bled couldn't help and suggested we try the main Porsche garage in the capital. So off I went to Ljubljana, while Brummy headed back to Bled in the Shogun.

The drive was unexpectedly enjoyable. It was liberating to cruise down the motorway at my own speed, with sunlight obscuring the warning light and the Shogun – and Laura – nowhere in sight. The scenery was equally pleasing, all forests and mountains and open countryside, sparsely populated and apparently arranged for maximum aesthetic effect. It was almost a disappointment when all too soon, the city erupted around me.

Within minutes, I was lost within it, but it wasn't too much of a worry. Ljubljana is even smaller than Plymouth, where we had been only forty-eight hours previously, so I was soon able to get my bearings and navigate through its blocky outskirts to the garage. Once the Porsche was confidently booked in for a check-up the following morning, I headed back to Bled and met up with the others in time for a spot of sightseeing around the lake.

I don't think I'll ever tire of wandering around Bled. The clearness of the mountain air and its perfect aesthetics captivate effortlessly. Everyone was in good spirits, except Laura who was understandably finding all the 'you should have brought a Shogun, you're not going to make it out of Europe' jokes a bit wearing. I didn't blame her. Louise and Laura were also both on the receiving end of much derision from Tom and Brummy, after they resolved to one day be the subjects of fairytale weddings at the dreamy church on the lake.

To save money we camped that evening. My motivation didn't stretch far enough to putting the finishing touches to our rooftop sleeping platform, so Laura and I pitched our tent on the ground in the traditional manner. Not for the last time on the trip, I regretted the decision we'd made months earlier, to share a single tent.

As if customary for the mountain paradise around us, day three began beneath a crystal sky. Laura and I rose and left early, bound for the garage in Ljubljana where we hoped our car worries could be resolved, enabling us to push on through the Balkans. We dropped off the car – 'come back at eleven' – and headed off for a much-needed coffee, followed by some shopping. The relaxed evening and a good night's sleep had gone a little way to breaking down the barriers between us, and conversation had flowed more freely than it had at any time during the previous few months. While the animosity was still there, we were both making an effort to break through it and to make the trip work. Perhaps the two of us could find a way to survive this after all? Whether our car could survive was the big question, however.

Eleven o'clock passed with no news and a definite air of lethargy hanging over the workshop. By the time the Shogun arrived I was beginning to get anxious, seeing long hours of waiting and big bills in my future. 'One more hour,' they said. I impotently wondered how it could take so long to unscrew a simple sensor and screw in a replacement. Brummy and Tom were less philosophical about the situation and expressed their opinions of Slovenian garages rather more forthrightly.

Eventually, the reason for the delay emerged. The garage didn't have an oil pressure gauge which fitted and hadn't been able to find one either. Graciously, they refused to charge for their efforts, an honesty that was mirrored everywhere we went in Slovenia. We thanked them, feeling slightly guilty for our impatience and went to a nearby restaurant for lunch, during which we considered our options. Time was of the essence. We had to meet Libby in Istanbul the following day and the ferry booking in southern Egypt was now less than two weeks away. The warning light may have got slightly worse, but the car still seemed to be running okay and there were no other symptoms. Maybe I was worrying about nothing? I had no experience of this sort of problem and my nerves had been shattered by the continuous tension of the previous weeks. Once again, I had little choice but to carry on blindly and see if things got any worse. After all, nothing had really changed – we were still in the situation where if the bearings were wearing out we wouldn't make it across Africa anyway. As always, all we could do was push on into the unknown, cross our fingers and hope for the best. And so, begrudgingly we did just that, heading south into Croatia.

Soon, we were cruising through a gently flattening landscape, the stunning mountains of the Slovenian Alps consigned to memory. Popping the headlights up into the dusk air, the outside world was lost in the shadows as we thrummed our way along Croatia's smooth tarmac towards the Serbian border.

Some countries sit comfortably in one's subconscious. You just like them, without knowing exactly why. Croatia is like this for me. Its plucky football team, apparent striving for closer links with other nations and beautiful coastline all paint Croatia as a welcome, unthreatening entity. Of course, the opposite is true for some other nations. For instance, China's human rights record, Tibetan genocide and culture of censorship leave me feeling somewhat negative and repelled, while Saudi Arabia's treatment of women generates negative connotations. Serbia is another nation whose perceived characteristics leave me cold. Once led by the somewhat abrasive Slobodan Milosevic, often in the news enforcing its will on relative minnows like Kosovo and apparently unenthused about relations with the West, Serbia was not a place I expected to feel welcome.

We exited Croatia quickly, its efficient border manned by smiling people, a rarity to be savoured. Serbia lay ahead. Brummy guided the Shogun up to the first window and handed over first the passports, then the car documents. An unsmiling forty-something border guard with the unmistakable face of a military man received them coldly. His features were broad and well defined. An officer's moustache perched above his lip and his pale Slavic skin was roughened with the aged patina of a life hard lived. A starchy, exaggerated collar and autocratic hat framed his intriguing, unwelcoming features. He was not happy. Few people who choose to argue with Brummy are. Empowered by his uniform, he studied the documents with an aura of grave detachment before passing back everything except one of the passports and gesturing the Shogun disdainfully away. And then it was our turn. I pulled up, handed over the passports and tried to crack a smile as the Porsche idled limply away. The cold stare I received back implied that a border crossing is no place for smiling.

'Green card,' he barked officiously.

'I'm going to buy insurance on the border,' I explained.

He looked at me disbelievingly.

'No green card, no Serbia!' was his curt response, theatrically holding up our two passports, before handing back Laura's and keeping mine for himself.

The implication of mistrust was clear.

I parked next to the Shogun.

'Welcome to Serbia!' I called out bitterly, to nobody in particular.

'Yeah, I wonder what he did during the war!' replied an angry Brummy. 'I showed him my insurance; it says green card, says Serbia, I spoke to the insurance company before we left the UK and they said it would be fine. What a bastard!'

I have to say I could only sympathise with how he felt, but didn't have the same grounds for feeling hard done by, as during the frantic last-minute preparations, I'd completely forgotten to bring my car insurance documents with me.

Energised by Brummy's anger, we went off in search of insurance. Behind some bland, apparently purposeless official buildings was a hardstanding crammed with sleeping trucks and, behind these, there were lights. We investigated and found a profusion of small, almost apologetic shanty-offices arranged in a long line, each one's dim lighting offset by an excessively bright sign advertising its services in finest Serbian. Even at midnight, they were all still open for business. Rotund truck drivers lingered by their entrances, smoking away.

By trial and error, we eventually found ourselves in an office that sold insurance. It was an uninspiring place, about two metres wide and overwhelmingly bland and white. Beige tiles covered the floor, while an uncoordinated assortment of 1980s furniture attempted to lend purpose to the space. A tall, dark haired woman with sharp, slightly sad features and a liking for black clothing occupied the office. I thought she looked like a widow. She explained to us in exaggerated though very welcome English that insurance cost a hundred and thirty-five euros, payable in the local currency. This price was for the minimum duration of one month. And that was that.

We went back outside and considered our options. To drive around Serbia would be more trouble than it was worth, and attempts to haggle down the price with other insurers were met with a dismissive, 'No hundred and thirty-five euros, no Serbia'. We would have been quite happy with no Serbia at that stage. We intended to transit the country in six hours, to not even see it in daylight, and were being charged a fistful of money for the privilege.

Begrudgingly, we accepted we didn't have a choice, so we headed to a nondescript shack purporting to be a bank, in search of money. Looking over the counter was like entering a time warp. The narrow room was glaringly lit, lined with ancient wood panelling and decorated with a selection of oversized ashtrays, an old fashioned typewriter, a banknote counter and a selection of document trays. Pride of place in the room went to a chunky old cream-coloured computer and monitor, which pulled the room from its 1970s pretence and rooted it firmly in the early 1990s. The bank clerk was exactly the sort of person you'd expect to work in such a place. Slightly built and unassuming, in a grey shirt and forgettable tie, his face was hollow and his haircut functional. Behind wiry spectacles, his dark eyes nestled shyly, as if scared. I felt sorry for him, alone in his midnight office in this thankless outpost of Serbia, surrounded by swaggering truckers and the slightly seedy undertones of many of the other businesses. I hoped he was happy, but felt his life was probably one of unfulfilled dreams and monotonous mediocrity. *Surely no one ended up in a place like this out of choice?*

Whatever his background, he dealt with us efficiently. Tom withdrew enough of the local currency to pay for the insurance, the notes counted repeatedly before being swiped from his Visa card onto a slip of tracing paper in a manner which had propelled Western economies through the 1980s.

Armed with cash, we returned to the widow-like insurance seller who painstakingly filled out the expensive documents for us, accepting our payment almost apologetically. It felt like Serbia was showing us that it did have a human side after all, struggling to escape from beneath a veneer of cold distrust.

We showed the poker-faced border guard our insurance documents and he evaluated them disapprovingly before passing back our passports with a grunt. We were in.

Even more so than Croatia, Serbia felt empty. The heavy darkness reached away to the horizon, where it merged imperceptibly with a starless sky. The Porsche felt like it was on a treadmill, continuously recycling the strip of road glowing in front of its headlights. Occasionally, another vehicle or a dimly lit village slid past, breaking the monotony. We stopped for fuel and coffee at a very modern, very generic petrol station, which advertised its location by shining a searchlight directly upwards into the night sky, making it visible for miles around. It struck us that everything we'd seen in Serbia so far – the villages, the cars, the people – looked either conspicuously shiny and new, or very old and dilapidated. The blended-in maturity of a landscape left to evolve gradually over generations didn't seem to exist.

Within minutes of reconvening our night-drive, Laura was asleep. Progress was mindless and as always in such a situation, my mind wandered, this time deciding to dwell on the conflict which had torn this region apart in the previous decade. The dark unseen countryside offered a blank canvas for my imagination to ponder the question: 'What happened here?' I turned up the music and fortuitously, the rock band 'My Chemical Romance' filled the night with lyrics of fear and war, duty and sacrifice.

As someone who grew up in the 1990s, my mind had come to perceive Serbia not so much as a country, but rather a combatant. Rightly or wrongly, its name conjured up barely remembered news reports of violence, of ethnic cleansing and of neighbour turning on neighbour. And so as I drove through its darkened hinterland, my mind, emboldened by the music, tried to relate its mental imprint of Serbia to the emptiness gliding past the car's windows.

It failed. The country was in fact little different to any other in the area. There were no more hostilities, thank goodness, only a moderately poor country striving to build for its future. I felt suddenly angry with myself for seeking truth in an outdated stereotype, rather than entering Serbia in an open-minded manner.

Gradually, as if to confirm Serbia's normality, the invisible countryside started to give way to the orange sodium lighting of settlements, before the outskirts of Belgrade swept in to envelop us. The road surface deteriorated as it cut through a coarse forest of crumbling apartment blocks before returning us to the countryside, where the darkness became complete once again. We slalomed down an unseen valley towards Bulgaria and as the night ticked by, the feeling of remoteness became greater than ever.

Just before the border, we passed through the town of Dimitrovgrad, which dripped forlornly down the side of a wooded hill.   An air of injustice hung over the place. Impoverished looking wooden hovels and shacks stood back from the road, often accompanied by a tractor, pickup or Lada, which invariably ranged in condition from the derelict to the soon-to-be-derelict.   Here and there, a mothballed petrol station or boarded up shop spoke of lost dreams.   Broken pieces of unrecognisable machinery lay around, suggesting that someone once believed in this place. Now, however, it was merely a run-down frontier town, strangely evocative of the Wild West; albeit with a Soviet slant which wouldn't go down too well in Texas.

By five in the morning, we were over the border and into Bulgaria.   We were exhausted, but pleased to be out of Serbia.   To be fair, our judgements had been made at the border and we hadn't given the country a chance to redeem itself. We hadn't seen it in daylight, and had spoken to few who lived there.   We couldn't pretend to have learnt anything of the place, but we had no choice. Our goal was to spend as much time as possible experiencing Africa, not Europe, and Serbia was an unfortunate casualty of this. We drove on, following signs for Sofia, Bulgaria's capital and willing dawn to break and end the long hours of darkness.

The first calm portents of sunrise hung over the horizon as we negotiated Sofia's ring road. The experience reminded me intensely of the long hours driving across Russia years before.   The road was a two-way strip of shiny, gripless tarmac, smooth and uniform as the Himalayas.   Its patchwork surface was melted into a confusion of torturous ridges and grooves, while the shadows hid bumps and potholes which pounded the Porsche rudely.   A steady stream of trucks came the other way, lights invariably set to dazzle and the horn sufficing in lieu of brakes. The exact location of the road's centreline seemed to vary depending on just how benevolent the oncoming truck driver was feeling, and whether he was busy making a coffee at the time. After driving through the night neither I, nor Tom in the Shogun, was equal to the challenge anymore. We pulled over for a driver change. My relief was immediate.

Sofia was soon added to our list of cities left sadly unvisited as we headed east through the countryside on improving roads. Rolling hills formed the perfect canvas for the crimson sunrise which built directly ahead. Valleys were flooded with a salmon mist, mirroring the colours of the shining clouds above. Hilltops thrust out of this molten medium – islands in a tranquil sea. At one point, the road swept down into a valley beneath a low ceiling of drifting pink mist, before climbing theatrically back into the drama of the coming day.

Or so Laura told me. It seems that sleeping through this most impressive of natural spectacles was my reward for staying awake all night, pushing across Serbia while trying to ignore the ever-present oil warning light. I wasn't bitter though; I needed the sleep a lot more than the sunrise.

Daylight revealed Bulgaria to be a beautiful country of flat plains hemmed in by modest mountains, which already bore the first traces of the winter snows. Occasionally an isolated, blocky town, factory or power plant rose from the flatlands, visible for miles around as we plodded along with the Shogun at fifty-eight miles per hour. These intrusions didn't really spoil the view however, instead serving to emphasise the beauty which existed in the rest of our field of vision. The sunlight washed out the oil warning light and soon we left the dual carriageway for a more intimate road.

Bulgaria closed in around us. Poor, poor dwellings lined the road as we endured the suicidal overtaking manoeuvres of the area's migrant truck driving population. Despite the poverty, rural Bulgaria seemed comfortable, at ease with its lot. People were starting their days with a smile, the sun was out and the temperature was already climbing fast. The pace of life was obviously slow and there appeared to be a sense of restrained pride among people, who didn't feel the need to point at our garish sports car, or even acknowledge its passing.

They had their lives. We had ours. Evidently that was enough.

Life was clearly tough however. Agriculture appeared unproductive and primitive, the soil unsuited to crops. People were restrained by their history and their diet; old folk bent double by malnutrition became a distressingly common sight. Soon enough, we overtook our first donkeys, braving the traffic to drag their carts like doomed anachronisms. Taking in our surroundings, we felt like the adventure was finally starting. The trappings of modern Europe were gradually being left behind; ahead lay the unknown.

It was nearing midday when we reached Bulgaria's south-eastern corner, where Sofia's authority comes to an end at the Greek and Turkish borders. Greece wasn't strictly on our route, but surprisingly none of us had actually been there, so we decided to nip across the border for lunch. The tarmac in the north of the country was deserted and fast, sweeping through rolling sandy countryside and villages which appeared to have been asleep for weeks. This made sense. Given the balmy temperatures, clear blue skies and smothering silence, I'd probably sleep for weeks at a time if I lived there. After fifteen miles of unsuccessfully searching for a restaurant, we pulled into an isolated service station and ate there, much to the distain of the local wasp population, which amused us greatly by singling Brummy out for attack.

Thanks to their European Union membership, we re-entered Bulgaria effortlessly and were soon wafting past a four mile long queue of lorries which terminated at the Turkish border. Drivers sat next to their laden steeds, playing cards, making tea, gambling and suchlike, anything to pass the days as they inched towards their chance to be cleared by customs. Western European borders must have been like this once, before the Schlengen Zone allowed trade to pass between member countries effortlessly. Eventually, we were past all the trucks and Turkey ceased to be somewhere over the horizon and in our dreams; it was just a few stamps and bits of paperwork away.

Our transit through the border was characterised by two unusual sights. Firstly the impressive mosque, which sat confidently in the middle of no-man's-land, generated a rather different atmosphere to the borders I'd crossed in the past. It was a grand sight, standing remote and proud from any other buildings, its heavy façade and slender minarets softened by the dusty air. The mosque injected symbolism to our passing, sitting as it did on the boundary between two very different worlds.

The second unusual sight consisted of a smiling border guard. In his twenties and of dark complexion, our new friend had the relaxed manner of someone playing a game and immediately set us at ease. Soon we had visas, our passports were stamped with a flourish and on we went to get the cars imported. Much to our relief, insurance cost about a third of the Serbian price, and half an hour later we were driving away from the border with our paperwork in order, another gargantuan mosque to our left and less than two hundred miles remaining to Istanbul. Since leaving Slovenia, we had been on the road for twenty-six hours straight, but the deeply satisfying feeling of making rapid progress across the map, combined with the promise of a beer in Istanbul, kept us pushing on through the tiredness. A few miles down the road, we passed our first Turkish town. Looking rather mystical in the oblique evening light, Edirne seemed to shimmer in a haze of dust, jewelled by three great mosques rushing skyward from its sea of urbanity. The sight stirred us as we cruised past, thrilled by the sudden transformation of cultures which crossing a line on the map had generated.

As we continued to crawl across the open countryside, sodden storm clouds rose all around, blurring mistily with the blue sky. The sun fell to the horizon behind us and a tired Laura could drive no more, so we swapped over. An inky blackness built over a landscape which was reminiscent of Bulgaria, but somehow bigger, more forbidding and unyielding. Maybe it was the weather. Maybe it was all in our minds. Whatever the reason, Turkey felt more serious than Bulgaria. As night became complete, the sodium glow of Istanbul's outlying satellites started to impede on the wilderness. Their density gradually increased until they merged into the homogeneous whole of the city's outskirts. Traffic levels on the main artery towards the centre, along which we were travelling, crept up resultantly.

We flowed along with the other vehicles, heading for the Sultanahmet area of the old city, where Libby was waiting for us. As Istanbul built all around, the traffic became more turbulent and I was forced to drive the Porsche quite aggressively in order to maintain my position behind the Shogun. To become split up would be a disaster, as we only had one map and would lose hours finding each other again. The worse the traffic got, the more aggressively I was forced to work the Porsche, staying within a few feet of the Shogun's rear bumper at all times and responding decisively to anyone who attempted to come between us. It was scary and exciting driving which kept me on edge, having to respond instantly to what was going on around me. Blinking wasn't an option and adrenaline helped my reflexes to overcome the fatigue and become equal to the task. Somehow, I felt like I had a sixth sense telling me exactly where all the traffic around me was and how roughly I could treat the other road users without causing too much offence.

As we left the dual carriageway and begin to penetrate the old city, the traffic congealed into a slow trickle and I had to fight more than ever to keep the convoy together, driving even closer to the Shogun and terrifying Laura in the process. Strangely, it felt good to be driving like this, the car and I both coming to life again after so many lethargic miles on the highways of Europe. I was glad that staying with the Shogun was occupying my mind fully, as it prevented me from dwelling on our various other problems.

At times, the traffic clotted to a halt and I was able to take in my surroundings; a lively, busy city, slightly reminiscent of the East. After the wide-open Turkish countryside, it felt both oppressive and exciting, towering over us and bombarding all our senses, energising us yet trapping us. Despite the late hour, Istanbul was bustling. People were out and about, shopping and chatting. Young lads rushed impatiently past us, pulling their carts, making urgent deliveries to various businesses. Older folk sat and talked beneath the garish neon signs, cigarettes in hand. Beggars eyed us opportunistically from beneath the window displays of expensive shops, the designer and the distraught separated by a sheet of hardened glass. This being the tourist heart of the city, we were also bombarded with questions: 'Where you from, England?' 'You need hotel?' 'Good price for you!'

Following Libby's directions, we stuttered ever closer until we found ourselves beneath the Blue Mosque. Libby was nowhere to be seen, so Brummy phoned her.

'I'm by a restaurant,' she said.

'So am I!'

'They're playing music…'

'They're ALL playing music!'

'It's near the big mosque.'

'Libby, the whole city is full of restaurants and big mosques. Any chance of a street name?'

While Brummy ran off in search of Libby, we took the opportunity to relax, my pulse rate slowly returning to normal after our heart-racing entry into the city. Around us, most of the passing Western tourists did their best to ignore the Porsche with its British number plates, hiding any interest by giving it only slightly embarrassed sideways glances.

Brummy reappeared fairly quickly, chatting excitedly to a relieved Libby about our progress so far. Her engaging smile alluded that she was happy to see us and more than a little surprised to see the Porsche.

'I can't believe it's made it here!' she said.

'Neither can any of us,' replied Laura.

Predictably, Libby had already made friends with the guys who ran a nearby hostel and she directed us there from the Shogun's now cramped back seat.

En route we passed several impressive mosques. The sheer scale of these structures is quietly impressive and their improbably tall yet thin minarets appeal greatly to my engineering mind – Islam can always be counted on to provide great architectural spectacles in its cities!

Wearily, we parked outside the hostel. It had taken thirty hours of forced driving to get there from Slovenia. Still running on the last drops of adrenaline from the drive in, we headed to the rooftop terrace for some food and a cold beer to celebrate our arrival. The following day, we would cross the Bosphorous, which separates Europe from Asia. A few days earlier, I couldn't even contemplate the possibility of making it out of Britain. In high spirits, glasses were chinked and relieved laughter reigned. The group buzzed as stories were told of our mad dash across Europe, of the Porsche's ailments and the Shogun's apparent invincibility.

Libby had made the same journey as us in about four hours, safely cocooned in a Boeing; a demonstration of how technology has taken the adventure and romance out of travel. A second round of beers was ordered as the banter continued but I was flagging, wiped out by the cumulative efforts of the previous three weeks. Halfway through my drink I could last no longer. Heavy eyelids shut out the world as I drifted off into an unavoidable sleep, while the chatter continued all around.

FOUR

FAIRY TOWERS

9th October 2008
Istanbul, Turkey

We sat on the hostel's roof terrace, breakfasting as the sun floated lazily above the city. A good night's sleep had transformed us. Cleaned and rested, a semblance of humanity had returned, in sharp contrast to the worn out, grimy people who had arrived in Istanbul the previous evening. Everyone seemed to have acquired a spring to their step and looked much more positive than before.

That morning, we split up. Tom and the girls decided to sample the unique form of relaxation dealt out by a traditional Turkish bath. However for Brummy and I, getting to Turkey had been punishment enough and so we opted for a less physical morning, repacking the cars before wandering over to the appealingly named Grand Bazaar. We planned to all meet up again for a visit to the Blue Mosque that afternoon, before hitting the road again.

While loading the cars, Brummy and I got chatting to an Italian guy, aged in his fifties and complete with artful accent and stereotypical hand gestures. The Porsche triggered a particularly passionate outburst.

'The Germans. Good cars, good beer, bad women! Cars and beer, these are the only good things to come from these people!'

Our friend's prejudice stemmed from a previous marriage to a German woman, and it seemed he had owned a similar Porsche while living there.

'They're pretty good at invading Poland too,' Brummy added, in his usual politically correct manner.

Once we'd repacked the cars and had yet another round of coffees we went for a stroll. The day had warmed up pleasantly and was just what we needed after a typically washed out British summer. We wandered around the seventeenth century Sultan Ahmed Mosque, more commonly known as the Blue Mosque, taking it in from all sides. Its design was audacious, almost an exaggerated caricature of the more modest mosques I'd seen before. Of humbling size, it sat with an assured supremacy over its surroundings, as if confident of its righteous purpose. Exquisitely blended domes and marble walls cascaded down in tiers of increasing size, while rapier-like minarets thrust up theatrically from the corners of the structure, adding an air of unassailable power, which I suppose is exactly what the architect was aiming to achieve. The overall effect was one of impressive boldness, if not blueness.

We left the mosque and set off across the old town, soon passing the dramatic mass of the Hagia Sophia. Built as a Christian cathedral in the sixth century AD, the building had acquired minarets and defected to Islam in the fifteenth century and now serves as a museum. As museums go it is rather impressive, a domed behemoth of similar proportions to the Blue Mosque. However it somehow lacked the former's effortless subtlety of design, the result of having evolved over centuries, rather than springing from a clean sheet of paper. The compound structures and taunt stances of both buildings gave them the appearance of a pair of giant arachnids, frozen in time as they tower above the city.

Our stroll across town then took us from the antique to the modern. The thoroughfares of this most touristy of districts contained all the high street names visitors would expect to see back home and pushy salesmen prowled among the ambling herds, seeking out the easily persuaded.

Fifteen minutes of walking brought us to the bazaar. Unfortunately, it wasn't the intimate local bazaar we were hoping for, appearing more like a themed shopping centre on first acquaintance. Eager to relive our experiences in the markets of Central Asia and the souqs of Morocco, we were somewhat disappointed, especially given that the prices would doubtless be inflated into the stratosphere. Following a cursory exploration, we returned to daylight in search of cheap food, but quickly realised we were in the wrong place, the roadside menus revealing that cheapness was at a premium in this very popular part of town. We settled for a quiet place in a side street, steaks were ordered and we spent a pleasant twenty minutes people watching. As we did so, every part of the Western world drifted past our table, in a fairly equal split of families and couples.

At one stage an American family wandered noisily past, the eight-year-old daughter wearing a T-shirt sporting the slogan 'Don't mess with Texas', backed up by an American flag, which was cropped into the outline of the lone star state. As unsubtle statements to make in a country bordering Iran and Iraq go, this one took the biscuit! While we waited, I honoured a promise I'd made back in Plymouth by phoning the garage which had put the finishing touches to the Porsche less than a week earlier.

'Hello, Oakdens Garage.'

'Hi there, it's Ben here'

'Oh, hello Ben. Have you left yet?'

'You could say that. We're pretty much in Asia,' I replied, barely believing my own words. 'Greetings from Istanbul!'

'Right. So how's the engine?'

'Well there are a few issues, but it seems to be as good as can be expected. We're off to Syria tomorrow.'

'Okay, well take it easy. Don't do anything stupid...'

The food arrived and was as good as it was needed. The previous night's kebabs hadn't really done the trick and neither had breakfast. However a juicy steak couldn't fail to lift someone whose eating patterns had, for the previous few weeks, been erratic at best.

After lunch, we wandered back and met up with the rest of the team, who looked flushed but energised by their experiences in the Turkish baths. Reunited, we headed over to the Blue Mosque for a look around the fine building's blue-tiled interior. As we approached through well-kept, uncrowded grounds, the mosque looked as stunning as ever.

Avoiding the advances of a wannabe guide, we climbed the steps into the courtyard and followed the flow of other tourists around to the entrance, where we waited for prayers to end. Once the worshippers had left, the sightseers began to file in. A stream of casual Westerners entering this bastion of Islam felt quite incongruous. Before entering, we removed our shoes as a sign of respect, and I followed a Japanese couple – who were enthusiastically photographing everything in sight – into the building. Once inside, the mosque came alive. Mirroring the building's exterior, tiers of balconies and overhangs flooded down from the central dome, all finely painted in pastel hues. Softened light poured in through a multitude of stained-glass windows, lending a rich depth to the spectacle. The graceful structure became even more impressive when viewed from within.

After visiting the mosque, Laura and I headed to the bazaar to purchase some fabric. One of the last-minute jobs which had gone uncompleted was to make sun shades for the car windows to prevent the interior from heating up like an oven when parked. We would need some fabric to do this, and hence we ended up with vague directions to a 'factory', tucked away in some nondescript side street. Eventually we found our way into a basement where cloth was made. It was a small, whitewashed room, about four metres square, with a low roof and protruding wooden supports. A makeshift cutting table took up most of the room, leaving just enough free space for a couple of sewing machines, which were operated by a pair of women in headscarves. Randomly, the room also contained about twelve rather playful cats and kittens, which alternated their time between chasing and dozing.

'Aw, can we bring Brummy down here?' said Laura, laughing. 'He'd love it.'

'Love it? He'd have a heart attack more like.'

Brummy is most definitely not a cat person.

We looked at a few different fabrics before bartering down the price of some heavy black cloth. Many handshakes later, we headed back up into the sunlight and found Team Shogun, who were waiting for us in a café.

It was mid-afternoon when we finally got back on the road, following the Shogun to Asia. It had been nice to spend the day as tourists, carefree and without the pressures of the journey constantly on our mind; however, once we were back in the car, feeling its ailments as we fought our way through the heavy traffic, the day's relaxed nature was soon lost. And then bad turned to worse. Frustratingly, a missed sign saw us make a wrong turn and we were soon adrift in a succession of one-way systems and traffic jams, overheating and seemingly clueless as to our whereabouts. It took over an hour before bearings were regained and we finally found the road to Asia.

The city of Istanbul is unique in that it straddles two continents. Running through its centre is the Bosphorus, part of an improbable series of waterways which link the Mediterranean to the Black Sea. This barrier between continents was easily crossed by bridge, and soon we were cruising through the rolling hills of southeast Istanbul with anonymous, depressing high-rises gliding past our windows. The sun went down as we left the city behind, our briefest of visits having whetted our appetites for a more thorough exploration in the future.

Two hundred miles of monotonous tarmac separated Istanbul from Ankara. About the same distance again would take us on to the village of Goreme, the modern centre of the ancient Cappadocian Kingdom and the eventual goal of the evening's drive. I was feeling thoroughly unenthusiastic about being back on the road. After a sunny day of carefree sightseeing, the dark, uneasy confines of the Porsche, along with the forced proximity to Laura, left me feeling depressed. Laura could sense this and so we ambled along in silence, willing the drive to be over. I wondered how I would cope with the rest of the trip; whether this pained existence was to last for the next two months. Would I complete the adventure of a lifetime only to look back on it with a regretful unhappiness? At that early stage of the trip, I couldn't see any other option. Fortunately, the Porsche's mood didn't seem to have got any worse following the long, rough hours of abuse it endured entering and leaving Istanbul, which made me more optimistic about its chances of reaching Africa. Despite this, during the long hours of darkness, the bright glow of the oil warning light still played on my mind. We were hoping to enter Syria the following day. The trip was about to get a lot more serious.

After skirting around Ankara, we left the smooth dual carriageway behind and pushed south on more modest roads. Turkey became strangely empty, with truck stops and cafés seeming to outnumber towns by about three to one. Their gleaming neon signs, lit up cafeterias and promises of coffee were enticing; islands of warmth and light in a sea of darkness. The road ran dead straight for mile after mile, its monotony punctuated by lumbering trucks and overnight buses.

The unending plod went on for hours before we reached the sleeping town of Aksaray, where we turned left and completed the final sixty or so miles to the night's destination. In the early hours of the morning, we found a campsite and set up our tents, while admiring the view of the village below; its crazy rock features lit up by floodlights. A few quick photos, then sleep beckoned.

We were gradually becoming accustomed to our sleep-deprived existence and awoke early the following day. An otherworldly landscape surrounded us, seemingly lifted from a Tolkien-esque fantasy and deposited in our reality. From the elevated vantage point of our campsite, we looked out over a forest of improbable bone-white rock formations. Hundreds of huge pillars and conical extrusions thrust dramatically upwards in a manner seldom associated with the natural world. Broad of base, the famous fairy towers all tapered up to an unfeasible point, like a field of witch's hats. Elegant, rounded cliffs fenced these unruly formations into their valleys, as if to prevent their escape to the more inhibited world beyond.

Following a lazy, unhurried breakfast, we struck camp and wandered among the surreal towers. Close up, we could see that almost all of them had been hollowed out to form living spaces and most were still inhabited. Phone and power lines stretched from cave to cave, while often a satellite dish would perch uneasily next to a residence, beaming the twenty-first century into these ancient dwellings. As we strolled aimlessly, marvelling at the mini-mountains surrounding us, we got chatting to one of the region's troglodyte inhabitants. Hatice was a motherly woman in her forties, with a dark olive complexion and a quick smile. She puttered into our lives on a quirky little moped, which coughed and smoked away in a charmingly eccentric manner. After exchanging pleasantries, we were invited into her cave for tea. She gave off the impression that she was fairly well practiced at engaging tourists like this, but we didn't mind. Her relaxed friendliness was quite disarming.

Hatice inhabited a twenty metre high pillar of rock, hollowed out at some stage during the last two millennia – she didn't know exactly when. Her home was contained only on the ground level of the monolith; however windows and openings scattered liberally up its entire height hinted at a rather denser level of inhabitancy in the past. Ducking under the low doorway, we entered the cave. Inside, it was noticeably cooler and quieter than the outside world. It was also not remotely what we expected a cave dwelling to look like, being a perfectly square room with wood-panelled walls and a fine Turkish rug on the floor. Electric lighting shone down from the low roof, sofas lined the walls and a television nestled in the corner. A picture of Mecca hung proudly on the wall. The only giveaway that we were in a cave was the chiselled, whitewashed ceiling, and the sense of deep isolation from the outside world.

'The Flintstones never had it this good,' joked Tom.

We chatted with Hatice over several rather good cups of apple tea. She used to work as a rug maker and would spend months crafting a single exquisite rug, all by hand. Now, her income came from tourism. She gave us a tour of the rest of her cave, which fitted in with our preconceptions of cave life better than the finely finished room in which we had taken tea. There were two more rooms, one a combination of bedroom and sitting room, the other a kitchen. Both had walls of chipped, whitewashed rock and electric lighting. Rugs hung decoratively on the walls, as did a shotgun – which presumably was not for decoration. The characterful kitchen contained a gas cooker and electric kettle, but was still satisfyingly minimalist in its appearance.

Over another cup of tea, we reached the point of our visit to Hatice's world. In an unpressured manner, various crafts apparently made by her family were offered for sale; tablecloths, rugs, dolls and headscarves. We all spent a little money on gifts for people back home before saying our goodbyes. We were rather touched by the warm welcome she had shown us, whatever profiteering motives lay behind it.

We left Goreme after lunch. As we climbed out of the valley, the Shogun belched thick black smoke from its exhaust. It had been doing this ever since we left the UK, the smokescreen gradually getting thicker as more miles were completed. We stopped and checked the air filter for clogging and looked for any other obvious signs of the cause, but found nothing. The general consensus was that it was being caused by a clogged particulate filter in the exhaust, a common issue with diesels and nothing to worry about, so we carried on towards that evening's goal, the Syrian border. Laura and I were quietly relieved that for once, it wasn't our car causing concern.

Southern Turkey offered smooth tarmac and spacious landscapes. Arid, wide-open plains stretched towards the horizon, where they rippled into gentle hills. The scenery had a grandiose drama about it which evoked images of battles and migrations. So often the meeting point between two contrasting cultures, it appeared to offer the perfect canvas on which 'civilisations' could settle their differences. We felt small as we drifted across it.

Tom had been rather reluctant to leave Goreme, having wanted to stay for another night in a hotel, to get cleaned up and recover properly from the gruelling drive across Europe. As time was still of the essence, this wasn't really an option and figuring a change was as good as a break, I suggested he join me in the Porsche for a bit. Unsurprisingly, Laura jumped at the chance of some time away from me and so off she went to catch up with the folk in the Shogun.

We chatted away as the sweeping landscape scrolled past us. Much like myself, Tom had been finding it difficult to relax and every noise and vibration the Shogun made seemed to play on his mind. He also spoke of a tense atmosphere in the Shogun, as his naturally cautious nature found itself at odds with Brummy's more carefree optimism. I imagined that Laura would be having a similar moan about the tension she had to endure in the Porsche's cramped cabin. However it was natural that relationships would be slightly strained. In a little over six days we had taken our steeds two and a half thousand miles across Europe and into the Middle East. Sleep had been limited and inadequate, while external pressures were continuous. Tom seemed to be feeling the strain more than the rest of Team Shogun and I hoped the day's change of company would help.

Equally, it was the first reasonable length of time in nearly a week that Laura and I had spent apart. Our friendship was still rocky and cold, alternating between businesslike tolerance and depressed anger, usually brought on by tiredness. Getting this far had been emotionally tough and physically gruelling, and we weren't even in Africa yet. I hoped for a mellowing between us, but I really couldn't imagine how it might happen. The bridges back seemed to have been burnt long ago.

The longer Laura and I spent together, tensely hoping the Porsche would go the distance, the more entrenched our differences seemed to become. I knew my animosity had gone way beyond what was justified. The stress and proximity had caused my negative feelings to be multiplied irrationally, but I couldn't bring myself to accept why. *Why can't I just move on, forget what happened months ago and rebuild our friendship?* I think deep down I knew, but couldn't admit it to myself. Every time she mentioned her boyfriend, it killed conversation stone dead. However my real feelings remained smothered by a layer of dull anger, which made it easy to ignore the obvious conclusion that could be drawn when our conversations ended prematurely.

On a straight section of road, I pulled alongside the Shogun to alleviate some of the boredom that invariably builds when following it for hour after hour. Louise peered down from the back window, her smooth, rounded face animating into a reassuring smile as our eyes met. She waved happily, looking at ease with the world, as if whatever the trip threw at her, a deep inner strength would see her through. I felt like my reserves of inner strength had already been exhausted and all that remained was a vague resignation to events around me. I'd only met Louise the day before we left, but she had already proved to be a caring person and had done all she could to try to cheer me up during the difficult times of the previous week.

In the Shogun's front passenger seat, Libby was sound asleep, while Brummy sat bolt upright next to her in his usual, distinctive driving position. Clean-shaven as always, with his fringe gelled down attentively, he looked more like someone heading to the supermarket than to Africa.

After crossing featureless plains for hours, the flatlands ended as the eastern fringes of the Tarus Mountains rose up in the distance. Initially hills, their smoothness crumpled into craggy peaks as they ambled higher. The road began to climb and the Shogun smoked away in protest. Soon, we were negotiating a rift between two peaks, a high pass from the plains of Turkey to the desert expanses of Syria, Jordan and Iraq which lay beyond.

Once over the high pass we coasted downhill, on the lookout for a place to stop for dinner. As we did, all the struggling lorries we'd passed on the way up overtook us suicidally, egged on by gravity and machismo. Somewhat frightened by this exercise in Russian roulette, we pulled into an anonymous-looking café. The owner, a relaxed young guy decked out in a shirt and tie, beckoned us round to the back of the building. The lush ground dropped away sharply as we filed down steps into an idyllic garden, bursting with fruit and greenery. A river burbled away at the bottom of the garden where the enterprising owner had set up a small fish farm among the leafy groves. Excitedly, he showed us his fresh trout, chatting to us in friendly, broken English. He reserved his friendliest patter for Libby however, whose trademark flirtatiousness is evidently none too common in this part of the world.

We sat down and enjoyed a beautiful meal, made all the better by the friendly banter which flowed between us and the owners of this most appealing of roadside cafés. The barriers between proprietor and customer quickly evaporated and a mutual friendship seemed to develop, with the offer of free board if we chose to stay the night.

Libby shed some light on the offer when she took me aside as we were walking back to the cars.

'I think we should leave now,' she said dramatically.

'Oh Libby, what have you done now?'

'Well, you know how they invited us to stay the night?'

'Yeah.'

'Well the full version the guy said to me was, 'you can all sleep here for free. You can sleep with me.''

'Well done Libby,' I said. 'Didn't he say he had a wife and kid?'

'Yeah, I don't think they're really on his mind right now.'

Ten minutes later, our laboured excuses for not being able to stay were accepted and we escaped the slightly sleazy company, descending a good mountain road towards the Mediterranean. Laura had rejoined me in the Porsche and we took it in turns to sleep our way towards Syria.

It was about ten in the evening when we reached the border, which we were pleased to find was still open. Devoid of traffic at such a late hour, we passed easily out of Turkey and soon the Porsche was chugging roughly away as it crossed the two hundred metres of no-man's-land to the Syrian border post. We parked outside the first building we came to, a nondescript concrete affair labelled 'Customs and Immigration'. Inside was a long, narrow hall, containing a different counter for each service which might be needed. Partitions divided the counters from one another and the occupants sat alone in their separate cubicles, looking generally disinterested. The hall was coldly lit and had an unwelcoming, anodyne feel to it. Passports were stamped first, our Syrian visas which had been acquired in London being accepted without question. Next, Brummy and I sorted out the car paperwork. Insurance and road tax for the Porsche came to around sixty-five US dollars, while Team Shogun were hit with an additional cost – a nonsensical 'diesel tax' which cost an another hundred dollars and led to a fair bit of mocking from the generally embattled Team Porsche. Taxes paid, our final formality before being let loose into Syria was to get the vehicle's 'Carnet de Passages en Douane' stamped. These documents, which had cost us so much back in the UK, provide a guarantee that if a car enters a country but doesn't leave it, customs duty will be paid on the vehicle. We had never used such documents before and so were relieved when the person in charge of customs, a slightly intimidating army officer with a fine handlebar moustache, talked us through the process in good English.

Soon enough, everything was completed and we headed out of the border post, through one last army checkpoint, and onto Syrian soil. It was midnight. It was also exactly one week to the day since I had exhaustedly guided the Porsche out of the garage in Plymouth, its untried engine tormenting me with failure.

FIVE

THE ARABIAN PORSCHE

11th October 2008
Near Aleppo, Northern Syria

Syria. We were in Syria. To most Westerners, the name conjures up some uneasy images. George Bush had somewhat sanctimoniously accused the nation of being a state sponsor of terrorism. Aspirations to weapons of mass destruction have been rumoured. The USA labelled Syria an 'axis of evil' state six years before our visit, wars and territorial disputes with Israel generally account for an unfortunately high percentage of headlines involving the country, while the implied dislike of the West is taken as gospel by most folk back home. And there we were, attempting to cross the country in a sickly British-registered sports car? At times, the surreal nature of our journey was all too clear.

We drove about a hundred metres beyond the border post, looked at the map, and decided to head for Aleppo to find beds for the night. However, the lack of signs meant we soon found ourselves on completely the wrong road, heading south towards Damascus. The northwest corner of Syria seemed very populated, flooded with lots of small towns which had swollen and sprawled into one another. It was late on Friday night and the streets were still busy, with plenty of people standing around, or walking in the warm darkness. We passed a few small discos, with loud Arabic pop music blasting out and disinterested teenagers hanging around out the front, amid a smattering of small motorbikes. They were reassuring. Maybe Syria wasn't as depressing as its image in the West suggests?
We soon stopped for fuel.

'Visa?' I said to the gap-toothed attendant.

He scowled at me blankly, as if I were some unwelcome apparition.

'Dollar?'

The scowl transformed into a grin and following some bartering on a pocket calculator, I was on my way with half a tank of the cheapest petrol I'd ever bought.

Having given up on finding a hotel, we kept looking for a place to park up and sleep, but were continuously frustrated by just how populated everywhere was. A quiet, secluded spot in which to spend the night just wasn't forthcoming and the endless requests for 'money money money' whenever we stopped did little to put us at ease. Plodding on south along the main road which runs the length of Syria, we eventually pulled over into a service station where we closed our eyes for a few hours before the sun rose. It was a nervous and uncomfortable night, wedged vulnerably in the Porsche as shifty-looking folk milled around us on the forecourt. With no other option we dozed fitfully, waiting for daylight to come. At seven o'clock, as the sun sat lazily on the horizon, a muezzin – the call to prayer from a nearby mosque – woke us, and we saw our surroundings for the first time. Syria looked dirty and unfinished. Sand blew around on the area of wasteland next to us, while noisy, smoking trucks growled disdainfully along the road. A few windowless breezeblock buildings rose from the dust nearby. There are certainly more welcoming places in which to awake.

'Welcome to paradise,' I said to Laura as she returned to consciousness.

Driving onward as the day warmed up, we added to our first impressions of Syria. Previously hidden from us by the darkness, the sudden increase in squalor was now clear to see. Banks of festering, stinking rubbish intermittently lined the road and reminded me of the poorer parts of India. Many buildings appeared to have never been finished and were gradually deteriorating in their incomplete state. The people we passed were generally unsmiling and morose. The few women we saw were covered from head to toe in heavy, dark wool burqas, with only a narrow slit for their eyes providing a connection to the outside world. We couldn't begin to imagine how they survived in such garb, roasting under the Middle Eastern sun.

Soon, our tiredness metamorphosed into a pressing need for coffee, so we detoured off the main road in search of a café. We found ourselves in a dilapidated neighbourhood, blown sand obscuring the road, while rocks and rubbish cluttered its unfinished edges. The buildings looked unloved, while ugly power and phone lines formed an oppressive web above us, shutting us in. Adults eyed us suspiciously, while the less inhibited children pointed and shouted. We felt unwelcome and untrusted. Sat behind the Shogun as it threw up clouds of dust, the view through the Porsche's windscreen bore an uneasy similarity to the ongoing footage from Iraq. I could understand why we weren't trusted. Soon, we turned around and returned to the main road, before the heavy tension in the air became more than just a feeling.

Syria is a fairly small country and we reached the town of Hims quickly, where a turn-off was to take us out into the desert, towards the ancient ruins of Palmyra. The lack of signs made navigating the unmemorable city an interesting experience but fortunately Brummy showed great enthusiasm in getting directions from the bored traffic police who lingered at every junction. They were unfailingly helpful, probably being surprised at actually having something useful to do for once. Leaving town, we found we were following signs to Iraq, a hundred and fifty miles distant. The enormity and absurdity of what we were slowly achieving was sinking in.

Once we were off the main road to Damascus, the grotty ribbon developments which had been lining our route were replaced with cotton plantations. The piles of rubbish vanished and the tarmac improved, while the heavy traffic thinned out, leaving us sharing the road with occasional army trucks, and soldiers zooming around on motorbikes.

Continuing inland, our surroundings dried up to form a proper sandy desert, the first of the trip. The Porsche celebrated by jamming its heater on the hottest setting and we were forced to open the windows wide to prevent us cooking. Arriving at a junction, we left behind the signs directing us to Iraq and instead followed those for Palmyra, still a hundred miles away. The dusty folk who inhabited the junction's café shouted angrily at Libby for photographing the Iraq signs in too obvious a manner. We didn't really blame them and, as one of them was brandishing a rather impressive, hungry-looking bird of prey, we chose not to argue. Extricating ourselves from the situation, we carried on through the dunes. Laura drove and I was happy to be chauffeured and to finally be visiting Palmyra. The ancient remnants of the Silk Road caravan town towards which we were driving had fascinated me since I'd first read about them while researching the trip. At its zenith in the first and second centuries AD, Palmyra exists today as an extensive sweep of ruins, whose great lines of columns and swathes of fine sandstone leave little doubt as to its former wealth and glory. It promised to be a cultural highlight of the journey.

Near our destination, we encountered our first camels, wandering in the desert. We stopped to take some photos of the proud beasts, enjoying the exoticness their presence implied.

'God, they're aloof looking things,' I said.

'Don't get too close, they spit,' replied Louise.

'If one of them tries that with me, I'll spit back,' Brummy said.

'Yeah, good luck with that,' Tom added sceptically.

As we continued east, the terrain gradually became more precipitous and soon began to sprout blunt rocky outcrops a little way back from the road. We drifted up among them and crossed a rise, which was guarded by the remnants of an ancient fort.   And then, stretched out below us, was Palmyra; a vast forest of ancient ruins floundering in the drifting sands. Great lines of noble columns stretched away into the distance, casting their shadows upon the parched ground, while vast swathes of blockwork lay chaotically in the dust where buildings had once stood. It looked like for centuries, the desert had slowly been flooding the city, returning the area to its natural state. The extent of the ruins was impressive, that such a large and wealthy city would be left to disappear beneath the sand hard to believe. Nothing is permanent.   Beside the ruins sat the orderly though instantly uninspiring new town of Palmyra.

The road dropped down between the two ages and at the first opportunity we turned away from the new town and headed along the cobbled road leading into the ruins. Ironically, our first impressions were of cleanliness. Compared to every other part of Syria where man has left his mark, the weathered remains of the old city were clean and dignified, the clutter and rubbish we'd seen in every other settlement pleasing in its absence. However, the ruins were not devoid of people. The instant the Shogun's doors swung open, its occupants were mobbed by an aggressive gaggle of opportunists hoping to profit from them in some way. On seeing this, our enthusiasm to leave the sanctity of the Porsche and explore the site took a sudden dive. The desperate way in which locals were hustling camel rides, tours, accommodation and souvenirs was saddening and at odds with the proud decorum traditionally associated with Arabs. In a shouted conversation with Team Shogun, we decided to leave exploring the ruins until later, so headed back into town for lunch instead. This was no problem for the Shogun; however some of the more industrious camel-mounted locals sprung a trap on Laura and I, teaming up to block the Porsche in and prevent us from leaving. Laura, still coming to terms with manoeuvring the car in tight spaces and unable to see out of the back window, was terrified of hitting one of the offending camels. It took several minutes – and a not inconsiderable amount of shouting at the locals – before we escaped their somewhat optimistic blockade and made it back into town. As memorable as having your Porsche parked in by camels is, it was not the arrival to this stunning historical site we had hoped for.

Evidently making an effort to appeal to tourists, the new town of Palmyra was relatively spacious and tidy. Some of the avenues and streets even had a cosmetic lining of trees. We parked in front of the first restaurant we saw, which had views back over the ruins. The place looked nice enough, and was obviously pitched directly at the tourist clientele. However unfortunately, it seemed to have been spoilt by its prime location, as the service was inconsistent and rather rude, the menu optimistic in its scope, the food average and the prices evidently flexible, creeping up when we attempted to settle the bill. We left and returned to the ruins, trying to sneak in as inconspicuously as possible to avoid being mobbed like before.

Our second attempt went much better and we made it out of our vehicles while being subjected to only a modest assault of hawking, as fortunately for us, a group of Japanese tourists presented a much more appealing target. We were not left completely to our own devices however and Brummy soon disappeared with someone claiming to own a campsite, predictably offered at 'good price for you'. Meanwhile, I got chatting to one of the camel drivers, who was evidently rather taken by the Porsche, enjoying its unusual styling from all angles and marvelling at its engine.

'In Syria, this car is eight thousand dollars for sure. Me, I give you ten thousand dollars for it, I don't care.'

I eyed him curiously, trying to assess his seriousness.

'How much for your camel? Maybe we can swap?'

'Three thousand dollars for a good camel. But I need them for my work.'

I wasn't sure if he had been making an offer or not, but felt pretty sure he didn't have the money in any case. If he was serious, I would have been rather tempted. I still had no confidence that the Porsche would get anywhere near Cape Town, and my actions in continuing were those of someone who had no choice. I still expected the car to fail at any moment, but had no option other than to push on regardless. It was reassuring to hear that the Porsche was still worth more than a camel however.

I also got chatting to a South African, a pilot who was in town chauffeuring the Qatari royal family on a day trip to watch the camel races taking place in Palmyra that afternoon. He shook his head as we described our plans, considering us a doomed mixture of bravery and foolhardiness. His description of most of Africa was particularly encouraging; a dismissive utterance of 'Shithole', in a broad Afrikaans drawl.

Brummy soon returned in the Shogun.

'Come on, I've found us a campsite on the other side of the ruins.'

We crawled along a dusty, potholed track lined with palm trees and blocky, ancient ruins. The campsite entrance was a steep drop-off on rough gravel, but the Porsche took its first real taste of off-roading in its stride and soon we were parked up in a pleasant wooded grove beneath a ruined first century citadel. For the first time since our arrival in Palmyra, silence surrounded us and we were left unharassed.

We had managed to reach our day's destination long before darkness, an unprecedented occurrence on the trip so far. Being able to relax for an afternoon was a refreshing novelty and so I did what I'd been looking forward to throughout the previous week. I took a beer from the Porsche's fridge and relaxed in the warm afternoon sun, enjoying my exotic surroundings. I had been dreaming of being able to do so ever since I envisaged the trip; pulling up in some remote desert, setting up camp and relaxing with a drink. Now, the dream was finally a reality. We weren't too far off the beaten track however and the girls took full advantage of the fact by whiling away the afternoon in the swimming pool, under the rather creepy gaze of the campsite owner.

I was happy to just sit alone, quietly sipping my lukewarm beer. It was nice to let my thoughts settle, but before long I felt guilty for my laziness and decided to spend my time more usefully by finishing the Porsche's roof platform, on which I planned to pitch our tent. I had been unable to complete the job in England as some sections of the structure could only be cut to the correct length once the whole eccentric assembly was attached to the roof of the car, and in the hours before our departure, there had been rather more pressing issues to overcome. Aided fairly ineffectually by the camel driver I'd been chatting to previously, I spent an hour or so sawing and cutting the final pieces of wood to shape. The camel driver appeared never to have seen a drill bit before and was fascinated to see how it penetrated the wood.

'How many camels for my co-driver?' I said as I worked.

'She is your wife?'

'No, it's a long story. Give me four camels and she's yours,' I joked.

'She is worth many more than four camels,' he said.

At dusk, I pulled myself away from my nearly-completed task and we all headed over to view the ruins in the evening light, where Libby took no encouragement to jump on the back of a stranger's camel and disappear off with her newfound acquaintance in a cloud of dust.

'She'll be pregnant next time we see her,' joked Brummy.

'If we ever see her again,' said Laura.

'She'll be fine.'

'She shouldn't just disappear off with strangers like that,' said Laura. 'And I wish she'd cover up more too. She's drawing attention like it's going out of fashion.'

'Libby drawing attention to herself? How unusual,' Tom said.

Laura's concerns came from her experiences of Syrian men so far. Despite the way she and Louise had been making an effort to honour local customs by keeping covered up, wearing long sleeves, skirts and headscarves, they had still felt a lot of hostility from the local population. Earlier, a man had spat at them in a petrol station and other men – we encountered almost no Syrian women – would hiss at them rather intimidatingly as they passed, seemingly for the simple reason that they were female and Western.

Louise and Laura both took issue with the general hostility, sometimes snapping back at their accosters. Louise in particular, who had lived in Arabic countries before, fearlessly chastised anyone who even came close to insulting her.

'You can't just let them do that,' she said feistily. 'I don't care what their culture or religion is, it's just wrong. No human being should spit at another person. Don't let them get away with it.'

As Libby vanished over the horizon on the camel, the rest of us walked among the ruins as the fading light brought them to life. They looked even more evocative of their past glory at dusk and it was obvious that in its prime, the city must have been spectacular. Epic lines of columns rose from the sand in grids, towering over the chaos of fallen blockwork. We milled about quietly in the spectacular atmosphere, trying to cast our minds back through the millennia and bring the great city back to life. After the sunset, some of the more notable ruins were lit up with floodlights and looked even more dramatic.

Eventually, Libby reappeared safely and we wandered back to camp through the still-warm night. Beers were opened by all and preparations for the evening meal commenced.

While the pasta bubbled away, I donned my head torch and finished the roof tent platform, before balancing my old mountaineering tent triumphantly on top of the car. Getting in and out proved tricky, as the entrance was directly above the car's fragile windscreen, but we quickly learnt how to complete the manoeuvre efficiently, if not elegantly

Soon the evening meal was ready and our collection of empty beer bottles was growing steadily. Everyone was in high spirits and the light-hearted mockery that always seemed to flow freely among the group at such times was reassuringly present, with much discussion about whether Laura and I would reach our untimely end in a collapsing roof tent during the night. Libby was mocked for running off with a bloke on a camel and Team Shogun were mocked for driving a butch, unadventurous 4x4, when evidently a tiny Porsche would suffice.

Eventually, there was no more beer left to fuel our revelry and we retired to our tents. For Laura and I, this was a nerve-wracking experience. Perched on the untried, slightly flexing platform on the roof of the car, we were loath to commit our weight at first, for fear of triggering its demise. Fortunately for us, the engineering proved to be sound; however that first night was a nervous one of avoiding sudden movements and willing it not to let us down.

Next morning Laura and I had planned to rise before sunrise; Laura to join Libby for a camel ride and myself for a spot of photography in the rich dawn light. Laura achieved her goal, but I was still prohibitively tired from the previous weeks and savoured my first guilt-free lie in for a month. It was blissful. I finally arose at ten, when the sun began to warm the tent uncomfortably. My first task of the day was to dismantle the roof tent platform, a job which fortunately turned out to be reasonably quick and simple. Once the tent was removed, the three-piece plywood platform concertinaed back to form the lid of the roof box, while the supports folded out of the way at the back of the box. Libby and Laura returned from their camel rides as we were finishing packing up and so, following another walk around the ruins, we were soon back on the road, hoping to reach Jordan that day.

Out in the desert, the roads were impeccable and smooth tarmac took us rapidly west towards Damascus. It was a perfect morning and Syria's rich elite were out in force, indulging their hobbies. Evidently, the hobby of choice for the fortunate few involved cruising along the desert highways in brand new, expensive 4x4s. We passed many convoys of such vehicles, generally eight or ten strong. The confident curves of the Toyota, Lexus, Audi and Range Rover SUVs flashed by in a display of ostentatious wealth which seemed wilfully inappropriate to us, given our experiences of Syria so far. The predictably male occupants generally appeared very well fed and wore Western-style clothing.

'They must be either terrorists, arms dealers or oil barons,' speculated Laura.

'Or politicians,' I said.

Whoever they were, they were completely unrepresentative of this country, which only the previous day had felt like it was struggling to survive.

Refreshed by sleep, Laura and I continued to chat as we drove. The further Palmyra receded into our rear-view mirrors, the happier Laura seemed to get.

'Thank goodness we're back on the road,' she said. 'I really wasn't comfortable there.'

'Why? All the desperate attempts to get money out of us?'

'Well there was that, yes. But it was more because of the campsite owner. He was so creepy and I felt really nervous around him. You know he just sat there staring at us when we went for a swim in the pool?'

'That must have been off-putting.'

'Yeah, and then he wouldn't go away when we wanted to leave the pool.'

'Didn't you go on a camel ride with this guy this morning?'

'Yes. Yes I did,' she replied coldly. 'And Libby knew I was scared, but disappeared off and left me alone with him anyway.'

'Ah good old Libby; never one to let anything get in the way of being alone with a bloke.'

'Well, a bloke and a camel in this instance,' laughed Laura.

After a cold drink at the stirringly named 'Baghdad Café', we continued towards Damascus, and the Jordanian border which lay beyond. We nearly ran out of fuel in the desert, but were pleased to make it to a junction where a stern-faced guy sporting distinctly Iraqi features filled the Porsche with cheap petrol. Once again in Syria, we felt unwelcome.

Nowhere is particularly far away in this small country and soon the clean, unpopulated wilderness morphed into the outskirts of Damascus, with all the negatives which that entailed. The road surface deteriorated and signs of first agriculture, then habitation reappeared. Litter also made an unwelcome return. Damascus claims to be the oldest city in the world, but judged purely on its outskirts, the rest of the world left it behind a long time ago. Like so much of Syria, everything felt unfinished and in a state of decay.

As afternoon turned into evening, we became lost in the maelstrom of heavy, dirty traffic. Weather-beaten old taxis and buses, homemade rickshaws and the occasional aggressive lorry thrust around us. Signs were conspicuous by their absence and the directions given by the many bored traffic police seemed to be permanently conflicting. Following the Shogun, our confidence in their navigation soon dried up and we were left feeling like a hamster on a wheel, frantically going nowhere. We lost two hours in Damascus that evening. After a frustratingly thorough tour of the city centre, we found ourselves heading back towards the north, the sun setting to our left. Following twenty minutes of futilely flashing my headlights, I stopped. Team Shogun got the hint and pulled over.

'The sunset is on our left. That means we've been heading north for the last twenty minutes,' I said.

'I know,' replied Tom.

'Well shall we head south? Jordan is south.'

'I was going to turn around.'

'Good. Let's do it.'

I often wished we could lead the convoy in cities, but the sluggish Shogun, with its less decisive drivers, would struggle to hold station behind us in heavy traffic, so in spite of the frustration which sometimes resulted, Shogun first was the best way to negotiate cities. In such situations, the most important thing was that the two cars didn't become separated and our tactics at least worked in that respect.

Nearing the Jordanian border, Libby took the opportunity to ride in the Porsche, and Laura needed no persuasion to jump in the Shogun. As we chatted away, Libby offered her opinion on the relative merits of the Porsche.

'It's bliss! It's way more comfortable, the music's better and it's just a much cooler way to travel.'

More worryingly, she also alluded that it was nice to be away from the long silences and tense atmosphere which sometimes existed in the Shogun, particularly when navigating through cities. This surprised me, as I'd assumed that most of the time, Team Shogun passed their days in a carefree manner, while Laura and I stewed in the Porsche, nervous about the car and cold towards each other. It was strange to think about how separate the two teams' experiences of the journey were, separated away in our little capsules. The world rolling past the windows was a constant for both vehicles, but the conversations it triggered and the worries and experiences which stemmed from it were very different.

Acutely aware of the deadline imposed by the ferry we were due to catch in southern Egypt – now only a week hence – we decided to get across the border and make some progress into Jordan that night. Darkness softened the harsh images of Syria's dirtiness and squalor, but our headlights still picked out enough unpleasantness to make us want to speed our departure as much as possible. Fortunately the miles passed effortlessly, the remaining cities didn't present too much of an obstacle and we arrived at the border at about half past nine. Departing Syria was straightforward, our passports stamped quickly under the superior gaze of no fewer than six portraits of Bashar Al-Assad, the country's president. Sometimes wearing military garb, at other times a businesslike suit, he stared down on his subjects with a slightly concerned look on his face. We were familiar with his appearance from the previous days, the dictator's solemn portrait having observed our journey through his country almost continuously, from billboards, houses, shops and even the rear windows of taxis.

With a sigh of relief, we were quickly stamped out of Syria. After crossing no-man's-land, we joined the back of a long queue where Jordanian customs officials were emptying and searching every car. Our hearts sank as we contemplated having to unpack our vehicles, but were lifted when we were directed over to a more exclusive lane, with a shorter queue. In the rarefied company of a Jeep and a Mercedes, we were through in about ten minutes. Once clear of customs, we parked and got stuck into the usual paperwork

First impressions were that Jordan was much more modern than Syria, with the border seeming like a well lit shopping mall in comparison to Syria's austere affair. We were able to get money from an ATM, buy fast food and take in the bustle and a sense of prosperity that was unheard of a few hundred metres previously. Soon insurance was bought, taxes paid and the cars imported, all in clean, well-lit offices whose professional décors seemed to be the ultimate in artistic flair after the starkness of the previous few days. Visas were purchased from the unenthusiastic clerks, passports were stamped and we were officially in Jordan. Firing up the cars – the Porsche sounding as sick as ever – we pottered over to the last checkpoint. Up went the barrier and we hit the road into Jordan proper.

The roads improved immediately and signs made a welcome return. Laura was asleep next to me as I cruised along, following Brummy towards Amman and I knew the Shogun's passengers would be sleeping too. I liked it when Brummy and I drove into the night like this. We had done so many times before, on the Mongol Rally, in Arctic Norway, around Europe and on the Indian Subcontinent. It was a regular occurrence in my life, cruising through darkness, alone with my thoughts while Brummy does the same nearby. I've always found it to be a reassuring constant.

Predictably, the signs dried up as we penetrated Amman, so we stopped at a petrol station to ask directions. The friendly folk were happy to chat and joke with us and drew us a map which we tried to follow, but promptly became even more lost. Remembering the satellite navigation gizmos that we'd brought on a trip for the first time, we turned them on and were able to find the road west to the Dead Sea with the help of their base maps.

We'd never used Global Positioning Systems before, preferring to navigate off old-fashioned maps. They proved their worth on this trip however and Brummy and I took back all the criticism we'd previously directed at them.

It was gone one in the morning but our destination was near. Leaving Amman, the road swept left and right as it dropped down towards the Dead Sea, the lowest dry-land point on the Earth's surface. Just before we hit Israel, we turned left and skirted along the shoreline, glimpsing the lake shimmering away beneath the full moon for the first time.

Given our proximity to the Israeli-occupied West Bank, we were not surprised when we encountered an army checkpoint. These checkpoints can often be a source of frustration on trips such as ours, staffed by bored soldiers who enjoy exercising their power. We approached nervously, sure our intentions to park up and camp by the Dead Sea wouldn't sit well with them. We were surprised, however, when the soldier in charge set our minds at ease.

'I am the commander of this checkpoint, and you are welcome to camp here,' he said, gesturing authoritatively towards a gravel area which bordered the sea. 'If you have any problems come and see me and I will do all I can.'

It was a nice contrast to our expectations and following handshakes and thanks we drove down and parked about a hundred metres from the lake, Team Shogun pitching their tents on the rough gravel floor, while Laura and I smugly erected our luxurious rooftop home. As our eyes adjusted to the darkness, the view of the Dead Sea became ever more impressive. Everything was a murky blue, lit by the full moon and a sky full of stars. On the lake's far shore, a few Israeli resorts glowed, their lights casting shimmering reflections on the water. We shared the beers I'd found in the back of the Porsche earlier that day and I took a few photos, while dwelling on the fact that we'd just driven to the lowest point on the planet's surface. We were over four hundred metres below sea level.

Six hours later, the sun gradually woke us, heating up our tents until we could lie there no more. We took in our first views of Jordan by daylight. The scenery around us was still impressive, though the dusty, broken landscape was washed out by the glare of direct sunlight in contrast to the unexpectedly subtle moonlit vista which had greeted us on our arrival. The world around us was painted from a limited palette, stocked only with tan and a few shades of blue. There were few signs of life, the lake's inhospitable salinity being illustrated by the beautiful sweeping waterlines of salt which lined on its shores.

Over breakfast we discussed the day's route. Our destination was Petra, about a hundred miles away. It could be reached fairly directly by taking the reasonable roads which traversed the Jordanian Highlands, or alternatively by a looping detour back the way we had come, up to the capital then down the main road south through the desert. The more interesting and direct route through the mountains was generally favoured, though Tom wanted to reduce the wear and tear on the Shogun by taking the easier route around the mountains. I had awoken in a bad mood and hence my reply to his reasoning was unfortunately terse.

'Well if you don't think it'll get over the little mountains here, how on earth do you think it'll get across Africa?'

The discussion was over. We would head through the mountains.

We packed away efficiently and made our departure. Childishly, I couldn't resist pulling a dramatic over-steering powerslide across the gravel as we left, and instantly felt rather silly. Overlooking us sat a desert-camouflaged Humvee 4x4, its machine gun pointing at the West Bank, its soldiers lazing in the morning sun. Evidently this wasn't really the place for such frivolous antics.

We were soon driving parallel to the Dead Sea, the road clinging to a broken slope which swept down to the waters below. After about ten miles of open, twisting tarmac, we were able to pull off the road for a swim and everyone except me headed down to the water's edge. My mood hadn't improved and I chose to stay with the cars, hoping a few minutes alone would improve my state of mind. I did a few odd jobs on the Porsche and listened to the others laughing and joking amid the improbable buoyancy of the lake. Soon their return signalled it was time to continue and so we proceeded along one of the lowest roads on the planet, while Laura excitedly recounted the strange sensation of eating breakfast while floating high in the saline water.

The Dead Sea is long – forty-two miles long in fact – but soon we were leaving its shoreline as the road took us into the desert. In a small, nondescript village, we turned left and headed towards the Jordanian Highlands. As we did so, we met two large motorcycles, each with two occupants apparently undertaking a journey similar to ours. The road swept dramatically up into the mountains and I gamely kept up with the bikes, whose number plates indicated their journey had begun in Poland.

On a straight bit of road, I pulled alongside one of the bikes, opened the window and greeted them in my finest English accent.

'Tally ho chaps!'

They smiled and waved back and together we swept up the mountain roads, around sweeping curves and hairpin bends, enjoying the freedom of the open road. The Shogun fell behind, but that wasn't a problem. There was no chance of getting lost and we would wait for them at the town of Al Karak, a few miles further on. It was so nice to be able to drive the Porsche as nature intended and let it sing its sports car heart out after thousands of miles in convoy with the plodding Shogun.

Soon, the bikers stopped for a rest and we continued alone, reducing our pace but still enjoying the freedom. The view back towards the Dead Sea was most impressive, the ground plummeting down from the plateau on which we found ourselves, into a rift which ran all the way from the Dead Sea to the Bay of Aquaba. Around us, talusy hills enlivened our progress and the road twisted sinuously along their contours. We were generally alone, save the occasional village or nomad's tent. After a while, Al Karak came into view, so we parked up to await the Shogun. Cliffs rose above us, topped by the snaking fortifications of a twelfth century Crusaders castle.

My spirits had been lifted by the exhilarating drive and Laura and I smiled and joked as we waited for the Shogun, the animosity between us lifting unexpectedly for the first time in the trip. Our wait wasn't a long one and the smile on Brummy's face suggested he'd enjoyed the challenging road just as much as I had. Tom's frown implied the opposite, however. I guessed that he wasn't particularly happy about how the Shogun had been rushed up the mountain and was also cross with me for leaving them behind.

Once again, the question of our route raised its head. We had two choices. We could either carry on east out of the mountains and then take the main road south, or we could head directly south along the historic 'King's Highway', which threaded through the mountains directly to Petra. The group consensus was that we were on this journey for adventure and had crossed enough countries via their boring main arteries already. The King's Highway it was!

We headed into Al Karak, as our route required us to transit the town. I led for once. Soon, the narrow, chaotic streets meant the Shogun fell behind and we were separated. Carrying on through the town, dodging errant taxis, donkeys and passers-by, I found my way onto the King's Highway and waited for the Shogun to catch up. My phone rang. It was Tom.

'Where have you disappeared to?' he asked, in an annoyed tone.

'We're on the road south just outside the town, waiting for you. There's only one road south, you can't miss it,' I said.

'Why didn't you wait for us when we got split up?'

'Because there was nowhere to stop, and it's only a small town anyway.'

'Well that's not very helpful, is it?'

'Well we didn't have much choice.'

'You should have waited.'

'I'm sure you can deal with it,' was my impatient response.

Tom promptly hung up on me.

We waited for a while and there was no sign of the Shogun, so we figured they must have taken a different road, maybe heading east out of the mountains to join the main road south. Sure enough, my phone soon beeped with a text message from Brummy, saying they'd taken a wrong turn coming out of town and were heading east. It wasn't a problem; we all knew we were heading for Petra, which wasn't that far away. Whatever happened we could meet up there. Laura and I fired up the Porsche and headed through the mountains alone.

What followed was one of the best driving roads I have ever negotiated. Fast sweeping corners flowed into one another and open valleys allowed a clear view of the road for miles ahead. The rise and fall of the terrain made it all the more exhilarating and for mile after mile we flew along through stunning hills and skirted around vast canyons. The road was empty and the tarmac good, and throwing caution to the wind, I put my foot down and pushed the car hard. My trust in the Porsche had grown greatly since it had survived the punishing city driving in Istanbul and Damascus, and I was finally willing to stop treating it with kid gloves.

I thanked the stars that we'd accidentally lost the Shogun, as this was just what I needed. Nearly three thousand miles of slowly plodding along dull roads at 4x4 speed had left me feeling cold towards driving. It had become a chore, rather than a pleasure. The chance to cut loose and fly along some beautiful driving roads made it a joy once again. I was in heaven, feeling the steering and chassis communicating with me in the corners, balancing the revs by dabbing the throttle as I changed down through the gearbox, listening to the ecstatic bark of the exhaust as we flew down the straights. There are few better ways to let off steam after a tough few weeks.

First mentioned in the Bible, the route along which we were travelling had conveyed migrations and conquests for millennia. The Crusaders, Byzantine Christians, Romans,

Nabateans, and Muslims had all left their archaeological mark on the thoroughfare. Their decayed fortresses and temples often flashed past our windows as we enjoyed the ride.

Soon, we reached Petra and relaxed while we waited for the Shogun, drinking lots of mineral water to stave off the desert heat. Our wait lasted only half an hour, but it was still too late to view the ruins that evening. We headed back into town to a hotel which allowed camping and set up our accommodation for the night.

I was feeling low as I walked through the fresh morning air towards the ruins. The rollercoaster of ups and downs which my mood had been riding had hit another one of its dips the previous evening, after the heady high of the day's drive. I knew the low would last all day and it saddened me as the celebrated lost city of Petra was another of the trip's tourist attractions which fascinated me. Feeling like anything but the intrepid adventurers we aspired to be, we purchased expensive tickets from the visitors' centre and headed past the multitude of Indiana Jones themed souvenir sellers towards the ruins.

Petra has one of the most spectacular settings any city has known. It snuggles deep in a natural stronghold within the mountains which form the east bank of Wadi Arabia, the valley running from the Dead Sea to the Bay of Aquaba. To approach it is to enter a fantasy world of unlikely proportions. The walk of over a kilometre to get there from the visitors' centre begins innocuously enough. A dusty track leads through a landscape of golden granite, bubbling up in domes and pancake formations all around. Some of the boulders had been eroded into surreal shapes by wind and water; others chiselled into ordered blocks by people long gone. I ambled along the gravelly track, consciously trying to keep my distance from the other visitors, alone with my melancholy thoughts. Occasionally, a tourist-spec donkey and cart ambled by, its occupants taking the quick way to the still unseen city.

I passed a particularly slight donkey. Its spindly legs looked perilously close to buckling and the look on its face was one of dour resignation. Perched on its bony back was a hugely overweight American. His stomach hung down bulbously from below his T-shirt and wobbled grotesquely as the donkey staggered onwards. He must have weighed at least twenty stone. He kept kicking the poor beast, while shouting angrily at its embarrassed master, protesting at how slowly it was struggling up the gentle incline, and demanding his money back.

It must have been partly due to my low mood, but I felt a worryingly strong urge to walk over and punch him squarely in the face.

After a few hundred metres, the granite domes to each side of the path grew ever higher and began to close in all around. Turning a corner, the path suddenly became the floor of a narrowing gorge, slicing improbably through the mountain. At times, the walls constricted to within four metres of one another and swept anything up to eighty metres overhead, their elegant, curving forms mirroring one another like a pair of dancers. The gorge continued its unlikely sweep through the dense granite, blocking out the sky with spectacular rock formations at every opportunity. Sometimes the sun streamed down and turned the surroundings gold; at other times the cool shade was total.It just went on and on. At every corner I expected the gorge to finish, to open out onto a more believable vista, but it just rushed on and on into the mountains for hundreds of metres, getting narrower and more improbable all the way, building to its grand finale as the cliffs nearly touched overhead.

Finally, the narrow cleft ended, and the dark shaded walls swept down tightly, framing the view ahead. Illuminated by sunlight, a slither of a golden colonnaded granite frontage was revealed. As I moved nearer, the view gradually widened until I could see the whole of 'Al-Khazneh' – the famous treasury. Standing over forty metres high and thirty wide, its façade was a sweep of pure drama. Columns, statues and gables had been cut into the rock face and stood incomparably within the natural arena where I found myself, which twenty-two centuries previously had been the glorious capital of the Nabataean kingdom.

Passing the treasury, I strolled further into the ruins. The cliffs around me stepped up in tiers, each peppered with a warren of doors and windows; dwellings from the past. At the base of the cliffs, a coliseum had been quarried, seating thousands in the Roman style. Temples and tombs vied for the prime ground level space to either side of me. Given the hardness of the granite, the excavations were an incredible achievement and despite my low spirits I was still hugely impressed by Petra – it would be impossible not to be. As I began to wander back I bumped into the others and we agreed to meet at the car park, so once again I walked alone, craning my vision upwards to take in the incredible rock architecture of the kilometre long entrance gorge.

After running the gauntlet of the souvenir sellers guarding the entrance to the ruins, I strolled into town to get some lunch. Everywhere was aimed at Western tourists, which was just fine by me. A pizza and a coke soon had my morale on the road to recovery.

We left Petra that afternoon, most of the day having vanished in our cursory exploration of the ruins. As usual with Jordan, the roads and scenery didn't disappoint. We swept across the diminishing mountains as the sun set, Libby once again joining me in the Porsche. Wadi Rum, where glorious desert vistas lay hidden in the night, was left behind as we sped onwards to the port of Aquaba, on the shores of the Red Sea.

Finding the ferry terminal involved more than a little hassle, but eventually we gained our bearings and located the port. The next ferry was due to depart at seven the following morning, so we bought tickets for it and parked up in the queue to await boarding instructions. It was about nine at night. After parking I noticed we'd sustained our first puncture of the trip. One of the rear wheels had slowly deflated, presumably after being cut during our drive around the port's untidy roads. I attempted to change the wheel, but one of the aluminium wheel nuts was stuck. It had disintegrated over the years and simply withered away as I attempted to turn it. While it wasn't going to prevent us from boarding the ferry, we wouldn't be able to get very far into Egypt until we'd fixed it.

While we were chatting, the bikers who we'd encountered the previous day arrived and introduced themselves. From Poland, they were undertaking a similar journey to ours and were hoping to reach Cape Town about three months hence. We chatted for a while, sharing our experiences so far, particularly of the coldness which had met us in Syria. A few refreshing Pepsis later, we decided to cook some dinner. Producing our tables, chairs and camping stove in the ferry terminal raised a few eyebrows, but we ate well before grabbing some sleep. Laura and I lay back in the comfort of our roof tent, while the occupants of the Shogun dozed uncomfortably wherever they could; Tom on a bench, the others in the car itself.

At five AM the sound of engines and the discomforting flashing of lights woke us. It was time to board the ferry. We got up as quickly as possible, took down the tent, pumped up the flat tyre – which held air for a few minutes at a time – and headed towards the vessel. It was still dark and our minds were blunted by sleep. It took nearly an hour to get the Porsche onboard; such were the predictable delays and inefficiency of the operation. It took considerably longer for the Shogun, however. Due to its height, it would be parking on the main deck, which at the time was occupied by a lorry pumping diesel into the ferry; hopefully enough to make it to Egypt. It was three hours before Team Shogun were finally able to come onboard and join us relaxing on deck, as the sun rose above Saudi Arabia to our east.

The Polish bikers and ourselves were the only Westerners on the ferry, and the general lethargy of the Arab majority told us that we shouldn't expect to be going anywhere soon. Such moments in travel are often welcome; unexpected down time when you can do nothing but simply relax and let the day go by. I couldn't even feel guilty for not working on the car, as it was tucked away in the vessel's hold. Time was marked by the coming and going of other ships and the regular announcements in Arabic regarding the delay. We understood nothing of what was said; however the blank expressions with which our fellow passengers greeted the news told us it wasn't good. We kept eagerly looking for some change in the status quo, some development that would facilitate our departure for Egypt – for Africa – but none was forthcoming. Lazily, the day passed. A smaller ferry berthed next to us, unloaded its cargo, was reloaded and set off again for Egypt. Around lunchtime, I thought I sensed movement, but it was only the container ship next to us casting off, its immense size filling our vision as it moved next to us.

As the afternoon progressed, we existed in a state of lethargic boredom, as there is only so much you can do to entertain yourself while sat on the deck of a ferry. We all dozed for a while. When Libby slept, lying across a bench on deck, three men came and sat opposite her. They stared at her disdainfully and regularly hissed their disapproval, spraying the air with phlegm. One member of the group took out a rather large knife and began to pick dirt from beneath his nails with it, whilst eyeing Libby in a rather unsettling manner.

Then three in the afternoon arrived and after eight hours of waiting, the ferry's big cargo doors closed and the deep harmonic rumble of diesel engines vibrated up through its structure. Amid shouts from the linesmen on shore and a restrained show of interest from the passengers, Jordan started moving away from us. We were underway. Next time we touched dry land, we would be in Africa. The adventure was about to begin in earnest.

SIX

PAST THE PYRAMIDS

15th October 2008
The Gulf of Aquaba

Ahead of us, the sun was setting over Africa. That morning, we had watched it rise over Asia. Our ferry wandered along an arbitrary line south between the two continents, heading towards the Egyptian port of Nuweiba. The Gulf of Aquaba is narrow and throughout our short voyage the parched mountains of Saudi Arabia to our left mirrored those of Egypt's Sinai to the right. As the sun dipped below the horizon, the sands of Arabia turned from tan to a deep orange, before a washed out, depthless grey preceded darkness. Meanwhile, the now shaded hills we were approaching were crowned with shafts of sunlight slicing through the sky. Beneath us, the sea lost its depth, its beautiful translucency giving way to an inky blackness. There was no dramatic salmon sunset. The air was too dry.

A tugboat came alongside and helped our unwieldy ferry onto its berth. Progress was slow and by the time the vessel was all-fast to the quay, darkness was total.

Nuweiba possessed the same semi-lit permanency that exists in all ports during the hours of darkness. It is a timeless atmosphere. Ships glide in and out almost silently, as tugboats dance attentively round them. Occasional trucks and cranes go about their night's work, interrupting the calm almost apologetically. The quietness and artificial lighting dulls the coarseness of the surroundings, the briskness of the day is gone and all is at peace. Permanence reigns. It is as if things have always been as they are and always will be. The dynamism required for change, for upheaval, could not exist in such a place. My job means I often visit ports during the hours of darkness and I always appreciate their air of interrupted serenity. It relaxes me and helps me to think.

I knew the relaxed atmosphere was an illusion, however. Egypt is one of the most fastidious countries on the planet into which to take an automobile. I'd heard the stories. I didn't expect an easy time at customs.

A garbled Arabic message crackled forth from the ship's loudspeakers, triggering movement among the understanding majority. We followed the crowds, leaving the vessel's deck and returning to our vehicles. The trucks were first to attempt to disembark. The ramp leading from the vehicle deck onto the quay was steep and caused the trailer of the first lorry to pivot up and jam against the steel latticework of the vessel's deck-head. Exposed girders dug into the flimsy structure of the trailer, wedging it firmly in place, halfway between ferry and land. My knowledge of Arabic swear words is hazy, but I'm pretty sure I must have heard them all during the lively exchanges between the lorry drivers and the ship's crew. Fortunately for Laura and I, our passage into Egypt was not completely blocked and we were able to slip past the stricken lorry onto Egyptian soil. The Shogun was not so lucky however, being stuck behind another dozen or so nervous trucks.

Once on the quay, we parked up, anticipating a long wait for the Shogun. It took half an hour for the falling tide to reduce the angle of the ferry's access ramp sufficiently to free the stricken lorry, allowing the Shogun to join us on dry land. As we waited, we attempted to remove the fragmented wheel nut which was preventing us from changing the Porsche's punctured tyre.Unfortunately, despite wielding chisels, pliers and drills with a lot of prejudice, the wheel had remained defiantly stuck.

'Why not let the person who's going to be a surgeon soon have a try,' Libby suggested, before confidently setting to work on the damaged wheel nut. As she picked up the hammer and chisel with a manic grin on her face, I felt a sudden jolt of terror on behalf of her future patients.

Unfortunately, the wheel nut defeated us all, so all we could do was pump up the tyre and head over to customs.

Once there, the punctured tyre wasn't the most immediate of our concerns. While we were pretty sure all our paperwork was in order, the apprehension that accompanies any potential pitfall built rapidly as we approached customs.

By night, it was a fairly unimposing place; a dimly lit swathe of tarmac, surrounded by anonymous offices and buildings. A crude framework of girders held up a corrugated metal roof, which provided shade to the customs officers as they inspected the vehicles. A seating area at one end of the hardstanding was piled high with garbage, which festered away repulsively beneath the sodium lighting. Beyond this, there was a toilet block. The toilets were so abhorrent that we came to almost appreciate the slight acclimatisation provided by the rotting garbage as we passed, as it made the nasal shock of entering the toilet block slightly less violent.

The border post was quiet and we didn't have to queue. We were greeted by a member of the tourist police as we parked, whose job was to guide visitors like us through the complexities of bringing a foreign car into Egypt. The irony was not lost on us – the Egyptians had managed to come up with an import system so complicated that we were not expected to be able to navigate it without full time assistance. Bureaucracy for bureaucracy's sake.

Hamid was a reassuring looking guy, paler of skin than we expected, with black hair gelled back in a confident sweep which stopped just short of an Elvis-like quiff. He wore a casual shirt and a black leather jacket. His relaxed confidence set us at ease.

He explained the procedure to us, but such was its complexity that we were left none the wiser as to exactly what was involved in getting the cars into Egypt. We were pretty sure, however, that it would involve copious amounts of paperwork and a depressing quantity of Egyptian pounds.

Sure enough, our first job was to obtain said Egyptian pounds. Not wanting to use up our valuable dollars, the border police were happy to let Brummy and I slip through the border into town to use the cash point. This unexpected relaxation of rules was a pleasant surprise. What followed was a continuous erosion of the pile of notes we'd just obtained. Our newfound friend led us from office to office, where, beneath harsh lighting, some clerk would process us disinterestedly. We would fill in some indeterminate Arabic form, hand over the requisite payment, and receive a receipt, which our assistant would routinely place in a folder. We paid to create a file about ourselves, for photocopies of all our documents, for our carnets to be stamped, for road tax, for customs tax and for insurance. Darting around the customs area in an illogical manner, the pile of receipts, photocopies and documents increased proportionally to the reduction in our finances. We couldn't keep track of where everything was. Our carnets disappeared for an hour or so, only to show up in a different office, as did our passports – or maybe they didn't, such was the confusion generated. This process went on for hours, the rest of the team settling in for a long wait as Brummy and I waded through the paperwork. It felt like we were being led down a production line, slowly preparing us to enter Egypt.

By one in the morning, we got the impression we were nearly done. The dossier of paperwork clutched protectively by our guide bulged like a Sunday paper as the customs officers carried out their checks on the cars. No, we didn't have any alcohol, drugs or firearms. Yes, we had a fire extinguisher for each vehicle. Another guy then appeared to take chalk rubbings of our vehicles' chassis numbers. *What sort of country wants to take chalk rubbings of the chassis numbers?*

Evidently Egypt is that sort of country and furthermore, we suffered for it. The Porsche's ownership documents contained an eighteen-digit number ending in '1327', while the metal plaque on the car's bulkhead contained only a seventeen digit number, identical but for the omission of the last number 7, which appeared to have been replaced with an asterisk. This discrepancy triggered solemn expressions on the faces of the customs officers present and even our tourist policeman's indifferent demeanour became suddenly tense. Heads were shaken, Arabic was spoken uneasily in hushed tones.

Obviously, we had a problem.

The matter was discussed with a series of people of escalating importance, before we found ourselves talking to the officer in charge of the border post.

'Exactly the same seventeen digit number appears on both the car and all the paperwork,' I said. 'The asterisk on the car is probably a reference to the number seven on the documents.'

'This is not important,' replied the somewhat tired looking official across the desk from me. 'The car cannot enter Egypt like this.'

'Do you really believe the paperwork is not for this car?'

'That is not important. The number on the carnet is different to the number on the car, so it cannot enter Egypt. You must return to Jordan on the next ferry.'

We left the office feeling rather frustrated.

'I'm guessing they're worried about it being mistaken for all the other British registered Porsches driving around Egypt,' I joked nervously as we walked back.

'Oh, I'm sure they've had three through already this week,' said Brummy.

The door into Africa had just been slammed in our face. Brummy and I explained what was happening to the others. As we explained, the tension in the air built up.

'Is there any way around Egypt?' asked a solemn Laura.

'Not really,' I said. 'There is a ferry from Saudi Arabia to Port Sudan, but it would be a right pain, and the Saudis aren't too fond of unmarried folk travelling together, so there would probably be issues there. Oh, and Libby's got to get to Cairo for her flight. Basically, I don't really think it's an option.'

'So if we can't sort this out we may have to just accept it and give up on Africa?' said Tom.

'Yep. The Shogun could go on but the Porsche would be screwed.'

'Bugger.'

'Anyone got any ideas?'

We talked our predicament through for half an hour. The Egyptians didn't seem too bothered about the car ownership documents. It was the carnet that they were uneasy about.

'Could we get a new carnet sent out from the UK?' suggested Libby.

'Are you paying?' I joked. 'Seriously, it's not likely. They don't hand them out too readily.'

'So basically, we're screwed,' said Tom.

'Pretty much, yes.'

'There must be something we can do,' said Louise.

'Not that I can think of,' I replied, already mulling over whether the Porsche could survive the long drive back to Britain.

We returned to the Egyptian authorities, who were rapidly tiring of our efforts. After an hour of deadlock and tempered frustration, we were finally able to hit on a possible solution. If, the next morning, we could get an official letter from the RAC – the issuing body for the carnet – confirming that the number on the paperwork was incorrect, but they would still honour it, we may be allowed to carry on with the border proceedings. It was a long shot, but it was also the best compromise we could get, so we agreed to wait until morning.

'So it's another night in no-man's-land! Second in a row.'

'Yep.'

'Well the Shogun is through okay; shall we get it across the border and wait for the Porsche at the campsite?' suggested Tom.

'No. We're all in this together,' said Brummy.

'But there's no point in us all having another bad night's sleep in customs. There's nothing we can do to help.'

Brummy became annoyed. 'We don't know if we can help the situation or not. If the Porsche has to go back this is the last time we'll see them. I'm not abandoning them just for a better night's sleep.'

'Fine,' said Tom.

I made a point of thanking Brummy later on. We were a team. Despite all our fatalistic joking, we had to stick together through thick and thin if we were to have any chance of making it across Africa.

The roof tent went up, the other tents were erected on the tarmac and a fitful sleep finally took us. It was half past two in the morning, and we had already been at the border for nearly five hours.

We were awake before seven the next morning, the noise of other vehicles moving around us being too disconcerting from within our tents to sleep through. It was already warming up rapidly as we emerged into the world. We made some breakfast on our stove and were given tea by a guard who felt sorry for us, as we awoke from our second night sleeping rough between international borders.

We had a long wait ahead of us. As Egypt is two hours ahead of England, it would be eleven o'clock before we could call Paul at the RAC to see if he'd be willing to fax us a letter. Brummy completed the import formalities for the Shogun, while the rest of us lounged around, chatting nervously about our chances of getting the Porsche into Egypt. It would be deeply ironic if the African Porsche Expedition was turned away at the gateway to Africa and never actually turned a wheel on African soil.

Eventually, the time came. The phone call which I had been dreading, the one on which our entire expedition now hung, could be delayed no longer. I dialled the number for Paul at the RAC.

'Hi Paul. It's Ben here, that idiot with the Porsche.'

121

'Oh, hello, how's it going?'

'Yeah pretty good, we've reached Egypt...'

'But?'

'Well there's one digit missing from the chassis number of the Porsche, and they won't accept the carnet. Any chance you could fax me an official looking letter on headed paper, confirming the correct number?'

'I don't see why not...'

And so our hopes were lifted.

It took about half an hour for Paul to get a fax through to one of the many offices at the border, where predictably I was asked to pay for the privilege of receiving it. However, once received its official appearance generated smiles among the paperwork-loving Egyptian authorities. The border formalities were recommenced, a whole new dossier detailing myself and the Porsche was assembled, my finances were depleted further in an incomprehensible manner and after a few tense hours the car was free to enter Egypt. The tension of the previous night receded to memory as we obtained our temporary Egyptian driving licences, rented Egyptian number plates and attached them to the cars, then joined the mêlée getting passports stamped at immigration. We were nearly there!

Goodbyes were exchanged with the people who had, for a short while, held the fate of the expedition in their hands, and we finally left the customs area. One last check of our paperwork at the port entrance and we were free to enter Egypt. It was forty hours since we'd been stamped out of Jordan, and our journey through Egyptian customs had taken seventeen hours, a hefty dose of stress and over a hundred pounds per car. All we wanted to do was relax.

Fortunately, if there's one place you can relax in Egypt, it's the coast of the Sinai Peninsula. We headed north for a few miles to the aptly named 'Soft Beach' resort. A cluster of wooden huts roofed with leaves sat next to a perfect beach, with the requisite number of palm trees completing the scene. This end of the Sinai, near the Israeli border, is very undeveloped in comparison to the Red Sea honeypots further south, and the resort was almost deserted.

On our arrival we were greeted by our four Polish biker friends, ordered a round of beers and collapsed on the beach.

'We didn't expect to be seeing you guys again,' they commented, having witnessed our predicament the previous night as they passed through customs.

The relief of making it into Africa was enormous, and the first round of beers didn't last long. Another round was ordered as we got on with the serious business of celebrating.

It turned out that the Poles were in a similar frame of mind and we were soon all high on stories of the journey so far, exchanging memories of border crossings, smooth tarmac and the unpleasantness of Syria. As we chatted, locals draped in white robes and headscarves drifted past along the beach, perched regally on their camels. Ships of the desert sailing on the shores of the sea.

The sun dropped behind the mountains of the Sinai for the second time as we headed intoxicated into the night. It was the first time on the trip where the beer had really flowed freely, greasing the conversation. After dark, we retreated from the beach into the bar, where the banter continued. We were all relieved to be in Africa, to have made it through the nightmare border crossing and to be able to relax, knowing full well just how close our expedition had come to a premature end. Our other problems, such as the Porsche's unfixable puncture, or our ferry deadline in Aswan three days hence, could wait until the morning. This was a release that we all needed.

Libby was the first to flag. After telling Alex, a South African who was working at the resort, about her exploits in the world of liver surgery, she passed out face down on the table, much to our amusement.

The rest of us weren't far behind Libby when it came to tiredness; the combination of stress, limited sleep and excessive beer proving very potent. We were all asleep long before midnight, Laura and I on the beach – where we were eaten alive by sand flies – while the rest of the group opted for their tents.

I woke before sunrise and sat alone on the beach as the pale sky prepared itself for the sun's arrival. I had no intention of doing anything that early in the morning, so dozed for a few more hours, drifting placidly in and out of consciousness. Eventually, I rose and washed, then set about rehydrating myself after too many days of hot sun and insufficient liquid, not to mention too much liquid of the wrong type the previous night. It was a balmy morning and everyone awoke later than normal, exhibiting the predictable lethargy of those finally allowed to relax.

Our relaxation was only temporary however. It was Friday morning. We had a ferry to catch in Aswan the following Monday. This gave us three days to cover around a thousand miles and hopefully see some of Egypt in the process. It wasn't long and we still had to get the puncture sorted before we could leave.

Fortunately, the Porsche had caught the eye of Eihb, one of the campsite workers. He was often to be found staring at it from various angles and was thrilled when I gestured him to sit in the driver's seat. The previous afternoon, before the beers had taken their toll, we'd had several conversations about the car as I checked it over and repacked the boot. He couldn't talk about it, or look at it, enough. The general consensus was that he had fallen in love with it. When I gave him a photo of the car and the bonnet badge from the donor car, he declared it one of the happiest days of his life. That evening, I'd told him about the problem with the wheel and he'd enthusiastically suggested we take it to his friend's garage the next morning.

We left at nine and headed back towards the town of Nuiweba. The garage was what I expected of Africa. A doorless frontage with space for two or three cars opened onto a dusty parking area. The work area lay beneath a rusting sheet metal roof, supported precariously by slender poles. Piles of old tyres and broken car parts dotted the floor. A few well-used tools lay around, forming a less comprehensive toolkit than the one I owned back in the UK. A hand-painted sign decorated the whole length of the garage; its indecipherable Arabic script presumably advertising the business.

The mechanic was quick to solve our problem. Using a welding set, he melted out the remains of the wheel nut, enabling the wheel to be removed. The puncture was soon fixed, and the now half-melted wheel stud replaced. All the while, my new best friend chattered away to the mechanics about the Porsche, as if it glorified him by association. However the mechanics didn't seem to care what sort of car it was; it was work all the same. In half an hour, the job was done. I paid the equivalent of ten English pounds and we headed back to the beach.

Our goodbyes to the Polish bikers and the folk at the resort were long and drawn out. Coffee was drunk, photos were taken and hands shaken. I liked the Poles and respected their carefree attitude to the trip. I then let Ehib drive the Porsche along the road that led into the resort. He was terrified at being entrusted with such a car, but the smile on his face after the experience said it all.

Eventually we dragged ourselves away, sad to be leaving such a relaxing place. We would have loved to stay for another night in paradise, but our schedule dictated against it. Our route followed the coast, sweeping along the slither of habitable land between mountains and sea. Laura drove. The road rose and fell as the mountains impeded into the coastal plain, twisting and turning as it contoured along the coast. It was a lovely ribbon of new tarmac. Stretches of deserted beach and secluded bays beckoned us to stop and relax, but we were back in our hurried mindset, intent on pushing on all the way to Cairo that evening.

In many areas, the unspoilt coastline was gradually being moderated by new developments. A holiday resort, or the bare bones of one under construction, never seemed far away. In the open landscape of desert and sea, these buildings had nowhere to hide, and no vegetation softened their outlines. They sat at odds with their natural surroundings, as if not caring about their almost offensive appearance.

I felt slightly hypocritical, taking issue with the development of the area after I'd enjoyed my time relaxing in a beach resort so much the previous evening.

This road of beaches and their profiteering eyesores could not carry on forever; soon the approaching Israeli border forced us to leave the coast and head inland through the mountains. Through, not over. The tarmac sliced into the ridges and precipices in a most improbable manner. Countless tonnes of rock and earth had been cut and blasted away to facilitate our progress through the fifteen miles of crags that guarded the open spaces of the Sinai Plateau. The broken cliffs shone golden in the sunlight as we flung the Porsche past them, marvelling at the effort expended in constructing the road.

Of course, what had driven the Egyptians to build such dependable roads here wasn't too much of a mystery. Twice in living memory, Israel had invaded and occupied the peninsula, and the border from which the invasions had emanated lay less than ten miles from us. The last Israeli soldiers had left the area in 1982 and the border between the two countries remained an area of tension. The smooth tarmac lining the bottom of the spectacular valley through which we were driving was being maintained for the Egyptian Army, not tourists in silly sports cars.

After twenty minutes of climbing through the dramatic mountainscape we emerged onto a desert plateau, the most abundant terrain of the Sinai. It was an otherworldly place, an empty Martian landscape of sand and crag which made a mockery of its history. Such a pointless place to fight over.

Ahead of us lay several hundred miles of this empty world. We stopped for fuel at a remote petrol station, all alone in the desert. A full tank in the Porsche cost the equivalent of twelve English pounds. I was beginning to like Egypt.

Back on the road, the sands rippled away from us in every direction. Small hills of no particular note were dotted around, their relief kept to a minimum, as if to maintain the anonymity of our surroundings. The hot sun beat down fiercely from the solid blue sky, flattening the landscape further through glaring overexposure.

Progress was good, the tarmac often stretching all the way to the horizon in a thick ribbon, beckoning us onwards to Cairo, then down to Aswan, then maybe – just maybe – to Cape Town. Occasional police checkpoints baked under the sun, their bored guardians generally waving us through in preference to leaving their shaded seats. On a few occasions, we stopped in the desert for a break, lost in the silence that engulfed us when the cars were allowed to rest. I always tried to catch a few moments on my own when we did.

There is something about being alone in an empty desert which stirs the soul. Perhaps it's to do with the smallness you invariably feel. Small in every way. It's impossible not to feel tiny in a landscape which stretches over empty horizons in every direction. You become just another grain of sand. You feel inconsequential when you remember that the landscape hasn't changed in thousands of years; reminded of your transitory nature by the heavy permanence all around you. You feel fragile, sweltering beneath the burning sun with no natural shade or water in sight. But through all this comes a clear lucidity. The lifeless simplicity of your surroundings provides perspective to the fleeting existence that life is; bringing it into a sharper focus through the contrast with what lies around.

I love deserts and the deeper level of self-consciousness their uncluttered vistas seem to trigger. I hoped the Porsche would make it to the open sands of the Sudan, Kenya and perhaps even Namibia. This particular wilderness was behind us all too quickly however. Thin eddies of wind-blown sand danced across the tarmac as we dropped down off the plateau towards Suez. The sun followed the same route as us that day, setting on the road directly in front of us. For a few minutes, it looked like the Egyptians had miraculously engineered a strip of tarmac leading straight to the heart of the sun, a road trip to end all road trips. And then it was gone, staining the horizon with a reddening smear that deepened to darkness. One red glow did remain however. The oil warning light continued to nag me, preventing me from relaxing. While I had accepted that the bearings weren't wearing out, it still unsettled me. It had become a symbol of all that was wrong with the car and continued to taunt me through the hours of darkness.

We coasted down through the dusk, descending to the Suez Canal, unseen below us. Soon enough, it was above us. The Ahmed Hamdi tunnel carried us swiftly beneath one of the great arteries of world trade, leaving us bypassing the town of Suez towards Cairo. We never did see the canal.

Even within a hundred kilometres of Cairo, Egypt was dark. The busy road cut through the empty night towards a slight glow in the sky, beneath which a city lay. It wasn't just any city. It was one of the great cities. Cairo. To me, the name is synonymous with adventure. Its location, surrounded by desert, straddling the Nile with the pyramids pressed up to its side, is perfect. Its mixture of colonial, Islamic and ancient influences promised to be an exotic fusion.

What a place to have driven to! It was two weeks to the day since that hopeless engine had been fitted and we had made it across Europe, through the Middle East, and now all the way to Cairo! Whatever happened now, I felt our achievements were finally gaining some respectability. We hadn't fallen at the first hurdle; we'd dug deep and made it to one of the great capitals of the African continent.

As with all the big cities we entered, the Shogun led while we followed. The traffic was just as dense as it was when we drove into Istanbul, but somehow more frenzied. I stayed welded to the rear bumper of the Shogun, weaving like a demented trailer. As traffic built, the road's single carriageway became two, then three lines of vehicles wide. We passed the airport and looped south towards Ma'adi, where we were to stay the night with Mike, a friend of Louise's family. It was hard work staying behind the Shogun. Cairo's taxi drivers seemed to take our proximity as a challenge to get between us and I was forced to employ some fairly aggressive tactics to prevent us being separated, darting pre-emptively at them whenever they lined up to slot into the non-existent gap. In this car-based game of chicken the locals always yielded first, taken aback by my unexpected aggressiveness. At one stage, I crashed into the back of the Shogun. We were only travelling at a few miles per hour at the time and a couple of small dents in the Shogun's rear bumper were the only resulting damage, but the sudden noise and the jolt from the collision certainly woke everyone up.

Rows of high-rise buildings and shining billboards lined our progress towards the evening's destination. Fortunately, we didn't have to drive into the middle of the city; instead we looped through the outskirts as we felt our way towards Ma'adi, about eight miles south of the centre. We reached the district fairly easily, having gained a healthy impression of the brooding size of the city, home to around eleven million people.

Ma'adi had a colonial air about it. Wide tree-lined boulevards glowed unassumingly in the darkness. The high-rise concrete of central Cairo was replaced by a less intense style of living, with villas and schools dotted around, basking in their spacious grounds. It was Friday night and people wandered idly, restrained in comparison to the frenzied, extrovert nature of a Friday night back home. Even the traffic seemed to have relaxed. I could see why the area was popular with Cairo's expatriate population.

Years previously, Louise had been a member of this expat population. When she was fourteen, her somewhat nomadic parents had moved from Tunisia to Cairo at the beck of British Gas, for whom her father worked as an engineer. Louise's nostalgic reminiscences of her time there made it sound like an idyllic upbringing. Since our arrival in Egypt we had heard tales of summiting pyramids, sneaking into illegal underground bars, diving in the Red Sea and having adventures in the desert. Unfortunately, however special the memories from those days may be, they didn't help us find Mike's apartment. Our traditional navigational faux pas meant it took us half an hour of driving around before Louise started recognising the surroundings and could guide us to our destination; at least this meant we got a good look around the area though.

Mike met us on the sidewalk and following brief introductions he beckoned us to drive into the underground car park beneath the block in which his apartment nestled. In his fifties, his ever-smiling face softened beneath a frizz of silver hair and a pair of wiry spectacles. He seemed genuine and his relaxed dress sense, easy smile and quiet self-assuredness spoke of someone used to success. He didn't look like someone I'd expect to live in Cairo, but any suspicions of ineligibility were completely unfounded. Born in Libya of a British father and Palestinian mother, he had known Louise's family since their days in Tunisia and was clearly very much at home in his surroundings.

We parked the cars carefully in the confined space. As usual, I felt embarrassed by the sick spluttering noises made by the Porsche's engine and so kept revving the engine slightly to disguise them. I was always very conscious among strangers of just how silly it must seem, purporting to be en route to Cape Town when the car sounded ready to expire at any moment.

Predictably, after parking the car I found that the electric windows wouldn't close; it took five minutes of fiddling with them before we could secure the car and head up to the apartment.

Mike lived with his Singaporean wife, their three children having all flown the nest. He clearly enjoyed his Cairo lifestyle – 'don't tell anyone, but it's absolutely fantastic' – and his work managing logistics for British Petroleum. His apartment was the polar opposite of our appearance, being clean, orderly and cared for, so self-consciousness reigned as we trudged in from yet another hot and dusty day on the road. In spite of the fine local furniture and pictures of ancient Egypt hanging from the walls, it was like being back home. The aura of comfort, cleanliness of surface and light, and the reliability of things around us put everything we were missing into stark relief. An order of home-delivery pizzas, cold beers straight from the fridge and BBC News24 on the television all added to the contrast.

It was surreal to watch the news for the first time since we'd left. For weeks, our world had been the trip. Everything else had receded into the background, replaced by thoughts of borders, progress and fragile vehicles. The so-called credit crunch had dimmed from our minds, but was brought back by headlines of falling house prices and failing banks. For all its stress and uncertainty, I much preferred our world to the one we had temporarily left behind. The evening passed quickly in a relaxed blur of beer and chat. Soon, one by one we drifted off to sleep, eager to be rested for the following day's visit to one of the wonders of the ancient world.

We oozed through the Cairo traffic as the morning gradually acquired its exotic warmth. The city cluttered in all around us, feeling busy and chaotic after the previous days' deserts. As we crossed a bridge over the Nile, the scruffy buildings receded and we gained our first panoramic views. On the east bank, a rash of lofty tower blocks merged untidily into one another, looking functional and unloved. Ahead of us to the west, Giza sprawled. And yet beneath the bridge, unflooded by the sea of urbanisation, there existed reminders of the fertile green lands which have made the banks of the Nile habitable since time immemorial. Lush fields, swamps and palm trees defiantly lined the great river, butting up against the dusty urban sprawl. The dwellings among the farmlands had a temporary, flimsy air to them, as if ready to be dismantled in retreat when the inevitable urbanisation reaches them. Occasional donkeys and livestock provided purpose to the scene.

Entering Giza, a sea of rough, unfinished blocks served by a web of power and phone lines coursed away into the distance and soon the reason for our visit made itself tantalisingly visible. Flickering into view behind the passing buildings, the dense bulk of the pyramids appeared, their gravity drawing us towards them seemingly involuntarily. As lesser buildings flashed past us at the roadside, cheapened by billboards and neglect, the pyramids remained stationary in our vision, by virtue of their distance from us. Even remote by many miles, flitting in and out of view, their presence was overwhelming.

As is often the way in Africa, the tarmac finished where presumably, the money had run out. A dirt track led us across a bowl of dust; the pyramids now in full view a mile or so away and unobstructed by the sprawl of the city. They jutted timelessly out of the swathe of sand, dulled by a smoggy haze which blunted the blue sky. No one else was around. We stopped for photos, riding high on the satisfaction of how far we'd come. It was important to indulge our inner selves like this. The trip was tough, hard work. Rewards like this moment had to be savoured, to build up our morale for the next challenge. We'd just driven to the pyramids! Jovially, we rejoined our vehicles and headed over for a closer look.

You don't simply decide to visit the pyramids. You are drawn to them by a strange compulsion. Their beckoning gravity is like that of a void, calling you from the edge of an abyss. As you get closer their gravity seems to increase, as if generated by their immense bulk.

They are an awesome sight. The unmistakable trigonometric outline is immediately familiar, seen in a thousand images already – in paintings, photos, films and replicas. But their simple beauty is cheapened by such hollow exposure. To see them for real is to cut away their devaluing familiarity and replace it with the dramatic reality. They were bigger than my mind's eye had imagined, bulky and powerful. Beyond them to the east, the desert stretched away into the distance, timeless and fitting.

It was surprisingly quiet that morning. The throngs of other tourists I'd expected to see hadn't materialised. We drove around the site, stopping regularly to bask in the sights. Like all who visit the pyramids, the construction methods which enabled such grand constructions defied our belief. Rocks weighing many tonnes had been transported hundreds of miles, shaped to millimetric precision and somehow elevated to their place in the structure.

The numbers are incredible. The Great Pyramid of Giza is made from over two million individual blocks of limestone. In raw terms, it is three million tonnes of rock, exactly aligned with an accuracy which would elicit respect in any century, let alone the twenty-sixth century BC. Its base covers over thirteen acres and had been levelled to within fifteen millimetres over its entire area before construction began. At its completion it stood almost one hundred and fifty metres high and was the tallest structure in the world for almost thirty-eight centuries.

But the figures are meaningless. Stood next to its immense bulk, the sense of awe overwhelms all. And the Great Pyramid of Giza is not in isolation. Next to it is the Pyramid of Khafre, a double take of similar proportions, while a few hundred metres away stands the Pyramid of

Menkaure, whose relative modesty is only due to the misfortune of its location, next to the grandest of behemoths. And then there's the Sphinx, reclining sublimely in its weathered splendour below. An incredible place.

Unfortunately, the millennia of dignity encapsulated within the Giza Necropolis does not extend to its current guardians. The tourist police prowled among the visitors, generally mounted on a bored camel. Their presence appeared to be more ceremonial than practical and they passed their days trying to get what freebies they could from passing Westerners. Whenever we parked up to photograph the Porsche in front of the wonders of the ancient world, we were inevitably hassled by one of these ineffectual characters. After a while I grew weary of their pestering and the conversations became monotonous and frustrating.

'Baksheesh!'

'Why? What have you done to warrant baksheesh?'

'You took a photo.'

'Yes and you weren't in it. Goodbye.'

Generally such reticence swiftly ended their advances, though on one occasion the policeman reacted somewhat persistently. Shouting at us as we returned to our car, he spurred his aloof beast into action and gave chase. Fortunately, our thoroughbred German sports car was more than a match for the camel and we were able to escape effortlessly. It's not every day you drive your Porsche past the pyramids, with a policeman on a camel in hot pursuit!

The pyramids marked the end of the adventure for Libby, so she departed in a taxi to catch the afternoon flight back to Britain. In her eleven days off work, she'd crossed Turkey, Syria, Jordan and part of Egypt, visited Istanbul, Kappadocia, Palmyra, Petra and the pyramids, and floated in the Dead Sea – quite an intense holiday by anyone's standards. She clearly didn't want to leave and cut catching her flight worryingly close. Too close, it transpired, as she missed it and had to wait until the following day to fly back to the UK. Fortunately however, she made the best of her situation. In true Libby style she was able to get a security guard at the airport to take her out for dinner and entertain her for the evening; a fitting end to her time on the expedition.

We left the pyramids early in the afternoon, and as we jostled through Cairo's traffic, the Porsche acquired a new trick. Overheating. The whole of Africa stretched out ahead of us, nine thousand miles to Cape Town. But here we were at the other end of the continent with a car that had found yet another way to conspire against us. If the engine ran too hot for too long, we were likely to destroy the head gasket or warp the cylinder head. Predictably, we had forgotten to bring any spare parts for these eventualities. We left Cairo with the heater blasting hot air into the cabin, trying to draw as much heat as possible away from the engine, and when the traffic died down and we were able to cruise at a reasonable speed, the extra cooling air going through the car's radiator stopped the overheating.

Cairo's southern suburbs petered out into a ribbon of agriculture and development, clinging to the narrow strip of irrigated land on the banks of the Nile. Thickets of palm trees and neat tended fields lined the road, while the life-giving river snaked in and out of view to our left. To our right, the sun dipped into wispy clouds, silhouetting the palm trees with a tropical-looking sunset. It was nice to finally be heading south. We'd made it to Africa and were now making inroads towards our ultimate goal.

As the sky faded to black, we settled in for another night on the road; hopefully our last, as once we'd reached the ferry at Aswan, the time pressures upon us would relax, allowing us to complete the remainder of the trip at a more sedate pace. Cruising through dimly lit villages, past outlandishly illuminated mosques and the occasional riverboat, we sunk into the night. All the while, Laura avoided conversation by pretending to sleep. The more things changed, the more they seemed to stay the same.

Reaching the town of Bani Suwayf, we stopped to buy some cheap Egyptian fuel. They filled the diesel Shogun first and when I asked for petrol, they produced the same nozzle. Evidently, we had a problem. Much shouting and hand waving ensued, until things calmed down enough to confirm that the diesel Shogun had indeed been filled with petrol. If we hadn't noticed and had started the engine, it would have resulted in its rapid destruction. We pushed the Shogun to the garage's inspection pit and Brummy scurried underneath it while I filled up the Porsche with petrol – definitely petrol, I checked a dozen times – then went back to see what was going on beneath the Shogun. A tiny screw provided a means to drain the tank, and Brummy was patiently holding containers beneath it as it emptied.

As usual, I offered support in this traumatic time by pitching a little friendly abuse Brummy's way. This only entertained for so long however, so soon Laura and I went off to seek alternative entertainment. We found it in the form of a Bajaj auto-rickshaw, of which there were many zooming about the dimly lit streets.

I have a healthy nostalgia for these little three-wheeled beasties, having taken one on a trip across India and Nepal a year previously. Driving them is quite unlike anything else, with their bike-like controls and enthusiastic engine buzzing away behind the back seat. Chatting to one of the auto-wallahs, I showed him a photo of me and my auto-rickshaw in the Himalayas and paid him a few pounds for the chance to reacquaint myself with their unique driving experience. Getting out of a Porsche into a rickshaw is rather surreal. The feisty Bajaj makes the most of its 7hp and is certainly the most fun way I know of to negotiate a city. As I blasted around, the memories flooded back as I remembered the finer points of controlling these unique little beasts. Laura's nervousness rose proportionally to my confidence however, and it was a relieved co-driver who climbed out of the back of the rickshaw when we returned to the garage. The Shogun was nearly drained by then and soon had a tank full of diesel, enough to reach the Sudan in fact. Following a spot of dinner and some shopping, we returned to the road, another potentially trip-ending error averted.

Egypt had an annoying system of convoys in place, a very visible attempt to provide a barrier between tourism – Egypt's biggest industry – and the latent threat of terrorism. Previous terrorist attacks in Luxor, Sharm-el-Sheikh and Cairo meant that the authorities were very keen to prevent further tarnishing of Egypt's relatively safe reputation. Soon, the roadblocks started. We would be pulled over, our papers checked and we would be made to wait a few minutes before setting off behind an escort vehicle, gun-toting soldiers peering out at us from within. There was always a slight tension at such official checkpoints, as things were temporarily out of our control; our fate in the hands of a few bored officials. Without fail, I have an empty feeling of guilt in such situations, however much I tell myself that I've done nothing wrong; as if my presence at the checkpoint is evidence enough of misconduct.

We were hustled from checkpoint to checkpoint by our armed guards, who generally rode in a blue pickup truck, or occasionally a police car. They all drove in the authoritative manner one would expect, their status giving them a greater claim to owning the road than anyone else. Despite the nuisance and uncertainty of the continuous stops, the convoy system did have its benefits. For a start, our escorts tended to know where the numerous unmarked speed bumps were, slowing down in good time and thus preventing us from pounding our vehicles into them on the unlit roads. They also knew the way through towns and villages and so eased our navigation somewhat. We accepted them as part of the journey and hustled along in their speeding tyre-tracks.

The night passed in a dream-like daze. Convoys and checkpoints merged into a blurred whole. Laura drove initially and then tired, so I took over for the long haul through the night to Luxor, four hundred miles south of Cairo. Our headlights occasionally illuminated glimpses of rural life in the Nile Delta, but the memories quickly vanished into the darkness. Driving standards were the worst so far. For the local populous, cruising along with only the dimmest of sidelights was routine, headlights being reserved for flashing warnings at oncoming vehicles to get out of the way. Often, we would pull out into the darkness to overtake a lorry, only to swerve back to safety when a pair of headlights suddenly appeared on the road ahead. Dicing with the locals often seemed to be assisted suicide, such was the aggression with which they wielded their decrepit steeds; but on the up side, at least the adrenaline from so many near misses warded off the urge to sleep. At five o'clock, I could take no more and Laura took over the driving. I was out cold within seconds of changing over.

Bright sunlight woke me as we cruised into Luxor's Valley of the Kings. It was going to be another scorching day. It was already hot enough at seven in the morning. We parked up among the myriad coaches and tour groups and became sightseers once more. Amid throngs of Westerners, we drifted in through the entrance to visit another of Egyptology's epicentres, but my heart wasn't in it. The few tombs open to the public were impressive, their hieroglyphics exquisite, but I was viewing everything through a veil of fatigue and felt removed from my surroundings. I had just driven through the night to get to Luxor, with only a few hours off, dozing in the passenger seat, but all I wanted to do was push on to the ferry at Aswan and a chance to relax properly.

Catching the Aswan ferry had become like a dream to me. That was the deadline. For the previous five weeks my life had been dominated by deadlines; to change the Porsche's engine before departure, to get the paperwork and last-minute preparations done in time. Once en route, the pressure to keep going in the face of uncertainty, to meet Libby in Istanbul and get her to her Cairo flight in time had all worn me down. And now we were fighting our way towards the final deadline – to catch the Aswan ferry. To miss it would mean a delay of a week; to catch it would provide a chance to wind down our pace and relax, maybe even to finally enjoy the journey. It would be a novelty.

We were only a few hundred miles from Aswan. The ferry left the following day. Firing up the vehicles, we continued south. Following the Nile, we passed turreted mosques and worn dwellings, cruised through palm trees and irrigated fields, from roadblock to roadblock, until there were no more roads. Beyond us lay Lake Nasser, hemmed in by desert and dam. We had arrived. Crossing the river, we located the overland travellers' campsite and pulled in for the evening, parking right next to a bright red double-decker bus. It sported English number plates, and purported to be the number 38 from Weymouth to Addis Ababa. It's a funny old world sometimes!

As soon as I stopped, the banter started.

'Afternoon. Come here often?'

'All the time. It only counts if you travel by bus mind.'

'Nah, look at all that space you've got. A Porsche is clearly sillier!'

It was going to be an amusing evening. We grabbed a drink and started chatting about adventures already had.

The bus, a portly Bristol model built in 1981, was being driven from the UK to Ethiopia in a similarly eccentric manner to our own expedition. Initially manned by eight intrepid adventurers, their numbers had withered to five by this stage, who gave us a tour of their accommodation.

Inside, there were bunks, a kitchen and even an open-air beer garden, formed by cutting the roof off the rear third of the bus. A toilet was installed, and a urinal which emptied directly onto the tarmac below. I was sure Brummy would have made full use of the feature at some of the border crossings we'd encountered!

It was nice to meet some fellow English eccentrics and to stop somewhere where we weren't the only weird folk for once. The campsite also contained a few impeccably equipped Italian and Dutch 4x4s, and a German Land Rover, all of which kept a safe distance from the crazy Brits. That afternoon, their owners had looked on in an uncomprehending manner as a big red bus pulled into the campsite and then had to double-take a few hours later when an overlanding Porsche appeared. It made us proud of our approach to things. The British sense of adventure which had driven people to the ends of the world, up the highest mountains and across the most treacherous seas remained alive and well. On that campsite in southern Egypt, it had simply been blended with a healthy dose of Monty Python-esque humour.

Sadly, our relaxed demeanour was short-lived. The ever-helpful campsite owner phoned the ferry company for us, who informed us that it would be virtually impossible to catch the ferry tomorrow – such was the weight of bureaucracy and paperwork to be negotiated before we left Egypt. Deflated by yet another obstacle, we responded in our time-honoured manner. The Shogun headed into town to find some beer and we hid behind our catchphrase, 'it'll be fine!' As the temperature dropped below a hundred degrees for the first time in hours, the Shogun returned with a few cans of precious, overpriced lager, and the bus guys announced they needed help consuming their alcohol supply before entering the Sudan. The die for the evening was cast. Tall tales were exchanged between Team Porsche, Team Shogun and Team Bus until late into the night and laughter filled the desert sky; not for the first time however, I couldn't share it. Tiredness and the continuous pressure I'd been under for the past five weeks had left me without the energy reserves for a party. I went to bed early after a couple of beers and lay awake, pleased to be alone with my own company. I wished I could share the fun of the moment, meeting fellow eccentric travellers in the midst of their adventure, but for over a month now I had been living in a state of continuous nervous tension. My joie de vivre had all but gone. The next day promised to be yet another race against the clock, a fight with officialdom and, quite frankly, I couldn't be bothered. Secretly, a part of me hoped we would miss the ferry and be forced to spend another week in Aswan, going nowhere. It would do me a world of good. I drifted to sleep listening to the laughter outside. Whenever I heard Laura laughing away, it annoyed me all the more.

We awoke early the next morning, to give ourselves a chance of completing all the required bureaucratic chores and catching the ferry. The first job of the day called for a trip to court, to sign a declaration confirming that we hadn't been involved in any road accidents during our trip across Egypt. We decided not to tell them about my little crash into the back of the Shogun in Cairo. Using the GPS, we navigated through the rapidly warming morning to an unlikely looking apartment block downtown. Outside, a local dressed in a white shirt and shorts was sat on the kerb, clutching some forms. Spotting us, he knew he had custom and one Egyptian pound acquired a 'Barra et Zimma', the document required by the court. So far so good. It turned out the undistinguished apartment block did indeed contain a court, in a shabby little office on the second floor. There, we were informed that we needed the signature of an officer who wasn't in the office yet. And so our plans began to unravel.

After an hour of waiting the clock ticked past nine in the morning. We were promised he would be in soon. Unfortunately, we couldn't complete the next stage of the paperwork without the signature. Sitting around intermittently in the hot street and the stuffy office, the momentum left the group.

Tom summed it up.

141

'If he's not here soon, we're fucked.'

He had a point.

'Okay, you guys take the Shogun to see the guy from the ferry company, Mr Saleh or whatever his name is and get the tickets sorted. I'll stay here and once the papers are signed I'll meet you at the traffic police's office,' I suggested.

'That makes sense, but what about Laura's photos?' I'd forgotten that Laura needed to get some passport photos printed for her entry into the Sudan.

'Oh yes. Right, you take Laura with you and try to get that sorted too. I'll text you if anything happens here.'

The Shogun and everyone else sped off and left me in the lap of the Egyptian authorities. I kept hassling the people in the court office, fairly half-heartedly, as I didn't believe that we could actually catch the ferry. We had continuously ridden our luck and survived, progressing through obstacle after obstacle by the skin of our teeth for weeks just to get here. Our good fortune must end sometime and by ten that morning, it seemed that moment had come.

Half an hour after the others left, an officious-looking chap finally entered the office and I was able to pester him into signing the forms. The Shogun pulled up just as I stepped outside into the bright sunlight. Brummy, clearly enjoying our frantic predicament, jumped out of the driver's seat.

'We've seen Mr Saleh. He's got the tickets and says just try to get there by midday. No photos yet though, there's no photobooth in this whole sweaty city. We took some on a digital camera and they should be printed soon. Hope they'll do.'

'Fair enough, let's go to the traffic police and give our Egyptian number plates back. We can sort the pictures afterwards,' I replied wearily.

'What if we miss the ferry? We'll be stuck in Egypt for a week unable to drive the cars,' Louise said, raising a concern that had been discussed inconclusively the previous evening.

'Well we'll just have to not miss it, won't we?' Brummy said. He could always be depended on to be positive in such situations.

We tore across town, locating the traffic offices with an hour remaining. Leaving Laura, Tom and Louise with the cars, Brummy and I sprinted off through a market to the office.

We entered a room which was divided in two by a glass screen, behind which an army of middle-aged women shuffled paperwork around in a disinterested, leisurely manner. Behind them, floor to ceiling shelves groaned under the weight of brown folders and faded papers, which surely dated back to Tutankhamen's time. On our side of the screen, Egyptian men jostled for their attention, trying to get some unintelligible form processed before the office closed in an hour's time. Evidently, the British pastime of queuing had not taken root in Egypt, so Brummy and I dived into the mêlée and managed to fight our way to separate windows, where we attempted to catch the eye of one of the disinterested ladies, who were oblivious to the power they held over our fates. It took fifteen minutes, such was their skill at avoiding eye contact with the rowdy mass behind the glass screens.

Eventually we were able to hand back our car number plates, Egyptian driving licences and court papers and received a customs document permitting the cars to leave Egypt. Brummy and I ran back to where they were parked. We had just twenty minutes to get Laura's photos and rush to the port. Unfortunately, we didn't know exactly where the port was.

A plan was made. 'Okay, you take the Shogun and find the port and get them to stay open, I'll take Laura to get the photos and we'll meet you there. The Porsche needs petrol too, before Sudan.'

The Shogun disappeared to the south, hunting for the ferry, while we raced back into town to get the photos. Predictably, it took a while, but eventually we had them. The petrol station had no petrol however, so we had to head to the port without filling up. They were expecting a delivery in half an hour, but we had no such time. Driving the Porsche harder than ever, I rushed south in the general direction of the lake. Soon, however, I was lost and the GPS was no help either. Desperate, Laura phoned Brummy. It was nearly midday.

'Brummy, are you there yet?'

'No, we took a wrong turn, but I think we're back on track now. Why aren't there any signposts in this whole damn country?'

'Yeah, tell me about it. Well good luck anyway, hopefully we'll see you there soon.'

Looking at the map, we figured out our mistake and set about correcting it. We rushed over broken tarmac towards the port, dodging left and right around potholes and imperfections. As usual, the Porsche responded to the change of tempo, feeling a lot happier than usual, barking in satisfaction from its baritone exhaust. It was a sports car once more. A few times, open corners appeared, covered in sand. I took them quickly and the back of the car slid around in graceful pirouettes, its oscillating mass balanced by applying armfuls of opposite lock to the steering wheel, as a cloud of dust billowed up behind. I revelled in the urgency our situation required, but felt empty at the same time. As the clock ticked past midday, I knew all was lost. We would be in Aswan for the week. Our luck had run out, and we had failed.

With further pointers from Team Shogun, we eventually careered sideways into the port. They had already met Mr Saleh and been informed that customs would be remaining open. That was the good news. The bad news was that we had to pay for the ferry in cash. We didn't have enough. I was given an arbitrary forty minutes to get back into town, get the cash, and return.

The whole port turned to stare as the Porsche spun around, laying down two thick lines of burnt rubber as it screeched away towards Aswan. We found a bank and I attempted to withdraw the money, but my bankcard wouldn't work. As it had been used in so many weird and wonderful locations, my bank had seen fit to choose this moment to lock it, as a precaution against suspected fraud. *Wonderful timing*, I thought to myself. Laura couldn't withdraw money either and all the dollars she'd brought along had gone already. I managed to take out just enough on my credit card, and filled up with fuel before returning to the port. We'd been able to withdraw enough cash to cover the ferry ticket, but if we couldn't find money when we arrived at Wadi Haifa, we would have real problems. That was a worry for the future however; we raced back to the ferry and paid for our tickets.

Departing Egypt was refreshingly uncomplicated in comparison to entering. Customs and immigration were cleared without a problem. No explanation of the anomaly involving the Porsche's chassis number was necessary this time, to which we breathed a sigh of relief.

Soon the cars were waiting down on the quay, parked next to a very plush Italian Toyota Land Cruiser, which we had seen at the campsite the previous day. We boarded the ferry and went to our cramped cabins, where we could at last relax a little. We had done it. Ever since the engine had broken, this ferry had been our ultimate deadline. Delaying our departure from the UK by a day had been no big deal. Missing this ferry would have cost us a week, with major implications for whether the trip could be completed in time for Brummy and Toms' flights home from Cape Town. Now, the time pressure was off, the air was cooling in the Nubian evening and the real adventure lay ahead.

It was after dark when we were asked to drive our cars onto the ramshackle barge that would transport them up Lake Nasser to Wadi Haifa, in the Sudan. They would be sharing it with wares of all descriptions, being taken from Egypt to be sold for profit further south. The bulk of the cargo appeared to be onions, leading Laura to christen the vessel the 'Onion Bargee' – a name that stuck.

At around eight that evening, the ferry started its engines, slipped its moorings and thrummed rhythmically into the night. The following day we would be in the Sudan.

SEVEN

THE DESERT

21ˢᵗ October 2008
Lake Nasser, Southern Egypt

The Great Temple of Abu Simbel sat solemnly, floating just above the shimmering lake. Its four huge statues, likenesses of King Ramesses II, stared out from a rocky bluff, as they had done for thirty-three centuries. But the years had not left them in dignified peace. An earthquake had felled one of the statues; its head and torso lay forlornly at its feet. Some early rising tourists were already drifting among them, cameras aimed upwards, fingers pointing, entering and leaving the temple at will. Even the temple's location is at odds with the eternal dignity aspired to by the ancient Egyptians. It was originally located sixty metres beneath us on the banks of the Nile, which had burst up to become Lake Nasser following the construction of the Aswan Dam. Fallen from ancient immortality, Abu Simbel had become a pawn in the history of modern Egypt, its retreat from the encroaching waters paid for by international donations in the 1960s. As the construction of the dam went ahead one hundred and fifty miles downriver, the temple had been carved up and moved, block by block, to its current location, safe from flooding.

As we passed the temple, many of the ferry's passengers laid their prayer mats on the steel deck and prayed to Mecca. Islam had reached Egypt in about 640AD, nearly two thousand years after the temple was built. Not all floods are of water.

Abu Simbel's grand frontage was not the only part of the landscape to have fled the rising waters. In a race against time, other temples and archaeological sites had been moved. Yet more were lost forever beneath the waves.

Many tens of thousands of Nubians had lived on the once fertile ground over which we floated. The rising waters forced their relocation. Even the town of Wadi Haifa, where we were to re-alight on dry land, had been moved years previously, its port and rail terminus reconstructed beyond the reach of the lake.

A line of floating barrels signalled our entry into the Sudan. We left the turbulence of Egyptian history behind and entered a very different nation, with a history all of its own.

Sudan had achieved its independence from Britain in 1956, fifty-two years before our journey. Bloody civil wars between the Arabic North and the black South had raged for thirty-eight of those fifty-two years. A separate conflict in Darfur, a few hundred miles to our west, was still smouldering away. These wars had taken the lives of several million Sudanese and, like so many African conflicts, relatively few had died on the battlefields. The civilian majority had borne the brunt of the attrition through disease and starvation. And still the country was divided. The North was being run by an apparently genocidal military dictatorship, while the South had been reduced to a stone-age existence by decades of conflict, isolation and pillage.

The port at Wadi Haifa was a ramshackle affair. A few transit sheds and buildings huddled near the shore, apparently alone in the sands. The main quay extended into the water like a finger of dusty tarmac, its rocky edges eroded over time by the lapping water. As it reached into the lake, the quay's level gradually dropped until it became submerged, as if trying to reach nostalgically down to the town's former location beneath the waves. Only abandoned lampposts hinted at its length, poking from the water like the masts of a sunken ship.

The ferry's captain gave the submerged quay a reassuringly wide berth as we swung in towards the mooring. Dressed in billowing robes and a light blue turban, he barked orders from the bridge in a manner which left no doubt as to his authority. His weathered face, contorted to a grimace by a life on the lake, hinted at a hundred untold stories. Lines were thrown ashore, first bow then stern, and much gesturing and animated chat brought the vessel lethargically alongside, its port side touching the dry land of the Sudan.

I already knew enough of Africa to realise we wouldn't be going anywhere quickly. Wadi Haifa is not exactly Calais or Dunkirk. Cargo took precedence over people during disembarkation, being hustled busily from the vessel's hold onto the quay, and it was over an hour before we could finally follow it off the ferry. We had no reason to hurry, however. Our cars, hopefully still lashed to the Onion Bargee, remained somewhere beyond the horizon, put-putting their way slowly south. We didn't expect them to arrive for another day. This time away from the Porsche and its multitude of problems was exactly what I needed. Despite the Sudan promising to be one of the most challenging countries of the trip, I was more relaxed than I had been at any stage since we left the UK. A good night's sleep, in the air-conditioned cabin which Tom and I had shared, certainly helped.

Once off the ferry, we filed through customs and immigration fairly quickly, having obtained visas in the UK before our departure. Sorting out the paperwork for the cars would have to wait until their arrival the following day. Outside the port, a proud fleet of old Land Rovers waited expectantly for custom. We bartered a ride and set off to the town, four kilometres away across a bleak dustbowl crisscrossed by an untidy mesh of tyre tracks.

I imagine that the old town of Haifa, nestled down on the banks of the Nile, would have been green and pleasant, surrounded by palm trees and agriculture, alive with birdsong. It may have been possible to move the town out of reach of the lake, but its character could not be saved and

149

had vanished beneath the waves. Dusty and forlorn, the new Wadi Haifa felt like the end of the world. As we approached, uninspiring single story buildings appeared out of the dust, marking the extent to which the new town had sprawled since its construction. Paint flaked from rough walls. Donkeys scavenged through rubbish left in the streets. Many buildings were roofed in corrugated iron, while still more remained unfinished. No greenery or trees softened their outlines; they rose unapologetically from the dead ground, the hard desert forming dusty thoroughfares between them.

We found somewhere cheap for dinner. The dining area consisted of cheap plastic furniture, heated by the desert sun. Alfresco dining, Sudanese style. The proprietor, a bullish man with greying hair and beard, declared himself Egyptian and announced that he had visited Liverpool in some previous career as a sailor. However, the animated bouts of abuse he hurled at various passersby and the lack of respect they accorded his comments made us somewhat wary of his various rantings. He cooked a mean camel though, reassuringly barbequed to destruction while we waited, chatting away.

'Welcome to the Sudan!' a jubilant Brummy announced.

'Absolutely.'

Celebrating, we chinked our bottles of Fanta over the table.

'Bring on the road to Dongola.'

'And a cashpoint, please.'

We had almost no money after paying for the ferry from Aswan. If we couldn't find cash in town the following day, we would be in trouble.

Money was a problem for tomorrow however. That evening, we could relax.

During our meal, a smooth-looking guy came over and introduced himself: 'Hi, I'm Mahid. I'll help you with customs. Here, fill out these forms.'

He proffered us some papers. In light of our uncertain finances, we couldn't commit to potentially expensive assistance.

'Sorry Mahid, I'm afraid we can't afford a fixer. We haven't got the money. Sorry.'

'Very cheap. Only forty dollars per car.'

'I'm sorry. Seriously, you have no idea how little money we have right now!' I said.

'Okay,' he replied, 'Well you keep the forms and if you decide you want help, we can speak then.'

Predictably, our paths were to cross again.

After dinner, we found somewhere to stay for the night. The Deffintoad Hotel purported to be the best in town, so we took our chances and checked in. The rooms opened onto a central courtyard and were secured like prison cells, the metal doors and slide-bolts being the most substantial parts of the entire building. Whether these were to keep undesirables out or stop guests escaping was open to debate. Inside the rooms, a bare concrete floor gave way to pockmarked walls, their white paint distressed and peeling, cracks and scrapes going unfixed. The roof was made from palm leaves and dust fell upon us whenever some rat or cat scampered across it. The soiled Turkish toilets doubled as filthy showers and repelled us all.

What more could you expect for a pound a night?

Fortunately, we were still very much in need of rest, so the sagging beds proved welcoming enough. We dozed the scorching afternoon away before climbing a small hill to watch the sunset. Mineral water sundowners would have to do, as we were off the tourist trail now. There would be no alcohol until Ethiopia, nearly a thousand miles away.

We watched from our vantage point on the summit of 'Jebel Haifa' as the sun descended gracefully towards the Lake. Just before it reached the horizon, it was extinguished by the dusty haze, fizzling out in a dull whimper of red. The oblique light of dusk brought out the colours of our surroundings. Beyond the town, the desert ceased to be washed out by the intense sunlight and tanned to a rich red, enticing us onwards. We gazed over the pristine sea of sand that awaited us, punctuated by modest hills and rocky outcrops which rolled away to beyond the horizon.

Beneath us, Wadi Haifa settled into the evening. Lights came on in shops, while televisions rested in windows, watched by groups of Arabic men sitting in neat rows. The TV schedules offered a choice between the two religions of the region: football or Islam. Donkeys took time out from foraging through rubbish to chase each other, while the occasional auto-rickshaw putted peacefully past. Above the tranquillity, the sky's blue became ever deeper.

'Look, a star,' I called, pointing above the lake.

'Well go on, make a wish!' Louise said, in her dulcet Scottish accent.

So I did. I wished that Laura and I could put our differences behind us and become as close as we had been during our New Year's trip, ten months previously. I felt we were getting there, but we still had a long way to go.

'Don't tell us what it is. Bad luck,' said Laura as the sunset painted her smiling face an autumnal bronze.

'Don't worry, I won't.'

She was quite safe there!

'Where's this star then?' Tom chimed in.

'Up there,' I said, pointing as best I could. 'I think it's a star, anyway. It looks a bit too high to be Venus.'

'Are you sure that's a star? I'm really not convinced…'

'It's definitely a star. What else could it be?' Laura answered for me.

'That's not a star. Nah, it's a carrier bag!' said Tom, convinced it had been carried up on the breeze and was catching the last of the sun's rays.

'Shut up!'

'It is. It's definitely a carrier bag!'

The debate raged backwards and forwards for a minute or so, before the fact it hadn't moved and was getting brighter resolved things in favour of the celestial camp.

Gradually, more and more carrier bags filled the desert sky, each one being pointed out to Tom in a joking manner. Whole constellations of them took shape, hovering convincingly in the murky blue.

'Oh grow up you lot, I really wasn't convinced, okay?'

Tom took the mocking in good spirits as we ambled down the hill into the pools of artificial light, which illuminated the town at the end of the world.

Despite the state of the hotel rooms, we all slept well and a predictably bright, hot desert morning was soon upon us. Brummy and I took an auto-rickshaw down to the port to await the arrival of our cars, hopefully still safely lashed to the deck of the Onion Bargee. The others went in search of cash and found out how to register with the police.

It was a peaceful morning at the port. A cargo of sacks was slowly being unloaded from a barge by a laughing team of Sudanese. Grain? Rice? Onions? We couldn't tell.

We hung around for a few lethargic hours. The only thing that happened rapidly here was the increase in the temperature each morning. Apparently, the Barge could appear anytime that day. Sometimes it came in the morning, sometimes the afternoon. *In'shallah* – God's will. Following a relaxing few hours of sitting around, we ventured back into town and joined the rest of the team to register with the police. Typically, this took about an hour, five separate offices, many bored officials of escalating rank and pomp, and about sixty dollars each. Eventually, each of our passports gained an expensive little sticker declaring our status as alien residents and we were free to go on our way.

Unfortunately, there was also some bad news. There was nowhere in town to get money, as the banks only dealt with local Sudanese accounts. As far as the Western financial world was concerned, we were off the map. Pooling what cash we had, there was just enough to pay for the police registration and import the cars, but precious little more. Fortunately we had plenty of fuel for both cars, maybe even enough to reach Khartoum, the capital. Rumours abounded of a bank which sometimes accepted Visa there, as well as the possibility of getting a money transfer from England.

The pressure was right back on again. First it had been the time and reliability concerns which pressed down on us. Time had now become less important, but reliability remained a big issue and was now joined by the threat of running out of cash – becoming stranded in some desert town, unable to afford fuel or repairs. We had to get to Khartoum without any unforeseen expenses and cross our fingers that we could find money there.

We split up once more, Brummy and I returning to the port in search of the cars. On the horizon, a vessel was approaching. Soon, its indistinct outline took on the shape of the Onion Bargee, complete with its precious cargo sat comically on deck.

Once alongside, all the other cargo needed to be unloaded before the cars, to reduce the barge's draft sufficiently for them to be driven onto the quay. This took hours of course, but lazing beneath the Sudanese sun isn't a bad way to pass the time.

There were three vehicles on the barge – the Porsche, the Shogun and the Italian Toyota Land Cruiser, owned by Giuliana, an Italian lady travelling alone. As the most forward of the three, Giuliana's big Toyota was first to gain dry land. The quay was about a foot higher than the barge's deck and the dockworkers optimistically crammed bits of wood, old tyres, inner tubes and sacking in front of the wheels, to make a vague ramp for it to drive up. An old hand at this sort of thing, Giuliana took it all in her stride and cautiously drove the big Toyota onto the quay, before breathing a sigh of relief. Brummy went next, the Shogun taking the gap in its stride, despite causing the barge to rock alarmingly as it regained dry land.

And then it was my turn. Because the barge dipped towards its aft end, the Porsche had to negotiate the biggest step up onto dry land. We packed a tyre in front of each front wheel, and then buried it with sacks, wood and old tyre inner tubes. I climbed in nervously, fired up the engine and was very relieved that the car hadn't decided to break down on its arrival in the Sudan. The ramp was climbed gingerly, creaking alarmingly beneath the weight of the sports car. Once the front wheels made it onto dry land, the sudden weight shift caused the barge to roll worryingly from side to side. I waited for its landward side to begin its upwards motion before gunning the engine and firing the Porsche ashore when the step up to the quay was at its smallest, then stood on the brakes before I flew clean over the pontoon and into the water on the other side. A few of the dock workers smiled and applauded. I breathed again.

Then we went to clear the cars through customs. How hard could it be? Very hard, naturally. Our experiences in Egypt had already answered that question for us.

We found ourselves going through the paperwork with a guy aged in his forties and dressed in flowing white robes, with a white turban protecting his head from the sun. His angular face was aged to leather, toughened by the continuous exposure to dust and sunshine. Everything seemed reasonably straightforward after Egypt and soon we were waiting for the inevitable rubber-stamping of our documents by someone with enough power not to be hurried.

Our papers came back to us in the savvy hands of Mahid, our fixer friend from the previous day. Pleasantries were exchanged; we thanked him and reiterated that we couldn't afford the services of a fixer. Everything seemed fine. He was helping Giuliana to bring her vehicle over the border and insisted he got our paperwork processed at the same time as hers. We once again reiterated that we had no money to pay for his services and would rather do everything ourselves if he expected anything from us. Once again he disappeared with our paperwork.

He was soon back.

'Okay, for each car I need sixty dollars to pay the port tax, customs tax and service costs.'

We had done our homework and knew about the port and customs tax. However, they came to nowhere near sixty dollars. The remainder, the 'service cost', was evidently his cut.

'We will pay the port tax and customs,' I replied diplomatically. 'They come to less than fifty Sudanese pounds. What is this service cost? We can't afford sixty dollars each.'

His reply was predictable.

'You accepted my help, I am a fixer. You must pay me for my services.'

'We told you yesterday we did not want to use a fixer. We told you we couldn't afford it. We told you again today we couldn't afford to use a fixer. Twice,' Brummy said agitatedly, holding up the requisite number of fingers for emphasis.

'But you accepted the help of my colleague.'

Evidently the guy in white robes we had done the paperwork with was a friend of Mahid.

'He didn't tell us he was a fixer. We thought he worked here. How are we supposed to know he's a fixer if he doesn't tell us?'

'This is how we do things here. If you come to Wadi Haifa, you need a fixer. You don't know how our customs work!' Mahid said, getting increasingly agitated.

'Look, in the past we've taken cars into Syria, Egypt, Russia, Uzbekistan, Nepal and Mongolia, all without using fixers. We know how customs work. Fixers are not a legal requirement.'

'This is the Sudan. This is how we do things. If you don't pay I will tear up these papers and you can start again yourself.'

A concerned Brummy turned to me as Mahid spoke and whispered, 'if he wants, he can completely fuck us here.'

Brummy was right. As far as the police and customs were concerned, any confrontation would be our word against his. He was the local, we were the outsiders. I didn't fancy our chances.

Brummy turned to Mahid and took out his wallet. 'Okay, you want to see how much money I've got? Here. A few euros, fifty four dollars and some other stuff.'

I got my wallet out. 'There you go. Seven dollars. Do you believe us now?'

Mahid saw where this was going. 'You have no more? Your friends also have no money?'

'We've got to get to a bank in Khartoum,' I said

Brummy was in full flow now, theatrically extracting us from our predicament.

'Look, you can see how much money we have. We told you this yesterday. We told you again today. Here, take sixty dollars. That's all we can give you.'

Mahid looked angry, but he understood. His attempts to barter us upwards had ground to a halt in the cul-de-sac of our finances.

'Take these too.' I passed him a few packs of Baksheesh cigarettes from the car, 'Marlboro – all the way from England.'

Mahid broke into a smile. He had got money out of us. He had won. 'Okay, I will take this paperwork and get it finished. You are already registered with police?'

'Yes.'

'Good. Ten minutes, we will be finished.'

Despite feeling angry at the time, I could see Mahid's point of view. Once a week, a ferry arrives and sometimes it harbours Westerners intent on adventure. To him, we must appear impossibly rich and sixty dollars per car should be nothing to us. Most people could be more easily coerced into accepting assistance too. The other Westerners on the ferry had accepted his services without question. His assistant had indeed helped us with the early stages of the paperwork. Whether or not he had made the terms of his assistance clear was irrelevant to them. We had been helped.

Soon, it was smiles all round. Mahid and his friend asked for lifts back into town but didn't get the joke when Brummy tried to charge them fifteen Sudanese pounds for the taxi ride. As we drove back, Mahid even offered us a free loan, which we could pay back to his brother when we reached Khartoum. Following our arguments, he had no reason to trust us. It seemed that helping out those in trouble was a way of life out there.

Back in town, we were reunited with Louise, Tom and Laura, and set off into the desert, the sun setting on our time in Wadi Haifa.

* * *

The Sahara is the greatest desert on the planet; its waterless crags and plains smother an area the size of Europe. We were halfway through our north – south crossing of its vastness. In Egypt we had barely noticed it, due to the linear anomaly of the Nile, its fertile banks leading us south on sealed roads to Aswan, where the ferry had gained us another few hundred effortless miles in the right direction. However now we had entered the Sudan, it would be impossible to ignore. Trapped between Nile and sea, the sands of the Sahara stretched away from us, sparsely inhabited and undeveloped, all the way to Khartoum.

Before darkness came, we put about ten miles of rough gravel tracks between Wadi Haifa and ourselves and then set up camp. This little corner of the Sahara is known as the Nubian Desert and at dusk it is stunning. Rolling, craggy hills rippled away into the distance. The tan of the desert and the black of the rocks combined monochromatically, the sandy colours slowly being overrun by shadows. As Louise and Laura started preparing dinner, I wandered off to be alone in the desert; to absorb its atmosphere. The sky overhead had already phased through washed orange to an inky blackness and the landscape took on a strange, translucent quality, as if distances ceased to be. It was totally silent; still and lifeless. I felt like I could reach out through the twilight and touch the hills in the distance as surely as the ground beneath me. I smiled. Such moments made all our efforts worthwhile.

Returning to camp, I chose not to share my ethereal musings with the group, for fear of being ridiculed by Brummy. Bubbling away on the stove, our evening meal was almost ready.

'How's dinner going?' I asked our fine chefs.

'Nearly done. Pasta mush again, I'm afraid.'

'Well if it's as good as last time, I'm not complaining.'

We ate beneath the Porsche's awning, chatting away excitedly about the challenges of the coming days. When we were researching the trip, two parts of our route had stood out as the biggest tests. The lawless plains of northern Kenya were one of these, while the other we would be attacking tomorrow. Finally, we were getting stuck into the adventure, camping wild in deserts, crossing them on tracks of gravel and sand. According to the map, over two hundred and fifty tough miles lay between us and the next piece of tarmac.

I felt that if the Porsche was successful here, I could relax a little. To cross the Nubian Desert would prove the journey wasn't some impossible, harebrained dream. Conversely, if the Porsche failed here, I would never hear the end of the 'I told you so' comments back in the UK. Much would be riding on our performance over the next few days, not least my pride.

We left early the following morning. The landscape passing our windows was composed of only three ingredients. Pale, dusty sand predominated and soon coated the Porsche's every surface. Black volcanic rock was cemented into crags or strewn as boulders, while floods of coarse gravel dominated the plains. The ingredients were stirred together and baked beneath a sky so glaring it was as if the colour had been bleached from it. For now, our route wandered just far enough from the Nile to make water an irrelevance to the recipe.

The temperature was something else. It soon reached the mid-forties, but inside the Porsche – the heater of which was still jammed on full – the thermometer was reading almost sixty degrees. Sweat poured down our faces, mixing with the ever-present dust to form a repulsive slime. The engine temperature remained acceptable provided we kept moving, forcing air through the radiator. However whenever we slowed it would shoot up into the red, just as it had done leaving Cairo. Unfortunately, going slow was the only option much of the time, due to the conditions beneath us. We were driving on rough tracks of sand and gravel which, until the Sudanese complete the long-awaited tarmac road through the desert, is about as good as it gets in this part of the world. Over the years, these tracks had become badly corrugated and threatened to shake the cars apart whenever we tried to make remotely rapid progress.

It is impossible to imagine just how frustrating a corrugated track can be until you experience one first hand. You are forced to crawl along, baking in the sun as your engine overheats, while both you and your car are shaken, quite literally, to pieces. Nobody has managed to come up with an explanation as to how corrugations form, but form they do, rapidly, on makeshift road surfaces. Consisting of horizontal ridges across the road, the effect is akin to driving across a washboard. The suspension is pounded up and down mercilessly, the vibrations being transmitted into the vehicle with a disconcerting machine-gun-like rattle. They are not constant. Sometimes they ease, lulling you into a false sense of security, only to worsen again once you speed up, hitting you harder than ever. On long desert tracks like those in northern Sudan, they are your near constant companion, continuously tormenting you and eroding your patience – and your car – to nothing.

Of course, the Shogun was designed for just this sort of punishment. Its big chunky tyres and beefy suspension absorbed most of the shocks, cushioning its sturdy body and chassis, while the over-engineered cooling system proved more than a match for the desert heat, keeping the engine as cool as it would be in Kent. Conversely, driving the Porsche was an exercise in damage limitation. Go too slow and the engine would overheat and break; drive too fast and the pulverising vibrations would cause some other part of the car to break. We decided to try to keep the speed up and cross our fingers that Porsche's legendary reputation for build quality would get us through the desert. We managed about an hour before the first thing fell off the car.

The corrugations had eased slightly and I was driving quickly to cool the engine. I saw the impact coming, but it was too late to avoid it. Directly in front of me, the passage of tyres had built up a mound of sand in the road. It wasn't huge; the Shogun would have sailed right over it. The low-slung Porsche, however, clattered its exhaust straight into the sand, far too quickly for comfort. I felt a jolt and slowed down, hoping I'd got away with my error. I found I hadn't when I attempted to speed up again. A deep baritone roar assaulted our ears, sounding like the roar from a Spitfire's Merlin engine in some old war film. The exhaust had been knocked off.

'Oops,' I said to Laura, looking slightly sheepish. Turning round, we headed back to where the Shogun had stopped. Brummy was holding up the exhaust with a gleeful smile on his face.

'Forgotten something? Or is the German Turd falling apart already?'

'Well, you know, I figured I'd save some weight, to make things better on the corrugations. We don't actually need an exhaust after all…'

'So you decided to knock it off on that mound of sand?'

'Yeah, that's right.'

It had broken just after the first silencer, about halfway along the car. We couldn't fix it properly without welding equipment, so the repair would have to wait until we stopped in a town. I strapped it to the roof – regretting my failure to fix the exhaust mounts before we left the UK – while Team Shogun laughed and joked merrily about what would fall off the Porsche next. After pointing out just how unadventurous it was to cross a desert in a chunky four-wheel-drive, Laura and I nonchalantly fashioned earplugs from bits of tissue and carried on into the heat.

Fortunately, the desert scenery was stunning enough to distract us from the pounding the Porsche was taking beneath us. Modest clusters of coal-black mountains rose up around us, encircling the gravelly plains and dunes of sand through which we travelled. Sometimes they came in closer and we snaked among them, kicking up plumes of dust in our wake. Often the mountains were conical, as if constructed by Egyptians less trigonometrically minded than those to the north. Now and then they swept along the horizon forming ridges and valleys, hemming us in. Signs of life were few, the sterility only broken by an occasional deep-rooted tree, clinging to the edge of existence. Human habitation was virtually nil. Who would want to live here?

And yet people had been living here for over five millennia. The Nubian people have a rich history, which stretches back just as far as their more famous neighbours further north. Like the Egyptians, they raised pyramids and temples along the Nile and traded their way to prosperity. And like so many other civilisations, they eventually fell. Since then, the area has seen the predictable ebb and flow of invading powers, the strong preying on the vulnerable. The region was last invaded by the British in 1899 and became part of Sudan after independence, in 1956.

Nowadays, the humanity in the area is sensible enough to predominate next to the Nile. Our route would join them on its banks in due course, but for now, we were alone in the desert. Like ants in some desiccated sea, we crawled on through the vastness.

Half an hour after the exhaust had fallen off, a clattering beneath the car signalled that once again all was not well. The remaining silencer section had chosen to part company too, rattling along the road barely attached to the car. We stopped and I removed it, Laura and I calling things a draw, as we had now both lost one piece of the car to the desert corrugations. And we had barely started to make progress towards Khartoum. How many other things would break? It didn't bear thinking about.

Progress was slow. We had hoped to reach a town called Dongola that day, two hundred and fifty miles from Wadi Haifa, where it was rumoured there may be a bank which could fix our lack of money. Due to the lack of cash, we had purchased minimal water and were forced to drink sparingly until we could get hold of more. As the day dragged on, we realised just how over-optimistic our plan had been, but had no choice other than to push on as quickly as we could. Miles from anywhere, our haste was shown in perspective. About thirty camels glided silently across the road in front of us, moving effortlessly in the shimmering heat. Their owner perched imperiously atop the leading camel. Despite their emaciated appearance, thick skin moulded to protruding ribs and joints, the camels could survive out here for days. If we were still here in a few days' time, the cars would probably have failed us and our self-sufficiency was nothing compared to these ships of the desert. We had to keep pushing on.

The corrugated tracks swept closer to the Nile, which appeared as a linear oasis of green, set improbably into the desert to our right. Dense groves of palm trees surged back from its banks, reaching about a hundred metres into the desert before being abruptly halted by the parched ground. Settlements became more common, dusty ribbon developments of single story dwellings lining the rough track. The men wore long white robes and went lethargically about their day, sometimes staring at us as we passed. In comparison, the young boys were more numerous in number and less inhibited in nature, and waved as we passed. When we stopped, they inquisitively ventured up to us in groups, asking incomprehensible questions, smiling and laughing, enjoying the unusual spectacle which we undoubtedly were. But where were the women and young girls? We saw almost none; such are the traditions in this part of the world.

By the afternoon, the temperature was firmly in the forties and the Porsche's engine temperature gauge was wedged firmly in the red. We stopped for a break, as we had done a few times before, to let it cool down a little. Tom looked concerned.

'Ben, take a look at this, will you?' he asked, beckoning me over to the Shogun's rear wheel.

'What? It looks okay to me.'

'There, on the chassis. It's cracking, see?'

'Oh dear…'

Tom had a habit of worrying about every little thing the Shogun did, be it a bit of smoke from the exhaust, or the fact that the engine temperature *didn't* shoot up towards the red like the Porsche's did (hence his conclusion that the gauge must be broken.) This time, however, his worrying was entirely justifiable. The pounding was indeed causing cracks to appear in the 4x4's chassis, spreading rapidly from where the rear suspension was transmitting shocks to it. With hundreds of miles of rough, corrugated tracks to go, it was inevitable the cracking would worsen and given the speed with which it had propagated so far, the Shogun was suddenly in very real danger of snapping in two before it made it out of the desert.

As usual, the seriousness of our predicament was defused with gallows humour.

'Serves you right for all the mocking you gave us over the exhaust falling off.'

164

'Laura, I really don't think that's very constructive,' replied an unamused Tom.

'So, the Shogun is actually coping worse off road than the Porsche? Ha, does this count as a breakdown?' I jibed, concerned but also relieved that for once it wasn't the Porsche causing trouble.

Our priorities were now changed. Rather than pushing on and keeping the Porsche cool by completing the remaining miles to Dongola as quickly as possible, we now had to concentrate on nursing the crippled Shogun out of the desert. Brummy led off slowly, while I followed in the Porsche, frustrated that we would have to drive slowly and overheat the engine even more. Despite the heater being on full, sucking heat away from the suffering motor, everything was still dangerously hot. Just ahead of us, the Shogun's rear bumper had begun to flap up and down worryingly as bumps in the track pounded its weakened chassis. Like a couple of injured survivors of some disaster, our vehicles limped on towards civilisation.

As the sun began to creep downwards, we were still around eighty miles from Dongola. The cracks in the Shogun's chassis were rapidly getting worse, but all we could do was hope it would make it through. Bored of following the Shogun and watching its chassis flex more with every mile, I followed a different route through the jumble of tracks which exited a small village; however the tyre marks I followed quickly petered out to nothing. Attempting to rejoin the main track, I tried to punch the Porsche through some mini-dunes of deep sand. It was a bad idea. As the front of the car hit the first mound of sand, it reared skywards, before plummeting into the second little dune and coming to an abrupt halt. The jolt threw us forward in our seats, stalled the engine and caused the roof box to fly forward from its mountings, landing on the windscreen with a heart-stopping crash.

I got out and surveyed the damage. The roof box was intact, but would need fixing back onto the roof. The clamps which held it in place were twisted and weakened. The bottom of the front bumper had been twisted backwards and the impact had cracked the windscreen. The Porsche looked forlorn, stuck in the sand with the roof box and the broken exhaust resting over the windscreen.

We set to work removing the weightiest items from the roof rack and refitting it. As we did, a standard-issue Toyota pickup pulled up on the track nearby. Its passenger, apparently local, looked our British-registered sports car over quizzically.

'You guys okay?'

'Yeah, we'll be okay. Are you from Dongola? How far is it?' said Brummy.

'Don-*gola*?' he drawled, 'gee, I'm from New Jersey! Say, where are you guys from?'

'We've just driven here from England,' Brummy replied, with more than a hint of smugness in his voice.

'Wow, you can do that?'

'Yep. We went around through the Middle East. Syria, Jordan. We're heading to Cape Town'

'That's pretty cool. Listen, are you sure you don't need any help?'

'No, we'll be okay.'

'No worries. Good luck to you, see ya around.'

And with that off they drove. It's amazing who you run into in the middle of nowhere!

Soon the Porsche was reassembled and a vague path was dug through the ridges of soft sand, back to the firmer ground where the Shogun was waiting. The Porsche's wide tyres proved just sufficient to keep it floating as I carefully negotiated the area of soft sand, trying to maintain momentum and keep in a high gear to prevent the rear wheels from spinning. The accident had been caused by my inexperience in desert driving, but I was learning quickly. Once back on firmer ground, I felt a bit of friendly banter was in order.

'See, who needs a 4x4 anyway? And to think that it didn't even nearly snap in two back there...'

As the sun set over the Nile, we pushed on, looking for somewhere secluded to spend the night. Unfortunately, the Nubian Desert appeared to have a sting in its tail. Tracks became rougher and less defined; often splitting up and leaving us with no clue which to take, or leading us into areas of deep sand. The roof box mounts had been damaged by the previous impact and it slid forwards several times, resting on the windscreen and threatening to crack it further, while the clamps holding it in place would be forced down, preventing the doors from opening. It was frustrating. Each time the box moved, we had to stop, climb out through the windows, drag it back onto the roof, and reattach it as best we could.

The soft sand meant we had to take more risks with the Porsche, which was now overheating more than ever, due to being worked so hard without enough cooling air flowing through the radiator. Sometimes, a partly concealed rock would thud into the car's vulnerable underside, bouncing it sickeningly up in the air. On several occasions I was convinced we'd cracked the engine's vulnerable, unprotected sump, but fortunately it was made of tough stuff. After sunset, Tom took the Shogun along a track where deep wheel ruts straddled a mound of sand in the middle of the road. I tried to follow, but with its minimal ground clearance, the Porsche bottomed out, becoming beached on the sand while its wheels spun helplessly. I swore aloud at Tom, cursing him for choosing a track which I felt was obviously too rough for the Porsche, then regretted my outburst straight away, feeling weak.

My frustrations were real. Things had got out of control and tempers were fraying. Our orderly progress had become a rout as we struggled to escape the desert before it finally dealt a knockout blow to one of our cars.

Darkness came quickly. We pulled away from the main weavings of dirt tracks and parked up for the night. While everyone else feasted on popcorn and prepared the meal, I set about working on the Porsche by torchlight, trying to give it a fighting chance of escaping the desert. It sat there looking forlorn, battered and dusty, with the familiar stench of smouldering oil wafting out from beneath its bonnet.

It had been a day of judgement. Despite the temperature, the overheating, the missing exhaust, the jagged rocks, soft sand, corrugations and dust, the Porsche had soldiered defiantly onwards. For the first time since I'd bought it years before, it had been called upon to dig deep and show some character, to fight its way through. It had done just that and more. It had come alive and battled its way through the pounding with flying colours.

Porsches tend to be aloof automobiles; their pursuit of engineering perfection leaving little space for the imperfections that constitute character in other vehicles. They are a bit like the school swot, frustratingly superior and believing in their unquestionable competence with conviction. The occasional breakdown aside, during our six years together it had nonchalantly done everything I'd asked of it. Today was probably the first time in its two hundred and ten thousand miles that it had been dragged out of its comfort zone and forced to dig deep. It had done. It became the school swot taking a battering on the rugby field, but fighting back bravely and giving as good as it got. Until that day, I had never felt much of an attachment to the Porsche. Huge respect, yes, but nothing more. That day, it had gritted its teeth and showed character and soul. As Daisy the Mini had done years previously in Mongolia, it had ceased to be just another car and come alive.

It still needed some help if it was to make it out of the desert though. I reattached the roof box, bending the clamps back into shape to hold it in place better. The radiator had been shunted backwards in the sandy crash hours earlier, so I removed the front bumper and bent the mountings back into place, hoping for better cooling the next day. The air filter was cleaned, as was the battered underside of the engine, which I checked for cracks. Fortunately, there weren't any. Nothing could be done about the broken exhaust at that stage, so it stayed on the roof. The rear dampers were leaking and the back of the car had sagged close to the ground. It would have to stay like that until we escaped the desert.

A glowing head torch floated over while I worked. I recognised it as Laura's.

'I made some popcorn but Team Shogun ate it all before you had any, so I've made a second batch just for you. Here you go.'

She placed a bowl next to where I was lying under the car.

'Oh, thanks Loz. You didn't have to though. I'll have some in a minute.'

'How's the car?'

'It's going back together okay. I'm surprised the overheating hasn't killed the head gasket yet, to be honest.'

'Yeah, it's not been good, has it? I'm going to get on with the cooking, see you in a few minutes.'

Dehydrated and covered in dust, I picked at the popcorn, before joining the others for dinner.

'So how far do we reckon it is to this Don-*gola* place?' I said, drawling out the place name in two distinct parts, as we all did since hearing our friend from New Jersey say it.

'Can't be more than about sixty miles according to the GPS.'

'Cool, an early start and provided nothing breaks down or snaps in two, we'll be there by lunchtime. How's the Shogun?'

Tom was clearly worried: 'The cracks are getting much worse. You can feel the whole thing flexing now when you go round corners; it's really vague, like steering a boat. I'm really not convinced it'll make it out of the desert unless we're careful.'

He showed me the cracks. They had worsened hugely in the last few hours of driving. The ladder frame chassis above the rear wheels was rotten and fractured for almost half a metre on both sides of the car. It was a terrible mess and must have weakened the vehicle considerably. Bits of painted fibreglass were cracking away where some unscrupulous previous owner had hidden the problem.

'I see what you mean,' I sympathised. 'But all we can do is treat it gently and cross our fingers. How much water is left?'

'We've nearly run out, there's less than three litres between the lot of us. Of course there's always the Nile, but even the locals don't drink that.'

'Ah. Better get out of the desert tomorrow then.'

I was exhausted, but slept curled up in the car that night, as once again the passenger window wouldn't close and despite being in the middle of nowhere, in the tent I would only lie awake worrying about security all night. For once, the desire for time away from Laura hadn't been the reason, as we were getting along much better since the adventure had started properly. Maybe it was because now we had a bit of a fight on our hands, uniting our focus and distracting us from our differences. Whatever the reason, for the first time in the trip I was genuinely positive that we would finish as friends rather than as solemn acquaintances keen to go our separate ways. I smiled, set my alarm for five the next morning and drifted away into an uncomfortable, irresistible sleep beneath a sky which dripped with stars.

Miles from any artificial lighting, sunrise in the desert seemed to last forever. As I stirred, a thin line of red highlighted the horizon, rising to silhouette the mountains and dunes to our east. Beyond the mountains, three hundred miles of empty, rugged desert stretched to the sea. A true wilderness, only a railway and a few rough tracks crossed it. I dozed fitfully for an hour as the big sky brightened, the horizon's red line easing to an electric

170

white. The stillness was overpowering. A dog's hollow bark echoed across from some distant village as the last of the stars were extinguished. It was time to make the most of the cool morning air and escape the desert. I turned the car stereo up, selected 'God Save the Queen' on my iPod, and woke the others with a patriotic morning chorus.

We departed soon after sunrise, but despite the cooler air, the Porsche's engine was overheating within minutes. The going was painfully similar to the previous afternoon – sometimes sand, sometimes gravel, always corrugated and rocky. At times, our route took us in close to the Nile, through villages and past crude irrigation schemes. On other occasions we found ourselves out of sight of water and structures, alone amongst the sand and rocks. Occasionally, a house-sized conical tomb flashed by, calling to us from the past. The morning light was predictably stunning, painting the desert more vividly than the washed out intensity of later in the day. The roof rack stayed in place, little was spoken for want of coffee and all around was peaceful – except for the barking rasp of our broken exhaust of course, which probably echoed all the way back to Aswan.

After a few hours of surfing along the sandy tracks, we came across signs of road building. A strip of bulldozed gravel appeared, slicing through the wilderness. Machinery was dotted around, working on the new road. Tarmac must lie ahead. Smooth, new tarmac. Soon, it was beneath our wheels. We beeped our horns and shook our fists out of the window in triumph. There are few things more blissful than finding yourself on a silkily smooth road after so many miles of suffering out in the corrugated desert, being pounded every mile of the way. Cruising along serenely at fifty mph, the Porsche evidently approved too, its engine temperature returning to normal. We pulled alongside the Shogun and grinned our approval, giving them the thumbs up. This must have tempted fate, however, because just as we did the silky tarmac came to an abrupt end. I hit the brakes as we clattered back onto the rough gravel surface. Evidently the road wasn't quite finished.

This happened several times during the final run-in to Dongola. Each time we would gain a few more effortless miles before having to work for our progress once again. When not on tarmac, we often found ourselves driving amongst the road workings, nipping around mounds of bedding gravel, dodging diggers and swerving around dumper trucks as they tipped their loads. Sometimes we were forced to climb up a steep dirt embankment to gain the new road, a manoeuvre requiring an aggressive approach and a sensitive right foot to stop the wheels from spinning uselessly. The Porsche took it all in its stride, but continued to overheat worryingly all the while. We split from Team Shogun at this stage, driving faster to cool the engine, while the Shogun slowed to protect its worsening chassis.

Soon, the tarmac became the norm rather than the exception and we cruised the last few blissful miles to Dongola, where we were to cross the Nile by ferry. Finding the slipway, we parked and turned off the much-abused engine. The roar of the broken exhaust died, replaced by a loud, ringing silence. We had done it. We had crossed the Nubian Desert – and the Sahara – in a Porsche. It was a wonderful feeling. The car may have taken a beating, we may have been dehydrated, caked in dust and craving a non-existent cold beer, but we had made it through. No one could take our achievement away from us and no one could now tell us we were stupid to believe the Porsche could do it. It was not a feeling of invincibility, for we were a long way from that, but one of great accomplishment.

The Porsche – and its untested scrapyard engine – had nervously exited the garage in England exactly three weeks previously.

Waiting for the Shogun to arrive, we gradually readjusted to life away from the wilderness. To refer to our surroundings as a ferry port would be somewhat optimistic. Hemmed in by apologetic buildings, a rubbish-strewn, dusty slope stretched down to the Nile. Ramshackle huts dotted it, stocked with the essentials of life. Water, bread, fruit and most importantly, phone cards and Coca Cola. Laura even managed to buy some yoghurt, but the desert heat had already turned it. The people hawking fruit and wares to us were nowhere near as aggressive as in Egypt, a pleasing indication of Dongola's remoteness.

Around us, men went about their days, sporting a mixture of long white robes and more Western dress; shirts and trousers worn loose against the heat. Battered white Toyota pickups came and went, heavily stylised with gaudy accessories. People were whiling away the midday heat, apparently waiting for something to happen. Our arrival in the burbling Porsche seemed to constitute 'something' and so the usual torrent of questions came our way.

'Where are you from?'

'What is this car?'

'Why?'

'How much for this car in England?'

'You want to buy Coke Cola? Come to my shop.'

'Which football team do you support? Manchester United?'

These questions were invariably aimed at me. Laura was roundly ignored and took offence when one old man asked me what her name was. She was stood right next to me at the time.

Following twenty minutes of relaxed waiting, chatting with the bored locals while swiping away the legions of flies, Team Shogun pulled up, looking relieved to have survived the desert. They had initially missed the sandy turn-off to the ferry and continued straight past Dongola, but they found us in the end. The ferry consisted of an ancient barge, with a makeshift bridge and space for a handful of cars. We scraped together enough money for tickets and drove onto its creaking wood-planked deck. The Nile's currents were strong, but soon we were heading off the ferry and up a steep earthen bank, into Dongola proper.

Downtown Dongola may have been dusty and littered, but it was also the closest we'd seen to a working town since Aswan. 'Working' is a relative term, however. Despite its status as a regional capital, there were no banks which would consider giving us money and even finding enough fuel to get to Khartoum was a struggle. To top it all, the rumoured good tarmac road, which stretched all the way to the capital, didn't actually start in the town. From what we could gather, it petered out in the desert somewhere to the south west and we would have to head out and look for it. We had heard rumours from other travellers of people taking days to locate it. We couldn't afford to do that, literally. We couldn't afford the fuel or food for more days in the desert. We had to get to Khartoum.

Heading vaguely to the south, we negotiated dusty, cracked tracks between the bleached walls of nucleated compounds, the northern Sudanese take on urban sprawl. Mosques studded this unplanned suburb, with walls of turquoise and minarets reaching for the sky. Occasionally, we were forced to break suddenly, when a morose donkey wandered into the road without looking. On one occasion, instead of a donkey, it was a child.

Whenever we stopped and asked for directions, the looks we received were incredulous. 'Khartoum?' was generally greeted with a bemused confusion; the same response you'd expect if you asked someone in Spain how to get to Berlin. On one occasion, we went to ask directions from a woman who was painting the wall of her compound. Before we even stopped, she ran around the corner into her house and locked the door behind her. The look in her eyes had been almost apologetic.

Eventually, following two hours of vaguely meandering south, never straying too far from the Nile, we crossed a sandy wasteland towards a promising looking embankment. It was the road to Khartoum. Perfect black tarmac sliced a

174

line of permanence through the sands, promising an easy run to the capital.

'That's what I'm talking about!' I shouted jubilantly over the exhaust.

We were all instantly in a celebratory mood. Sweeping briskly along the wonderfully smooth surface, we were thrilled to have put one of the worst sections of the trip behind us and to be making easy progress once more. Louise drove the Shogun for the first time, despite not yet having passed her test back in the UK. Soon she had the unusual claim to fame of having driven more miles in the Sudan than in her native Britain. And as we drove, we were treated to another stunning sunset over the desert, destined to be our last for a while, as we were leaving the Sahara. The sands around us gradually started to harbour thorny shrubs and tough little trees. Grasses made a reappearance. We were entering the Sahel, a region of hardy vegetation and uncertain rains which separates the desert from the green forests and plains of Sub-Saharan Africa.

After four hours of tarmac, we reached the outskirts of Omdurman, one of the three cities which make up Greater Khartoum. We proceeded with trepidation. Barely six months previously, the conflict in nearby Darfur had spilled over into the area, when rebels from the 'Justice and Equality Movement' had audaciously overrun Omdurman and briefly held it from government forces. For several days, helicopter gunships had prowled the skies above while machinegun fire raked the very streets we were driving through. We expected to encounter tight security and a degree of suspicion, at the very least.

We were pleasantly surprised. A couple of lightly manned roadblocks were present on the main road into the city, but gave us no trouble, a flash of our passports and the fact we weren't in a gun-toting 'technical' being sufficient to speed our progress. Soon, we were enveloped by the sights and smells of three million people crammed together in poverty. Groups of traditionally dressed men stood beneath dim streetlights chatting, begging or picking at kebabs. Smoke from cooking and exhausts billowed everywhere, while dust was stirred up from the sandy streets. It was still oppressively hot. The pungent odours of rotting garbage or rancid meat would waft suddenly through the Porsche, before disappearing just as quickly, leaving us primed for the next assault.

Traffic was a nightmare. Crammed Toyota pickups, wizened buses and smoking minibus-taxis drove and stopped pretty much wherever they pleased, often choking traffic by pulling up three or four deep at the side of the road in the more lucrative locations to prowl for business. There was no easy passage, no quick way through, and the engine overheated worse than ever in the baking air. I felt condemned to spending the whole trip worrying about the car. First there was the oil warning light and then, as soon as I learnt to relax and believe that it wasn't an issue, the overheating took its place. Crawling along with the Shogun, it took over an hour to inch our way through to the sturdy cantilever bridge which would take us over the White Nile into central Khartoum. There, we planned to make use of the camping facilities of the Blue Nile Sailing Club, a wonderfully named institution that harks back to the long lost days of colony.

Where Omdurman was cramped and poor, central Khartoum was spacious and deserted. We swept along parallel to the waterfront, down boulevards lined with palm trees. To our left, the two Niles were merging together peacefully. What an emotive place! The Blue Nile had flowed nearly a thousand miles from Ethiopia; the White Nile more than double that from equatorial Lake Victoria. Khartoum stood sentinel over their unification, and saw the river off on its slow passage north, through the Nubian Desert, Lake Nasser and Egypt, all the way to the Mediterranean.

'Laura. We've just driven to the confluence of the Nile. In a Porsche. How amazing is that!'

'It's pretty special, isn't it? I can't believe we've made it this far.'

'Definitely. It really didn't seem possible back in the UK. Remember heading through the drizzle towards Dover, or that stormy ferry crossing? It all feels like so long ago.'

'A lifetime ago. I really hope the Blue Nile Sailing Club has beer. We've so earned it.'

'It would be nice. I'm not holding my breath though.'

'No, me neither. They'll have a shower, though. That'll be blissful enough.'

The sailing club was reached without too much trouble, save a slight navigational error which saw us trying to drive straight through the front gate of the Republican Palace. A youthful soldier on guard duty stopped us.

'Erm, is this the way to the Blue Nile Sailing Club?' Laura asked sheepishly.

'You speak Arabic!'

'As salaam alaikum. That's pretty much all the Arabic I know. Blue Nile Sailing Club?' I replied.

'You speak Arabic!'

'You speak English!' I barked back

'Speak Arabic!'

Brummy interjected: 'Well this really isn't helping anyone.'

Fortunately, a passer-by fluent in both of the Sudan's official languages bridged the language gap and we were soon aware of our faux pas. We were on our way with directions in no time.

The sailing club was still open when we arrived. Sudanese families and friends were busy enjoying a pleasantly warm evening on the banks of the Nile, laughing away beneath glaring artificial floodlights. It was a pleasant spot, looking across to the relatively peaceful, undeveloped northern bank of the river. Correlating this relaxed place to the city in which it nestled, home to one of Africa's most notorious regimes, was difficult, but such thoughts didn't seem to matter at the time. The round of beers we ordered

177

arrived promptly. They were predictably non-alcoholic and tasted strongly of chemicals, but it didn't matter.

'Welcome to Khartoum,' Tom said.

'Yeah, welcome to Khartoum,' we all mumbled in agreement, chinking our bottles together triumphantly.

EIGHT

HIGH EMOTION

25th October 2008
Khartoum, the Sudan

Khartoum was not a very attractive city in its early years. Founded in the third decade of the nineteenth century, its original purpose was as an outpost of the Egyptian Army, from which it evolved to become a centre of regional trade. Its strategic location provided the rationale behind both roles. A sorry place, tan hovels and tattered mosques hunkered down in a mesh of dusty streets, which floundered and disappeared as they reached into the desert. Nearby, the two Niles merged and then wandered off disinterestedly. It must have felt like the uttermost end of the world.

Few people in Europe had heard of Khartoum in its early years, but that all changed towards the end of the nineteenth century, when the city became the evocative stage for a drama which captivated Britain. A twisting plot, played out by a cast of rare charisma, focused public interest on this sandy outpost of the empire.

The first character of the story was doted upon by all of Britain. General Gordon was a man of rare gravity. Standing not quite five and a half feet tall, his disarming smile and piercing blue eyes had an enchanting effect on all he met, while his beard was magnificent even by the high standards of the time. A devout Christian, famed for his adventures in China, Palestine and the Crimea, he was the very definition of the eccentric imperial adventurer.

Gordon arrived in Khartoum in early 1884 at the behest of the British Government, ostensibly on a quick fact-finding mission to precede the empire's abandonment of the Sudan. Despite repeated orders to return to Egypt and a hostile army bearing down on the city, he was strangely reluctant to leave and remained in the presidential palace even as opposing forces moved in and began their siege. These forces were under the command of the second charismatic character in this imperial drama, the enigmatic Muhammad Ahmad, better known as the self declared 'Mahdi', a prophesised redeemer of Islam. Gordon was the sole European in the city for the majority of the siege and an admiring British public became collectively aware of Khartoum's existence for the first time through his plight. To them it was a simple story of good against evil, a civilised noble standing fast against the savages. Despite the government of the day wanting nothing to do with the Sudan, the pressure generated by a spellbound public resulted in a relieving army being dispatched from Egypt as the siege tightened. In January 1885, a year after Gordon's arrival in Khartoum, its paddlewheel gunboats tentatively approached the Presidential Palace – the same palace which we had inadvertently tried to drive into on our arrival in Khartoum. No Union Flag fluttered defiantly against the dusty sky. They were just three days too late.

On the 26th January 1885, the city's defences had been overwhelmed, and General Gordon was killed while fighting defiantly on the stairs of the Presidential Palace. The army sent from Cairo returned having failed to save Gordon, and the newly imperialistic British public went into a communal mourning for the loss of a favourite son. The humiliation at the hands of the Mahdi wasn't forgotten however, and just over a decade later the indefatigable General Kitchener led a force twenty-five thousand strong up the Nile towards Khartoum. The conquest was deliberate and methodical, an advance as slow and unstoppable as an incoming tide. In over a year of campaigning they inched south, before their final victory took place at the battle of Omdurman in 1898, where ten thousand members of the Mahdist army were massacred, for the loss of only twenty-eight Britons. Pride was restored.

Such a margin of victory could only be made possible by the technology of empire. Britain's engineering was the best in the world, making it the superpower of the time. The Sudanese army of 'savages' may have been no match for the maxim guns, breach loading artillery and the rifles of the invading force, but perhaps the most pivotal of the weapons fielded were the Nile gunboats. Built in the Shipyards of London and transported to the Nile in sections, these vessels enabled the transportation of much of the expeditionary force up the Nile and brought unimaginable firepower to bear on their enemies in the region. Ten of these dominating vessels were eventually at General Kitchener's disposal, leading assaults and ensuring the logistically vital Nile remained under British control. Nowadays, only one survives intact – the T.S.S. Melik, residing in the Blue Nile Sailing Club. We had parked the Porsche next to it on our arrival in Khartoum.

The old boat was a sorry sight, sitting forlornly in the sand, thirty metres from the sluggish Nile. Its paint was crazed and peeling, while its aged metalwork was frozen in a permanent state of decay. The big gun on its bow pointed upwards, no longer holding the Nile to sway. Drifting sadly towards dereliction over the course of the twentieth century, its last belated voyage had taken place twenty years previously, when powerful floodwaters had floated it from its moorings and swept it ashore. In spite of its fall from grace, there was still a proud air about the vessel, as if it had contracted General Kitchener's Victorian spirit through association. During retirement it had found use as the clubhouse for the Blue Nile Sailing Club, its presence in central Khartoum an anomaly that speaks volumes for the Sudanese middle class's continued affinity with the British way of doing things.

The similarities between the gunboat and the Porsche parked next to it made for a fortuitous encounter. Both had made the long journey here from England. Both had faced their moment of judgement in a distant desert and both had proved their mettle. Finally, both were now in quite shocking states of disrepair and would need rather a lot of TLC in the very near future.

The dappled shade provided by the trees kept my tent cool until well after sunrise. I dozed blissfully, enjoying the unaccustomed luxury of not being in a hurry for once. We would be in Khartoum for a few days at least, restocking, recovering and repairing. It was past ten o'clock before Louise's offer of a nice cup of tea finally tempted me to join the outside world, where I breakfasted on the deck of the gunboat. My first shower in a week then revived me further, not to mention turning my skin several shades lighter.

So it wasn't a suntan, after all.

That lazy morning set the tone for our three days in Khartoum. We couldn't go anywhere quickly, as we had arrived on the Friday night and would have to wait until the Monday before we could get our Ethiopian and Kenyan visas and arrange a money transfer from back home. Over that lazy weekend, I got to grips with the backlog of jobs which needed to be carried out on the Porsche. The exhaust was welded back together and refitted. Our overheating problems were traced to a faulty cooling fan, so I swapped it for the spare one we'd brought along. I had a proper look at the oil pressure sensor and found it had been incorrectly wired. Once rectified, the engine gave a pressure of two bars when ticking over. Not brilliant, but at least acceptable and a weight – finally – off my mind. In between these tasks, I relaxed at the sailing club. Working and living in the constant heat generated an insatiable thirst and so for three days we lived off the endless supply of cold Pepsi sold there. It was pleasant to sit out on the grassy terrace above the moorings, sipping a cold drink as the Blue Nile slowly meandered past to meet its white counterpart, while the city's muffled sounds drifted faintly over to our tranquil haunt. Sunsets were dazzling, enriched by the dusty air, while at night the technicolour lights of a newly constructed suspension bridge just downstream cast long reflections in the peaceful waters, which danced hypnotically amongst the ripples.

The Shogun's wounded chassis desperately needed attention, so Tom and Brummy took it next door to a dusty waterfront yard where a group of industrious Sudanese had set up a welding business. Their equipment was primitive and their safety precautions non-existent. In lieu of a welding mask, a pair of fake Oakley sunglasses protected the eyes, while gloves and protective clothing were shunned in the heat. Fortunately, they didn't do themselves too much lasting damage as they cut out the rotten metal from the chassis and welded angled bits of steel in place to reinforce the areas where the cracking had spread. It was about as crude a repair as could be imagined, but there was little else that could be done. As the extent of the damage became apparent, we realised just how lucky we were to have made it out of the desert.

We could have fared much worse, however. Two days after our arrival at the sailing club, Guiliana's big Toyota 4x4 arrived. She was visibly shaken, and flamboyantly described how in the middle of the desert, one of the rear wheels had come off her vehicle and jammed itself in the wheel arch. Unable to budge it herself, she had to wait half a day for someone to arrive, who then summoned help from a nearby village. Jacking up the stricken Toyota revealed that the studs holding the wheel onto the axle had sheared at the wheel spacer, allowing it to come adrift. A repair had enabled her to escape the desert after two days of uncertainty, but her confidence was evidently dented. She dented our confidence in turn, by recounting how she'd come this way years previously and found the rough tracks of northern Kenya to be a much tougher test than those of the Sudan. Given how close the Nubian Desert had come to finishing off our vehicles, this did not bode well.

Another overland traveller was also staying at the sailing club. Volka, a German native, had been living in Cape Town for years, working as a handbag designer of all things. He was slowly heading north in his rather impressive Land Rover, aiming to be back in Germany for Christmas. Volka showed an almost childlike enthusiasm for our roof tent arrangement – *on a Porsche* – and couldn't get over the bottle opener fixed permanently to the roof box. He also bore warnings of what we would encounter in Ethiopia.

'The children are terrible. They run into the road right in front of you to ask for money. Some of them throw stones at passing cars too. Don't let them get away with it. One kid threw stones at me, so I stopped, jumped out and chased him. When I caught him, he cried and peed himself.'

All in all, quite an advert for the next country on our journey!

On the Monday, after several abortive attempts, Louise and I were able to arrange money transfers from the UK, ending our financial worries. Finally, we could afford to pay for the campsite, the endless Pepsis, the welding and the visas. We made several visits to the Ethiopian Embassy, a rundown structure a couple of miles to the south of where we were staying, and obtained visas from the disinterested officials who inhabited a grimy office. A taxi ride out to the airport area was made to visit the Kenyan Embassy, where – by contrast – visas were purchased from a smiling, well-spoken chap in a pristine, air-conditioned office. With money and visas obtained and the cars fixed, we were ready to leave.

Despite there being nothing particularly wrong with central Khartoum, after three days there we were all pleased to be leaving – and not just because of the city's lack of beer. The place was nice enough, if rather bland. High-rise buildings lined clean paved avenues, while a wealth of ambitious construction projects dominated the skyline. The sidewalks were quiet, being shaded by well-tended trees and feeling perfectly safe. A sense of realised prosperity was apparent, as if Khartoum was only just awaking to a newfound wealth and was preparing to enjoy its time of fortune. Traffic was dense, battered yellow taxis jostling with typically African cars and a disconcerting number of brand new 4x4s, which more often than not sported the insignia of some aid agency or NGO on the door. The sheer number of agencies operating in the area was astonishing, but understandable given the uncertainties in the south of the country and the horrors being perpetrated in Darfur, less than five hundred miles to our west.

I didn't see much of Khartoum during our stay there. I saw more of the Porsche's underside than the shantytowns scattered around the city limits, where over two million people displaced by war and poverty live, and witnessed Omdurman's slums only through darkness. However, my impressions of central Khartoum were real enough and were not what I was expecting from an internationally isolated capital which had been waging expensive and catastrophic civil wars for thirty-eight of the last fifty-two years. By rights, the city should be impoverished and run down, struggling to survive. But, over the previous decade, development has been pushing forward vigorously, fuelled by the petrodollars pouring in from the oilfields to the south.

It is saddening to think that the Sudan's embezzling elite and its military – the strong arm of its perfidious government – are receiving almost all of the benefit from the windfalls. The richer parts of Khartoum float like islands of wealth upon a sea of poverty and injustice. Richest of all are those closest to the government of President Omar al-Bashir, under whose leadership the Sudan exists as an oppressive, authoritarian state. Since taking power in a coup in 1989, Bashir has pursued his unique brand of politics through such policies as providing a safe haven for Osama Bin Laden, fanning the flames of

Darfur and roundly ignoring all the accusations of genocide and war crimes which have been levelled against him.

Meanwhile, aid agencies continue their efforts to drag the impoverished Sudanese people out of the dark ages and provide them with a means to survive, while the government, more often than not, serves only to hinder their efforts and profit from their presence. To them, the aid agencies are just another source of money to be leached dry.

The road from Khartoum to the Ethiopian border stretched out before us. It shadowed the Blue Nile for a hundred miles or so before heading out west through scrubland for another few hundred miles to the border town of Gallabat.

The day was already roasting hot as we left Khartoum. Suburbs, organised agriculture and light industry gradually gave way to a simpler, rural way of life. Traffic was manic, but our experiences in Egypt a week before had acclimatised us to the madness and it felt almost normal. The Blue Nile flitted in and out of view to our left, providing irrigation for the adjacent farmland. After a few hours it was crossed and left behind, and aridity became the dominating force in the landscape once again.

All around us, the earth was baking. We were crossing a vast plain, rocky and featureless. Nowhere to hide. Occasional hills and crags flecked it, while little tracks often beckoned us into villages of circular mud huts with attractive conical straw roofs. The drama of the landscape was contained within its monotony; hour after hour of the same shrubby openness, dwarfed beneath the huge blue dome of the sky. Mostly we were alone, crawling along the tarmac which spanned the primeval plain, feeling insignificant. Sometimes, a herd of camels would interrupt the solitude.

Every so often, the timeless illusion was shattered by a police checkpoint, which typically consisted of little more than a tin hut, cooking its occupants unsympathetically in the heat. The routine was always the same and very predictable, to the point where we grew bored of it. Names, dates of birth, passport numbers and occupations were asked for and then entered into a weighty book in Arabic script. Generally, the folk manning the checkpoint didn't understand much of what we said and entered the same indecipherable scribble for each of us. Even when Tom and I, bored, declared Brummy to be a 'computer geek' and Laura a 'professional netball player', they just wrote something solemnly into the book, confirming the uselessness of the procedure.

The sun began to drop as we neared the Ethiopian border. Villages had increased in their density and life-sustaining arable agriculture was all around. Livestock was scarce and it was an unusual occurrence when we were stopped for five minutes by cattle crossing the road in a village. Beneath the darkening sky, young boys came running and gazed at us inquisitively from a safe distance, until we beckoned them closer, breaking the ice. Proudly dressed in sandals and clean shirts, they laughed and cowered amongst themselves, embarrassed by the attention they were receiving, yet captivated by our appearance. Before long the cattle cleared the road and we were able to continue. We didn't get far.

Out of the dusk, two men saw our approach and flagged us down, their AK47s and combat fatigues marking them out as members of the Sudanese Army.

'No pass. You wait here.'

'Why?' we enquired. 'We're going to Ethiopia. Its only fifteen miles away.'

'Wait here.'

Eventually, we gleaned from the commanding officer of this remote outpost that there had been a lot of shifta activity in the area; outlaws living in the hills and robbing anyone who happened to be passing through. Because of this, we would have to wait until a convoy left to safeguard our passage to the Ethiopian border.

'Just our luck,' Brummy said. 'We get within fifteen miles of our first beer in a week and the killjoys won't let us push on.'

Settling in for a long wait, we dug out the cooking gear and rustled up some popcorn, followed by a meal of spaghetti bolognese. The sun set as we cooked. A proper African sunset, it dipped into the Sahelian bushes rapidly, the dramatic reds generated by the dust further north being replaced with soothing salmon clouds draped across the sky.

We had an inquisitive audience as we cooked and ate by the light of our head torches. The Sudanese who sampled our dinner smiled politely, but failed to convince us that they really enjoyed our basic interpretation of Italian cuisine. All of them were surprised that we ate separately from our own plates, as the custom in this part of the world is for everyone to tuck into a single, communal dish.

Before we'd finished, an army jeep led a convoy into the checkpoint and promptly turned around ready to depart again. Cookers, pans and dinners were quickly thrown into the vehicles as we joined the convoy and were escorted safely through the darkness.

The border town of Gallabat was dark. Very dark. Little artificial lighting punctured the weighty blackness. Along its single street, which led into Ethiopia over a stagnant creek, lorries were parked up waiting to cross. Down a steep verge to one side of the road, the Sudanese customs officials inhabited their offices. We were soon stamped out and ventured across a shambles of a bridge into Ethiopia, where everyone related to officialdom was sleeping. We would have to wait until morning to complete the paperwork. Evidently they took their border security very seriously!

'They probably assume the shiftas will get anyone who makes a run for it during the hours of darkness,' suggested Laura.

So unofficially, we were in Ethiopia. There was only one thing to do. We went to the pub. While the pubs back in

England ape their long lost past relentlessly, in Ethiopia they do *ye olde medieval inne* properly. A wooden framework had been sealed with weathered mud and straw to make the walls, which were punctuated by tiny windows full of darkness. The straw roof overhead was as effective as any thatch and the choice of beer was sublime, being named in honour of St George. The outside toilet was positively medieval too, albeit not something you'd find in a retro pub back in the UK. Hints of modernity were few. A dim light bulb hung apologetically from the ceiling, while a few locals huddled around a tiny, flickering television, watching as an Ethiopian soap opera attempted to break through the static. Outside, a well-worn pool table floated in a circle of light, tucked beneath a corrugated iron roof.

Cold beers were promptly bought, our first since Aswan. They disappeared quickly, but their appealing taste lingered. Predictably, another round was on the table within minutes. We were all so happy to be there.

'This is so nice after the Sudan!' exclaimed a happy Louise.

'Anywhere with beer is nice after the Sudan,' said Brummy.

'Indeed. Funny how we're not even stamped into Ethiopia yet, but we're already in a bar.'

'Yeah, trust us, our first act as illegal immigrants is to crack open the beers!' Laura said.

'Rather fitting,' observed Tom.

'Have you noticed them,' Laura whispered, gesturing towards the window, where a pair of pouting women were peering in at us.

'Yeah, what are they all about?' asked Tom.

'Prostitutes,' said Louise.

'Yep, that's the AIDS crisis happening right there,' spat Laura.

She was right. Frontier towns like this, with their poor residents and transitory populations of bored truck drivers, provide plenty of opportunities for the human immunodeficiency virus (HIV) to spread, propagating along the continent's arteries as efficiently as those of its victims. The epidemic sweeping Africa can in part trace its potency to small transit villages such as the one we were in and it was a sobering thought that HIV/AIDS had crossed Africa along the same roads we were using.

Our epiphany diluted the thrill of the evening somewhat. We chatted over a few more beers then set up camp and went to sleep.

My first ever African memories are of Ethiopia. It was 1984 and I was four years old. I remember seeing television news reports of horrific famines gripping the nation, in which children looked on from among the dying, too weak or helpless to swipe the flies away from their hollow faces. Some of them had grotesquely oversized stomachs, the result of water retention brought on by the advanced stages of starvation. My brain wasn't yet mature enough to understand how they could be hungry when their bellies looked so big, but it was mature enough to realise that those children were *my age* and that something terrible was happening in this place called Africa.

Up to a million Ethiopians died in the famines of the mid 1980s and many of the defining images of that decade – and of Africa – stem from those horrors. I wasn't sure what to expect from the country which to people my age, seems to epitomise the suffering of a continent more than any other.

I awoke with the comforting familiarity of a slight hangover, my first for nearly two weeks. Ethiopia had already been awake for hours, rising with the dawn, and the border town of Metema bustled chaotically. Its main thoroughfare had become a turbulent flood of humanity, the likes of which we had not yet encountered on our journey. People were dressed down after the Sudan, austere white robes replaced by grubbier Western-style garb. Donkeys, goats and chickens were stirred into the commotion and occasionally a lorry edged cautiously through the flood. To the sides of the main street, makeshift pontoons spanned stagnant drainage trenches, providing access to rustic shacks of wood and corrugated iron, which propped each other up like a chaotic house of cards. All were selling wares, aiming to profit from the passing traffic and the prohibition of the Sudan. The air was thick with dust, moisture and a multitude of festering smells. Sweat, fumes and rotting debris took it in turns to assault our timid noses. It was all refreshingly anarchic and alive after our time in the Sudan, the self-conscious reticence of the Arabs being replaced by a dynamic extroversion, the anodyne desert giving way to a bustling frontier town. The atmosphere buzzed with laughter, chatter, purpose and energy. I felt energised by it.

Immigration was tucked away obscurely off the main thoroughfare. A stroll down a path through some grassy wasteland, with a dusting of litter and grazing goats, soon saw us there. Hiding aloofly within its own compound, beneath a fluttering Ethiopian flag, it turned out to be a structure similar to the previous evening's bar. Characterful mud walls and a straw roof provided the basics of the shelter in which formalities were conducted. Chickens scavenged within the compound's grounds. Inside, the walls had been pockmarked by time and a variety of promotional calendars clung decoratively to them, detailing years long gone. The room was divided by a large desk, behind which a young man and woman treated their tasks with aloof seriousness, which bordered on comical given the surroundings. Following half an hour of sitting around in their office as they expertly avoided eye contact, they graciously deigned to process our passports. This initially involved them scanning through a long list of handwritten names in a well-thumbed book, a process which seemed to take forever. The faint whiff of comedy never left as they completed their scan, which confirmed we weren't banned from Ethiopia, before laboriously recording our details and stamping us into the country. Leaving the wattle and daub hut into the sunlight, we were illegal immigrants no more.

Eager to be underway, we changed the last of our Sudanese money and hit the road into the Ethiopian Highlands towards Gonder, our goal for the evening. Once we had inched our way out of the seething mass of humanity in Medema, the day's entertainment presented itself. Rough and gravelly, the track rose rapidly beneath pleasantly cloudy skies. Bumps, potholes and corrugations were once again our ever-present companions, while sometimes streams crossed the track, forcing us to ford the waters. The Shogun would cautiously wade through first and the water was never too deep for the low-slung Porsche to follow.

The landscape had changed completely from the flat plains and sand of the previous day. Thick vegetation crowded in around the gravel track, while the horizon was a permanent sweep of dramatic hills. Everywhere was a lush explosion of green. Trees, bushes and grasses carpeted every inch of ground, while pleasant cumulous clouds jewelled the sky. It was as if the sandy emptiness of the previous day had been denied entry at the Ethiopian border and stayed obediently in the Sudan. We barely saw another vehicle, but the track still had plenty of users. Children herded smiling goats and emaciated cattle along it, the livelihood of the family under the playful supervision of its four-year-olds. Men strolled from village to village or sat at the road's edge, watching the world go by. Reactions to our passing varied. Children would sometimes wave, but more often than not would point and shout precociously, 'you, you, you,' or 'give me money.' Sometimes they greeted our passing with a strange, gorilla-like dance, the significance of which we never quite got to the bottom of. They never threw stones at us. Maybe we were lucky. The grown-ups often waved, sometimes grimaced and always retained an indifferent dignity.

As we climbed higher, the scenery became ever more dramatic and precipitous. The temperature fell to comfortable and occasional raindrops hit the Porsche's cracked windscreen. After a few hours of gravel, tarmac reappeared, indicating we were nearing Gonder, Ethiopia's tourist capital, perched over two kilometres up in the foothills of the Simien Mountains.

It was a pleasant place. Clean by the standards of the trip so far, fairly relaxed and pleasantly cool by virtue of its elevation. Following their GPS's instructions, Team Shogun drove straight through the town and started heading off towards Eritrea. With no way to let them know their mistake, we gave up following and returned into town. They'd get the idea and be back soon and, given that Gonder seemed to be set up with the explicit goal of extracting money from tourists, we were quickly able to find a nice coffee shop in which to wait for them. As usual with such places, we weren't left alone for long.

'Hi, I'm Dan. Where are you from?'

He was tall and slight, and wore a cream denim jacket. His young face was relaxed and trustworthy.

'Dan? That's not a very Ethiopian name?'

'You can call me Dan. What's your name?'

'I'm Ben and this is Laura. We're from England.'

'England, nice. Do you need help with anything? I can take you to a hotel or a garage if you like?'

'Maybe later, we're just having our dinner now and our friends haven't arrived yet.'

'Okay, we can talk later.'

'Maybe.'

Every town frequented by foreigners seems to have people eager to help, people who intuitively know how they are going to profit from your visit the moment they clamp eyes on you. Dan was a very smooth demonstration of this. We wanted a garage where the Shogun's chassis could be checked over? His uncle had a garage. We wanted to take a trip to the Simien Mountains the following day? Of course he could arrange it, with lunch included naturally. Laundering? Predictably yes, he knew someone. I respected his brash approach to making a living and given our tight schedule, it was easy to simply bow to his local connections and let him take his cut – after all, he'd earned it for his cheeky initiative alone.

Team Shogun took forty-five minutes to find us, eventually noticing we weren't following them anymore and retracing their steps. We had sent them the GPS co-ordinates for the café, but there was a mistake in there somewhere, as they'd ended up at an expensive hotel on the side of a hill, overlooking the town.

'At least the views were great. You should head up there,' reasoned Brummy.

'Can we finish our second coffee before we go?' Laura asked, savouring her caffeine fix.

Tom wasn't sharing the joke. Team Porsche had once again abandoned them and didn't outwardly seem to care about the fact. Fortunately, the two children who had begun to take an interest in us quickly defused the tension.

Ethiopia is overflowing with children. Nearly half of the country's eighty-two million citizens are under the age of fourteen. Wherever you are in the country, it seems you can't escape the gaze of a group of precocious kids. Round faced, their expressions alternate from smiling to serious, but never approach bored. The two children who adopted us couldn't have been more than five years old. Their clothes were filthy and ragged, but were overshadowed by their beaming, saucer-like faces and shining eyes, full of the joy of being alive. When not being chased away from the café by one of its attentive waiters, they seemed to love little more than 'guarding' the Porsche, or accepting the chips we clandestinely offered them when the waiters weren't looking. Often, they would chatter excitedly to us in their native language. Obviously, we couldn't understand a word, but this didn't seem to matter in the slightest.

After dinner, we spoke to Dan and quickly arranged a touristy excursion to the Simien Mountains for the next day, while the cars were booked into Dan's uncle's garage for some work at the same time. We then went to book into the Belengez Pension, which offered reasonable accommodation, low prices and somewhere secure to park the cars. The guys we'd met on the red bus in Aswan were already there, so logically, there was only one thing to do. We all headed into town to swap stories over a few drinks. Of course, Dan knew just the place.

The red bus had arrived in Wadi Haifa the day after we left, on a much larger barge than we had used. Running well behind schedule, they had been forced to drive in shifts and not stop in Khartoum like we had; hence they'd arrived in Gonder a day before us. Dan had struck again and their bus was already in the garage our cars would be visiting the following day, having a series of urgent repairs undertaken. This didn't bode well for them however, as they were due in Addis Ababa two days later, for a rugby match against the Ethiopian national team. As they were missing half the members of a team, they invited us to join them and we quickly agreed to take part in this most unlikely of international fixtures.

The night rolled on, starting with some traditional Ethiopian music before descending into a drunken haze. We met up with Dan and his friends for a few drinks and the contrast with the Sudanese couldn't have been more dramatic: 'The Sudanese? We call them FANTA. It stands for 'Foolish Arabs Never Taste Alcohol.''

Eventually we ended up in a pitiful nightclub, where a few locals danced to painful Ethiopian pop, which blasted forth with enough bass to shake the very structure of the building. Conversation was impossible. Team Shogun headed off to bed first, leaving Laura and I to walk back alone. A chill breeze chased along the deserted alleys as we wandered back, whistling spookily in the night. We spoke little, but our silence was laden with messages nonetheless.

The uneasy weeks together, not discussing our dysfunctional coexistence, had been building up the tension between us.

The swirling wind buffeted our roof tent as we lay in our sleeping bags. Laura seemed uneasy.

'Are you okay?' I said.

'Yes, I think so.'

'Are you sure? It's not the beer is it?'

'No, it's not the beer.'

'Seriously Laura, is there anything you want to talk about?'

'Well, not really.'

'Laura, it's me. Come on, what's up?'

She was lying facing me, her glistening eyes fixating on mine. It was light enough to see tears on her cheeks. She took my hand as she spoke.

'Ben, I'm so sorry for hurting you. I never intended for it to happen. I'm so sorry.'

'Laura, don't be silly,' I replied uneasily, feeling suddenly sober. 'Neither of us intended for things to end up like this. You just did what was right by you. Don't blame yourself. What happened, us falling out, it isn't your fault – it just happened, that's all. I don't blame you.'

'It's just that all this tension between us, the not getting on. I feel like it's my fault.'

She was sobbing ever so slightly. The sudden release of pent up emotion was somewhat unexpected. I felt a lump appear in my throat.

'Please don't blame yourself dude. It's my fault too, what's happened is down to both of us.' I placed my hand on her shoulder, attempting to add some sincerity to the words.

'I liked you too, you know that? It's just that I met Alan and it all seemed so right.'

'In that case you did the right thing. Don't worry about me; you have to do whatever is right for you. If it felt right then you shouldn't have any regrets.'

'I just thought he would be better for me. I was so confused about what I wanted back then. I don't know, I think I was just scared of getting involved with you.'

'Why?'

'I didn't realise what a sensitive person you were. I thought you'd talk me out of finishing medical school, drag me away from my career to travel and go climbing all the time.'

'Seriously?'

'It sounds silly I know, but it's what I thought. Medicine means so much to me and I didn't know you as well back then as I do now. I know how stupid it sounds now.'

She held my hand tighter.

'It's not stupid,' I replied. 'You made your decision based on what felt right at the time, and you stuck with it. I respect you for that,' I replied, feeling somewhat awkward as months of coldness were unexpectedly stripped away.

'I don't know. Now I know you better, it's made me realise how little I knew you before.'

'Laura. Rightly or wrongly, your decision was based on what you knew at the time. You've got to believe you did the right thing. Honestly, don't worry about me.'

'I'll try. I just hope we can sort out our friendship and go back to how things were before it all went wrong. I hate being angry with you.'

'Yeah, I hate being angry with you too. Probably because I liked you so much before and things were so good between us.'

'They were!' Laura raised her voice, adding conviction. 'We used to get on so well. Remember how much fun we had last New Year?'

'Yeah, we got on so well then. I just want to put all this behind us and enjoy the rest of the journey. And you know what? I think we've just made a huge step towards that just from having this conversation.'

'I'm sure you're right. I'm so glad we're finally talking about things, getting them out in the open,' Laura said, smiling for the first time since we began to talk.

We chatted for over an hour and as we did, the distance between us eroded to nothing. Gradually, we talked aside our differences from the past few months and began to understand each other for the first time in the trip. Laura had been finding our cold proximity just as difficult as I had and on that moody night in Ethiopia, in a buffeted tent perched on the roof of a Porsche, we finally ended our mutual solitude and reconnected with one other.

* * *

The Simien Mountains swept up to a height of over four thousand metres above the plains of the Sudan. We stood on the edge of their dramatic precipices, our lungs gasping for air as the vista rushed away towards the horizon. Vegetated, broken crags fell away beneath us, drawing our eyes to the shaded valleys below. To the north, the Sudan stretched back towards our journey's origin, while the awesome granite domes of Kasalla were just visible through the dusty haze, defiantly punching for the sky. The precipices rising beneath our feet were topped with swathes of undulating grasslands, like heavenly fields in the sky. Life was everywhere. Goats and cattle grazed on the idyllic heights, while troops of monkeys foraged peacefully. The area's human population lived in circular mud huts and nowhere in the mountains was very far from a group of beaming, filthy, inquisitive children. The cool, breezy air and abundance of green hills were a welcome contrast to the sandy plains of the previous weeks. Laura and I said nothing of the previous night's conversation, but the tension between us had finally lifted. We would return to the subject when the time was right. We both needed time to let our emotions settle after our heart-to-heart beneath the stormy Ethiopian night.

I thought about our chat during the day's excursion. We both clearly still felt something for each other, a strange attraction which had fuelled the animosity between us and allowed it to continue for so long. Now the animosity had lifted, I was nervous of where our proximity, combined with our new-found mutual understanding, might lead us. We were becoming closer, but Laura had a boyfriend waiting for her back home and I had no desire to wade in and split them up behind his back. The remainder of the journey promised to be rather interesting.

Back in Gonder that evening, we collected the cars from the garage, where they had spent the day receiving a bit of much-needed T.L.C. Predictably, they tried to overcharge us grossly for the work – a bit of welding on the Shogun's chassis and a new rear shock absorber for the Porsche – and so our evening began with a heated argument. Thanks to the amount of practice we'd had arguing at Arab border crossings, we won and were able to barter the garage owner down to a more reasonable price. That evening we went out for a meal, intent on sampling traditional Ethiopian cuisine.

The national dish of Ethiopia is certainly an acquired taste, and one which I spectacularly failed to acquire. A large, communal plate hid beneath a horrendous grey pancake which looked and tasted very much like a manky piece of some old, well-used wetsuit. Atop this foamy delight sat – not very encouragingly – a spicy mush of mince, sauce and vegetables. In lieu of utensils, it is customary to tear off parts of the foamy, rubbery pancake and use it to scoop the stew into your unsuspecting mouth. The taste and texture of the pancake were repulsive, but as the saying goes, when in Rome, you have to try the local rubbery delicacy – however much your common sense tells you it can't end well. The meal was finished by all and was washed down with a few beers before we retired to bed.

Laura and I had forgotten to take our malaria tablets that day, so we took them before going to bed. As lying down within an hour of taking the acidic doxycycline pills generally results in a violent illness, we sat up and chatted pleasantly for a while before going to sleep – a little too early as it turned out.

I gently phased in and out of consciousness, vaguely aware of the discomfort slowly building in my stomach. I knew what it meant, but tried to sleep through it anyway.

It's only a tablet. It'll pass.

By about one in the morning, the discomfort had become a sharp pain, impossible to ignore. I curled up in a foetal position in an attempt to minimise the discomfort, but it continued to worsen. Sometimes a sharp, acidic taste drifted up from my stomach, causing me to retch sickeningly.

It really isn't going to pass.

My luck had run out. I had to get out of the tent, quickly. Very quickly, in fact. Fighting with the zips in the darkness, I just about got the door open, but then promptly became tangled up in our light's power cable as I attempted to escape. Panic built within me. Not a moment too soon, I extricated myself, narrowly avoiding falling through the Porsche's windscreen in the process, and dashed to the toilet.

The doxycycline tablet had dissolved in contact with the side of my stomach, causing a frankly sadistic reaction. For the first time in my travels, I was violently sick, the fluorescent yellow gunge tasting inconceivably acidic and sharp. It was disgusting. I shakily returned to the tent about ten minutes later, feeling weakened by my exertions and with a terrible taste in my mouth that no amount of toothpaste could remove.

'Are you okay?' a drowsy Laura asked.

'I will be. I've just been Doxy'd.'

'Oh no, it's horrible isn't it? I had it happen in Peru last year.'

'Yeah, I'll admit it's not my favourite experience, but don't worry. I'll be alright.'

I dozed off again, but unfortunately my stomach chose to remain awake. Another hour meant another dash to the toilet was required, where I threw up until there was nothing left. I then threw up a bit more for good measure, retching up only liquid while feeling cut through by the acrid taste and smell of the doxycycline.

'Ah well,' I told myself, 'at least the sharp taste means I don't have to taste those horrific pancakes for a second time.'

It was scant consolation. Following twenty painfully memorable minutes, I was utterly destroyed. I felt weak and exhausted, in need of sleep and water but fearing them both.

Once back in the tent, the sharp pain in my stomach finally decided to leave me be, stepping aside to make way for a duller ache from somewhere lower down. I raced to the toilet for a third time. *This isn't going to be fun.* Evidently the doxycycline wasn't the only thing having an effect on me. I thought back to the manky pancakes and floods of nausea washed over me.

As the upper levels of my digestive system were already empty, the bottom half had evidently decided to violently purge itself in sympathy. My body hadn't quite got bored of vomiting just yet however and hence the two disparate ailments conspired cruelly to make me suffer. It felt like a lifetime of straining and discomfort. So delicate was I that there was no way I could leave the bathroom, so for hours I was trapped there, answering my body's masochistic whims while reflecting on the glamorous side of driving across Africa in a Porsche. When the torment subsided momentarily, I would pass out sitting on the throne, drifting in and out of sleep with my sweat-soaked forehead resting on the adjacent sink. I wondered whether it was by design that the sink was located in such a position that you could be sick into it while sitting on the toilet. When I was finally able to go back outside, the sun was already up.

I may have regained enough composure to leave the toilet, but there was no way I was about to risk returning to the roof tent, so I put on my down jacket and passed out on a chair in the courtyard, feeling weaker and fainter than ever before. The contrast between the high emotions of our first two nights in Gonder could not have been more pronounced!

We had planned to leave for Addis Ababa that day, but my condition meant there was no way we were going anywhere. My body didn't seem able to accept it was empty that morning, enforcing many more trips to the toilet, which produced only excessive suffering for little result and sapped my energy to nothing. In between these outbursts, I collapsed immobile behind the Porsche on a large foam crash mat, which had been brought along in the Shogun for use when rock climbing. Eating and drinking were not even options. I must have cursed Ethiopian cuisine a thousand times.

By the afternoon, I was once again able to sit upright and was managing an hour or so between trips to the toilet. Desperately run down, I tried to drink. It took me half an hour to manage a few mouthfuls of Pepsi, which resulted in one of the biggest challenges of the journey so far – keeping the sugary liquids down. Predictably, I failed. Doctor Laura produced a mixture of water, rehydration salts and honey, but the curdled appearance of the drink alone made me ill. Following a day that seemed to last forever, drifting in and out of an uncomfortable consciousness, I retreated to an ensuite room, hoping to be well enough for the journey to Addis Ababa the following day.

I came around twelve hours later, feeling weak and lethargic. I hadn't eaten or drunk anything for thirty-six hours, but fortunately the need for uncontrolled dashes to the bathroom appeared to have stopped. The others were up already. I wandered over to Brummy, who was loading up the Shogun.

'Morning.'

'Why hello! How are you this morning?' he asked enthusiastically.

'Completely drained, but way better than yesterday morning. I haven't been sick for at least ninety minutes.'

'Excellent. All set to head to Addis then?'

'I suppose so. I'm game for anything which involves getting as far away from here as possible.'

'There may be a problem there. You know Laura slept on the floor of my room last night?'

'Yeah?'

'Well this morning she said, 'I've just eaten. Why am I hungry?' Then she suddenly looked rather worried and added 'hang on a minute, that's not hunger,' and dashed into the bathroom. I think she's been Uzbek'd too. It seems Gonder has it in for Team Porsche.'

'Nice. Makes a change, everyone but you coming down with it.'

'Yeah, I think my immune system got the workout of its life on the Mongol Rally. Anything else is a doddle compared with Uzbekistan.'

Just then, a pale-looking Laura appeared.

'Morning Laura. I hear you've been Uzbek'd?'

'Yeah, I don't think it's as bad as yours though,' she replied shakily.

'I hope so, for your sake. How are you for travelling?'

'I'll give it a go. Can you drive though? I've got no energy at all. Would that be okay?'

'Yeah no worries. I should be able to manage that. Just give me plenty of notice if you need me to stop.'

Brummy was just beginning to feel the effects of Ethiopia's cuisine too, but fortunately Tom and Louise were free from illness, so we left as soon as the cars were ready. I felt exhausted from fatigue, hunger and dehydration. Addis Ababa lay five hundred miles away. It was going to be a tough day.

'Seriously, stop the car.'

There was a hard-edged seriousness to Laura's request which told me everything I needed to know. I pulled over on the outskirts of one of those linear villages that invariably sprawl along the roads in this part of the world. Within seconds, Laura had rushed off hastily into the undergrowth. When she reappeared, her previously pale face was looking a lot more flushed.

'That was horrible, I ran into the trees, only to pop out into a field on the other side. I couldn't stop myself. I nearly threw up in an irrigation ditch with a family watching.'

We made it a few miles up the road before the Shogun screeched to a halt in a village. The usual inquisitive crowd flocked towards it as it stopped, but then retreated aghast when a door flew open and Brummy's head bowed out, paused, and then threw up violently at their feet. Within ten seconds the Shogun was underway again, leaving behind a group of bemused Ethiopian villagers glancing disbelievingly at each other. A few minutes later, it was our turn to feel bemused, as a wiry local came jogging down the road towards us, completely naked.

It was going to be one of those days.

Ethiopia offers many things. For us, two of its offerings turned out to be mutually incompatible. Firstly, the illness which now affected sixty percent of the group and secondly, a population density unmatched by the desert countries to the north, and the resulting lack of privacy in the face of our illness. We were rarely out of sight of the kaleidoscope of life which exists in the highlands, which is great if you want to experience a country, less so if your agenda gravitates more towards being randomly sick in privacy.

Humanity flowed up and down the main road, an artery which cuts north from Addis Ababa, crossing the highlands and linking the capital to the country's most populous region. As we had come to expect from Ethiopia, pedestrians and their livestock outnumbered vehicles a hundred to one. Donkeys and oxen hauled carts to market, driven by their indifferent owners. Adults ambled along, generally clutching a fine wooden stick, used by some as an aid to walking, while others carried it lying horizontally over the shoulders, arms stretched out along its length with hands draped nonchalantly over the ends. Rough shawls generally sufficed for clothing, while some folk sported jaunty green outfits, reminiscent of Robin Hood and his band of merry men. Beneath the clothing, thinness reigned, accompanied by a sense of strength. This thin yet powerful appearance carried an efficient dignity about it, the dignity of those who take pride in their tough existence, suffering staved off only through hard work.

The scenery was equally as epic as that of the Sudan, but it was also the polar opposite. Whereas the Sudan was defined by sand and flatness, Ethiopia's green and precipitous lands offered a welcome change. The hills continued all the way to Addis Ababa, crisscrossed by rivers and balanced with the occasional lake. In the north, dramatic lava towers sometimes thrust improbably up from the earth, climbing hundreds of feet to their inaccessible summits. Further south, these distractions grew fewer and our interest was instead drawn to the derelict tanks or armoured cars abandoned near the road. How long they had lay there was anyone's guess, given Ethiopia's turbulent history of uprisings and conflicts over the past forty years.

As we neared Addis Ababa, a broad gash opened up in the landscape, sandstone crags plummeting a thousand feet down to the river below. We had reached the Blue Nile Gorge, where the fledgling river passes on its way to Khartoum, about six hundred miles distant.

Climbing out of the gorge caused the car to overheat badly once again, eking yet more life out of the engine's delicate gaskets. A bodged hill start, brought on by an impenetrable wave of livestock descending the hill towards us, then stretched all the remaining life out of the handbrake cable, leaving us without such a luxury. Near the top of the gully, a fine sandstone boulder presented itself by the road, its overhanging faces looking out spectacularly over the gorge. It was the perfect place for a rest, a bite to eat and maybe even a spot of rock climbing on the overhanging face if our weakened bodies allowed. I missed climbing, having not indulged in the hobby for several months due to the trip.

Sure enough, the Shogun pulled over. However, a pale-looking Brummy promptly leapt from the back seat and disappeared urgently behind the boulder, toilet roll in hand.

It was settled. Climbing could wait for another day.

As we completed the day's drive, a storm erupted all around us. The cloud base fell; driving rain pounded our vehicles and lightning lashed into the hills all around. Far away to our left, a bloody sunset glowed on the periphery of the storm, lending an apocalyptic drama to our passage. The Porsche's wipers, whose actuating mechanism was held together by cable ties and elastic, struggled to clear the deluge from the windscreen, while the headlights provided only cosmetic assistance.

It was dark when we dropped down onto Addis's broken tarmac and found a hotel, amazingly without getting lost even once – evidently our navigation was improving. Sleep came quickly, tired as we were from the five hundred miles we'd covered that day, with our bodies in their variously weakened states.

The following morning brought sunshine and the night's sleep seemed to have given everyone a bit more energy. The jokes and banter, which had been unusually absent for much of our time in Ethiopia, began to return. Following an unchallenging breakfast, Louise, Laura and I were loading up the cars ready for the day while chatting away light-heartedly. Brummy was still unsuccessfully trying to finish his breakfast when Tom returned from his hotel room with a mischievous smirk on his face.

'You guys will love this. You know Brummy asked to use the toilet in my hotel room because he'd already checked out of his?' Tom said, grinning.

'Yeah?'

'Well I just went in there and there's a discarded pair of pants in the bin,' came the gleeful reply. 'I don't think he's well at all.'

We all tried not to laugh. We all failed.

'Ach no,' summed up Louise.

'Aww, poor Brummy. He always ends up like this, every time he goes abroad,' Laura said.

'He was doing pretty well until Ethiopia. I thought he'd finally sorted things out, but no. It always gets him in the end!' I said.

'You know what he told me in Gonder?' Laura said, giggling.

'Go on.'

'He told me that he has a routine for this. What he does when he's feeling delicate is he folds up a few sheets of toilet paper and uses them to line his pants.'

'An insurance policy?' Tom suggested, as we all laughed.

'Yeah, exactly. He's very proud of his little routine.'

'Well it can't have worked very well, given the pants in our bin,' said Tom.

'Aww, bless,' said Louise.

Just then Brummy ambled down the stairs, having given up on his overpriced breakfast. We all gave him sideways glances and tried not to laugh. Eventually, I couldn't resist any longer and broke the silence: 'How are you feeling Brum?'

'Marvellous. Never felt better!' came his upbeat reply.

'So there's nothing you want to tell us?'

'No, why?'

'You're not feeling a bit delicate this morning?'

'No, I feel absolutely fine.'

'So why has a pair of your pants appeared in the bin in Tom's bathroom?'

'Erm, I don't know. They're not mine anyway,' he muttered with a sideways glance, before striding off towards the hotel room, in as dignified a manner as possible. We all burst out laughing as he went.

Through his trouser seat, a hefty bulge was clearly visible, hewn from sheets of toilet paper. Evidently he was taking every precaution that day!

We left Addis Ababa that morning, conscious of slipping behind schedule and wanting to escape the culinary minefield that Ethiopia seemed to have become for us. There was also a feeling of growing anticipation in the group, as we were nearing the biggest remaining challenge of the journey – the notorious Moyale to Isiolo road in northern Kenya. This make-or-break dirt track was now looming over us, about five hundred miles distant. We wanted to get to grips with it and put it behind us as soon as possible.

The road out of Addis was worse than broken. It hadn't even been built yet. We weaved in and out of the bumpy workings through the congestion, the Porsche overheating enthusiastically while its back end constantly bottomed out on the uneven ground. This went on for about two hours, before first the concrete blocks, then the houses, then finally the shantytowns were behind us. We emerged from the chaos into a landscape of flat grassy plains, dotted with proud trees and the occasional coffee plantation, while the horizon beyond was a ripple of unassuming hills. Our route was taking us down the Great Rift Valley and, while it would be an exaggeration to describe our surroundings as a valley, the string of spacious lakes lining the road gave us at least an inkling as to the geological rift which lay beneath us. The tarmac was good, the weather was pleasantly warm and our surroundings were beautiful. The Porsche's scrap yard engine purred along dependably, having won our trust over the previous six and a half thousand miles, while the breeze from the open windows kept us cool enough. About halfway through the day, our passing startled an enormous stork, which took flight just in front of us. We passed beneath it with only a couple of metres to spare. Its wingspan easily eclipsed the width of our car, while its vast shadow shaded us for the shortest instant.

I was rather relieved that it didn't hit the windscreen.

We stopped early that evening, pulling into the town of Awasa with plenty of daylight remaining. The usual group of children approached the car.

'You, you, you! Give me money!'

The children's palms hovered outstretched, while big, milky eyes focussed intensely on mine, drawing attention away from the rest of their quizzically beaming faces.

It was the standard greeting used by children everywhere in Ethiopia.

'Why?' I asked them teasingly.

'Money, money, money,' came the reply, its pitch raised ever so slightly higher for emphasis.

On our arrival in Ethiopia, this aggressive begging had repelled us all, before we quickly became accustomed to it and it started to melt our hearts. The begging seemed to be a rehearsed greeting for tourists like us, taught by parents or picked up from other children, rather than an outright plea of desperation. We were never asked for food.

I pointed at the most precocious looking kid.

'You, you, you! Give *me* money!' I said.

They giggled, beaming brightly as they held an excited discussion in Amharic. Then their faces became suddenly more serious and they offered me money, thrusting a one Birr note and a few coins towards me.

I blushed, suddenly feeling rather silly. I tried to decline their offer, but they would have none of it. With little choice, I took the money they gave me, tripled it and handed it back to them. My opinion of the precocious children of Ethiopia went up a lot in that moment.

Next morning, we pointed the Porsche's chiselled snout south and headed out of Awasa. Just out of town, a somewhat suicidal hawker watched us approaching before stepping out into the road, directly in front of the Porsche. He was trying to sell us vegetables. Laura panicked and only just managed to swerve around his frail frame. She was rather shaken and I was instantly angry with the guy for scaring her. My reaction was a little aggressive. Punching the horn with my right hand, I leaned out of my open window and shouted 'out of the fucking way!' as we swerved. He looked at me in a confused manner, as if cars were an unprecedented occurrence on the roads around here. This was fairly typical of our – and other overlanders' – experiences of Ethiopia, where looking before crossing the road is sometimes a novel concept and one of the most popular responses to an oncoming vehicle is to stand in the road and stare, rabbit-like, as it bears down on you.

Up in the highlands, altitude had lent the climate a temperate feel, cool air and adapted vegetation giving the region an appearance strangely reminiscent of some of the hillier parts of northern Europe. We spent our last morning in Ethiopia negotiating the hills to the south of Awasa and for a few short hours the temperate climate changed to tropical and the general ambiance became all the more African for it. Our first taste of rainforest was a vivid experience. Broad-leaved ferns crowded together, mixing with densely packed trees to form an apparently impenetrable, improbably lush backdrop to the road. As everywhere in sub-Saharan Africa, circular huts of wood or mud clustered along our route, often next to a stagnant, mosquito infested pool of standing water. The sky became moist and brooding, as if we were driving across a boundary, passing from the more familiar highlands to the threatening equatorial plains, where the sky has the energy to unleash heavy weather whenever it pleases.

Laura and I took in our surroundings as we drove. Village after dilapidated village drifted past our windows. Despite the apparently bountiful surroundings, poverty had a vice-like grip on the area and the lives of the people we saw that morning often appeared to have an unshakable lethargy about them. As with the suicidal hawker earlier that morning, we simply weren't on the same wavelength as the people living in the area through which we were hurrying. Passing from village to village, we tried to understand the lives of those who lived here, but all we could discern was a relaxed apathy. Amongst the men in the villages, sitting around appeared the most popular way to pass the day, while standing around chatting came a close second. The stresses of the past weeks had left us frustrated with the African way of doing things, where – possibly because of our own lack of understanding – a set task generally involves three times more hassle and waiting around than it would in Europe. Perhaps because of the anger we felt at the inefficiency and inequality all around us, we got rather animated about people's apparent lack of get-up-and-go.

Laura gestured to a guy sat on a stool outside his circular hut.

'Look at him. He's sat there doing nothing, when the roof on his hut blatantly needs fixing. Why doesn't he stop sitting around and spend the day fixing it?'

'Because that would interfere with his routine of sitting around?' I ventured sarcastically.

'Yeah, about right.'

'I know what you mean though,' I said. 'There seems to be so much time spent doing absolutely nothing. I know people often walk miles every day to fetch water, or sell firewood, but it's usually the women doing that. Don't the men ever think, 'I know, I'm not going to just sit around today. I'm going to make my life better'?'

'I don't get it. I couldn't simply exist, without striving to make things better for myself and my family. Instead of lingering, they could be planting crops, making things, bettering themselves.'

I pointed at a dishevelled dwelling. 'If I lived in that rundown hut there, I'd be striving to improve it, to get my house up to the standard of the smarter one next door.'

'I guess people here simply aren't as materialistic, or as competitive, as we are in the West,' Laura suggested.

'I hope for their sake that they're not. That doesn't mean they shouldn't aspire towards having a roof that keeps out the rain though, or windows that work.'

'And a means to pay for a more comfortable life too. Instead of sitting around all day, why don't they start some sort of business?'

To a large degree, we knew the answers to our questions already and our conversation was simply a way of letting off steam about how tough life appears to be in such rural areas. People did work hard. In many of the areas through which we'd travelled, water had to be fetched and things bought and sold, many miles from home. Crops and livestock were tended without any recourse to the mechanised methods taken for granted back home, and poor diets left people little energy for action which wasn't absolutely required. Even a loan for enough grain to sow a field, or buy a bicycle and begin a hawking business, was out of reach of the average rural African. How do you raise fifty dollars if you have nothing to sell? It is impossible to secure a loan on your house in the majority of rural Africa, as land ownership isn't enforceable by law, so banks have no guarantee of getting their money back. And who else is going to lend you the money? The poorest don't even have addresses. How can you expect to get a loan without an address? If the key to a sustainable income is fifty dollars of grain and fertiliser, how can you save up the money? In much of Africa, people cling to existence, subsisting on only a few hundred dollars a year. It would take years to accumulate the required capital in such a situation.

Rural Africans often exist in a cruel Catch-22. Not only does day-to-day survival often involve pushing themselves hard, but even if they wish to show initiative, it is often nearly impossible for them to raise the capital to break out of their lives of subsistence. Even their own governments are often indifferent to their situations. An uneducated, poor and tired populous is easier for a dictator or totalitarian regime to control, while a slightly more healthy and well-off rural population is more able to voice its complaints and stand up against ineffectual rule. As many of the continent's governments are ineffectual at best, there is little incentive for them to help their poorest citizens achieve gains in their quality of life.

Often, African governments employ policies which are positively destructive for their rural populations. In Ethiopia, for example, the communist dictator Mengistu, who was in power from 1974 to 1991, would force farmers to sell quotas of their grain harvests to state officials at a hugely deflated price, to ensure sufficient cheap food was available for the army and the urban centres. Often the farmers were left without enough grain to feed their villages and themselves, let alone to produce the next crop. This legalised robbery contributed directly to the famines mentioned earlier in the chapter, as did a war against rebels in the region north of Gonder, where starvation was actively used as a weapon by the government – to such a degree that the Ethiopian Army prevented foreign aid from reaching the three million people living in areas where rebels were at large. With policymaking like that, it's not surprising that rural poverty remains a perennial problem for the continent.

Storm clouds were gathering as we neared the border with Kenya, lit up obliquely by the sun's dying rays. The landscape had toughened to a bleak plain, punctuated by jutting termite mounds and hardy trees. Heavy raindrops fell from the brooding sky as we drove into the dusk, exploding on the tarmac with miniature drama. We arrived at Moyale late; too late to cross the border. We set up our tents and the Porsche's awning and cooked dinner in a cloud of mosquitoes. Then we retired nervously, dreaming of Kenya's muddy tracks, as the rain drummed ominously on the canvas.

NINE

MUD AND RUTS

4th November 2008
Dida Galgalu Desert, Northern Kenya

Coarse drum and bass rhythms thundered out from the Porsche's stereo as we left Moyale, a synthesised voice chanting monotonically over a blur of hypnotic beats. Background accompaniment was provided by the Porsche and by Kenya. Wide tyres scrabbled on the saturated mud track, making a guttural sucking noise as the rubber separated from the mud, which became a dull buffeting sound as the heavy muck was sprayed against the car's underside. A staccato drumming sounded out as the unwelcome rain hit the windscreen only a foot from our faces, while the wipers squeaked with their futile attempts to clear it. The exhaust droned away in the background, sometimes stealing the show by barking urgently when the revs built against the slipping clutch while powering out of some water-filled pothole. Finally, the whistling wind tickled our ears through the open windows, which were letting in cooler air to counteract the heater, still jammed on full heat.

We were in the middle of the adventure. The crux. The eye of the storm. Even in the dry, northern Kenya had promised some of the toughest and most dangerous terrain of the trip. The rains had arrived four days before us and turned the rutted dirt tracks into an unforgiving mush. We would not see tarmac again for over three hundred miles – the distance from London to the Scottish border. It was going to be an interesting few days.

As well as the challenges of the terrain, northern Kenya also threw up some more sinister obstacles. Sparsely populated and beyond the reach of the law, the area is a haven for those who play by their own rules. The porous Somali border is nearby and banditry is rife, with shiftas targeting vehicles on a worryingly regular basis. Veteran travel writer Paul Theroux was shot at when he travelled this way and when Ewan McGregor and Charley Boorman, along with their support crew, passed through during their 'Long Way Down' expedition, they had armed guards travel with them in their big four-wheel-drives. We had no such luxuries – only crossed fingers. Armed robberies and carjacking are a way of life here and have given the area an intimidating reputation, as well as an irrational allure.

As well as the shiftas who prey on folk passing through the area, northern Kenya is also a hotbed of inter-tribal conflict. The area's sparse natural resources and limited water sources are barely able to sustain its meagre population, so in times of hardship conflict between tribes often arises. In the good old days, these squabbles would leave a few unfortunate warriors worse off from encounters with spears and machetes. Today however, the ubiquitous Kalashnikov machine gun makes disagreements considerably more serious. These tribal battles are seldom reported in the Western press, being fought between combatants who care little for outside opinion, but despite this, occasionally news of a tragedy creeps out. In 2005, around sixty members of the Gabra tribe were killed when a school at Turbi, near Marsabit, was attacked in revenge of a previous theft of goats and cattle. Shortly after our visit to the area, over three hundred died in a pitched battle near Moyale. But more often than not, the news never reaches the outside world. This part of Africa is truly one of the last remaining lawless wildernesses, seldom penetrated by governments or journalists.

Our time in northern Kenya had begun innocuously enough. A pristinely presented customs officer greeted us in perfect English, offered us a cup of tea and made us feel most welcome.

'England? I was there once, ten years ago,' he said longingly. 'London. It was wonderful. I walked the streets for two weeks and never had to clean my shoes once. So different to here.'

He silently gestured outside, where the rains had turned the road into a river of mud.

With the border formalities completed, we headed into town and found ourselves in a queue of about ten lorries waiting to make the journey south in a heavily armed convoy, courtesy of the Kenyan army. We were more than happy to join the convoy.

While we were waiting to leave, a slightly agitated group of locals grew around the Porsche. After a few minutes, the crowd had grown to number about twenty. A few of them chatted pleasantly to Laura and I in the usual manner of such meetings; however most gossiped urgently amongst themselves, the group gradually working itself up into a concerned, agitated jury.

Eventually, one guy was nominated as the group speaker. He fixed me with a serious stare and talked very slowly, adding a dramatic emphasis to his words.

'This car cannot make it along the road to Marsabit. It is impossible.'

Twenty drawn faces hung on my reply. All background noise seemed to stop as the statement suddenly put me on the spot.

'It'll be fine,' I replied, as nonchalantly as possible. 'We've already driven it from England, across the deserts of the Sudan, through Ethiopia. It's proven itself already.'

Another bout of nervous chatter ensued, dying out slowly, before the spokesman replied: 'This is Kenya. No vehicles have made it through from Marsabit in days. It is very dangerous. There are shiftas and the rains have made the ruts very bad. This car will not survive.'

'We'll give it a try. We can always come back if the road is impassable.'

217

I sensed the futility of trying to make them believe in my confidence, which strangely wasn't shaken by their gloomy appraisal of my chances. I was relieved when the group gradually lost interest in the discussion and gently dissipated. They seemed to feel it was their duty to warn us of our stupidity and having done so they drifted away, their collective conscience clear.

I can think of more confidence-inspiring conversations to have before heading off down a muddy track through bandit country!

At about eleven in the morning, the soldier in charge of the checkpoint beckoned us to the front of the armed convoy, ahead of the chunky lorries and just behind a Land Rover reassuringly packed to the gunnels with soldiers and firepower. There were no other cars. In front of the Land Rover, planks of wood with rusty six inch nails hammered through them lay across the sodden track, preventing anyone from leaving town without an escort. We were solemnly asked to enter our details in the checkpoint log and at eleven o'clock the planks of wood were moved from our path. We were away.

Unfortunately, so was the rest of the convoy.

The Land Rover swiftly disappeared into the distance and so did the lorries, aloofly showering us with mud as they overtook at a speed we couldn't hope to match in our fragile steeds.

'So much for the safety of an armed convoy!' Laura said.

'Yep, looks like we'll be fending for ourselves,' I replied.

Except for the occasional mud hut, soon we were all alone, heading into the unknown beneath a brooding gunmetal sky.

In the past few years, I've pitted my mediocre driving abilities against many a tricky challenge. I've driven hundreds of miles on the sheet ice and drifting snow of the Arctic Highway, in a pitiful Fiat 126 city car. I've coaxed a spluttering auto-rickshaw over gravel mountain passes high in the Himalayas and explored the sandy deserts of Nevada in a convertible Ford Mustang. I've even survived Friday rush hour on the M25, armed only with a slightly rusty Peugeot saloon. However nothing from my past quite compared with trying to control the Porsche on the rutted soup roads of northern Kenya.

'Soupy' is possibly the closest adjective we found to describe the surface on which we were driving, though Brummy thought soapy was more apt. Either way, the mixture of gloopy mud and standing water stretched a hundred and fifty miles away from us to Marsabit, the next town of any significance. These conditions were not exactly what the designers back in Stuttgart had in mind when they created the Porsche 944. Butch off-roaders have four-wheel-drive, torquey low-revving engines, all manner of differential locks and lots of ground clearance for good reason. All the Porsche could bring to northern Kenya was rear wheel drive, pointlessly wide wheels and a bit too much power. The thick mud soon clogged the smooth tyres, meaning grip was non-existent. Whenever the accelerator was depressed even a few millimetres too much, the rear wheels would spin and the back of the car would attempt to pirouette off into the undergrowth like a spinning top. To make matters worse, the recently broken screen wash system meant visibility was often non-existent.

It was character building, to say the least.

We were eased into the difficulties gradually. Leaving Moyale, the track sliced straight and wide away from us, nothing more than a thirty foot wide strip where no vegetation grew. Thick scrub stretched away to either side of us, while the occasional tree stood clear against the churning sky, serving to emphasise just how monotonous the landscape was. I eyed the scenery nervously as I drove. The soil around us – and hence the track beneath us – was initially the attractive clay brown colour so evocative of Africa. This made for a fairly solid surface, so initially the ruts and potholes weren't too bad. However after a few miles, the soil changed, becoming ominously blacker as the rain began to sheet down apocalyptically.

'Well, I hope the rain means the shiftas stay at home,' said Laura.

The pouring rain and black mud are not what Porsche drivers generally want to encounter on their holidays. Not only was the track now less pretty than the red-brown soil, but it was also softer, so the previously acceptable road surface deteriorated accordingly. Broad, deep potholes appeared like traps, filled with water and soft mud which could easily swallow a Porsche and prevent it climbing up the sides to escape the slippery trap.

Even worse, the ruts made an appearance. Often hundreds of metres long, sometimes over a foot deep and filled with water, they had been created by the churning passage of lorry tyres and pushed the Porsche – not to mention the Shogun – to the limit. As the lorries were wider than our steeds, the ruts they created were wider too. This meant that the only way to progress along the road was to drive with one side of the car sunk into a rut while the wheels on the other side rode high on the mound of mud which had been pushed up between the lorries' tyres. It must have been a strange sight to the few people who witnessed our passing, a pointy sports car scrabbling along, tilted over at a crazy angle with one side of the car partially submerged in the mud and standing water while the other side rode high on a mound of dirt.

This sort of driving required a lot of forward planning. Once we'd committed to following a rut, it was difficult for us to climb out of it again. If it deepened too much, to avoid bottoming out we were forced to bounce the car out of the rut and into a shallower one. This was an unsubtle manoeuvre which required getting a bit of speed up before spinning the steering wheel to ram the muddy wall we were attempting to climb, while hoping we didn't simply dig in and get stuck anyway. Once out of the rut, we had to be careful to get the steering wheel turned back the other way as soon as possible, otherwise we would find ourselves spearing off the road into the vegetation.

After about thirty miles of wrestling with the conditions, this is exactly what happened to the Shogun. Brummy had been trying to turn right but the butch off-roader was having none of it, choosing to slide along trapped in a rut instead. Suddenly, the wheels caught and spun them round, sending them flying off the road, down a small bank and into a conveniently placed bush. I found somewhere reasonably solid to stop the Porsche before wandering over intent on mocking them. However once I got there, my input appeared unnecessary.

Tom was sat in the back with a stern frown on his face, slouching forward and sighing with despair. In the driver's seat, Brummy was beaming, loving the crazy roads and the randomness of northern Kenya, while not exactly concerned about his minor indiscretion with the local scenery. Louise was sat in the front passenger seat, happily filming away.

'Oh cock,' said Brummy, laughing as his attempt to reverse back up the muddy bank was met only with spinning wheels.

'And we're fucked,' sighed an unamused Tom.

'We're not fucked. We've come off the road, that's all,' barked back Brummy, as he fiddled with the Shogun's complicated gearboxes.

'Well if you'd stop dicking about…' said Tom, oblivious to any comedy in the situation.

'It's just a bit of mud, that's all,' growled back Brummy.

Evidently the atmosphere in the Shogun wasn't taking kindly to northern Kenya. Unfortunately, Louise and Brummy's approach to the trip was very different to Tom's. They greeted everything with a laugh and a joke, trying not to get too bogged down with the seriousness of situations, instead preferring to muddle through irreverently with smiles and humour.

Tom took things a lot more seriously. Here he was, in the middle of bandit country, facing up to the unknown in a Shogun which they'd bought for a few quid off the internet and had been slowly snapping apart ever since. To Tom, it was not a place for fun and games. It was a serious situation which called for a serious attitude.

Neither camp was wrong in its approach, but unfortunately there wasn't enough space for the two polar attitudes in the Shogun's cramped cabin. This led to both camps gradually losing patience with each other as the trip went on and occasionally, when the going got bad, feelings would boil over.

While Brummy revved up the Shogun, I pushed on the bonnet to help it up the bank, while keeping a nervous, watchful eye on the dense scrubland all around. The car made it back onto the road and as it leapt backwards up the bank I came within an inch of toppling face first into the mud, raising a laugh from everyone. Even Tom. After suggesting to Brummy that he learn to drive I returned to the Porsche, happy that in our car at least, the atmosphere and understanding between Laura and I was now practically perfect.

Somehow, we covered another few dozen miles of treacherous ruts, gaping potholes and gloopy mud before Brummy's over-exuberance meant he repeated his little off-road adventure. This time, rather than leaving the road at right angles, he slid off at a more acute angle, leaving the Shogun beached in a ditch, unable to climb back out onto the road. As I drove past the stricken vehicle to reach firmer ground, I couldn't resist the urge to shout, 'the four-wheel-drive's stuck again, is it?' through their open window.

The rise blocking the Shogun's path back onto the track wasn't particularly big or steep, but it was very slippery and there was no way Brummy could build up enough momentum to climb it. Clouds of black smoke belched from the exhaust as he tried repeatedly, but the Shogun remained resolutely stuck. There was only one thing for it. Out came the shovel.

As there was only one shovel and it was Brummy's driving which had put the Shogun in the ditch, it seemed only fair that he should dig it out again. He attacked the job with his characteristic humour, while the rest of us formed a supportive audience.

'Well done Brummy, I'm enjoying watching you shovelling your piece of crap out of the crap,' I said constructively.

'I know what we'll do to solve this,' he laughed back, gesturing vaguely with the shovel. 'We'll just move this bit of Africa, over there.'

Laura was now videoing away intently, unable to restrain her laughter.

'Is there anything you want to say Brummy?' she asked.

'Yeah. I wish I brought a Porsche!'

'You hear that Ben? He wishes he brought a Porsche!' Laura shouted over.

'Yeah, I heard that. You do realise, if this doesn't work, I'll have to tow your 4x4 out of the mud with my sports car?'

'It'll be fine!' Brummy chimed back, borrowing one of my catchphrases.

After a few minutes of shovelling, a vague ramp was formed, leading back up to the dirt track. Brummy climbed in and fired up the Shogun. The first attempt to regain the road had it scrabbling along tantalisingly close, but not quite able to climb the ramp. On the second try, however, the tyres gripped a little better and the Shogun leapt back to join the Porsche on the quagmire 'road' to Marsabit.

We'd lost about fifteen minutes to Brummy's latest indiscretion and had laughed and joked our way through the delay. Tom had looked on in an unimpressed manner as we clowned around. Clearly it wasn't the time or the place.

As they returned to the Shogun, I heard him say, 'Right, I think it's my turn to drive now.'

'I don't think so; I'm having too much fun,' Brummy replied.

At times, it was impossible not to sympathise with Tom!

Our surroundings changed little from hour to hour. An endless plain, bordered by unmemorable hills, covered in samey bushes and carpeted with fresh, hardy looking grasses. The greenness around us was probably only due to the recent rains, as in theory, our incompetent progress was taking us across a desert. It was just our luck that the rains had arrived four days before us.

'Well, at least there aren't any corrugations,' I said to Laura, searching for a silver lining.

There were virtually no permanent settlements along our route and the few which did exist possessed an overwhelming aura of failure and decay. Sprinkled out in the bush, they existed as small clusters of circular huts, their grass roofs appearing woefully inadequate in the face of the rains. These settlements were rare however, and dense undergrowth was our more usual companion. I continued to eye our surroundings nervously as we drove, worried about who might be hiding out there, and making sure I was ready to take evasive action at the first sign of an ambush.

By early afternoon, we had covered well over half the distance to Marsabit, the halfway point of our three hundred mile marathon of mud. The conditions beneath our tyres had been awful, but through a mixture of determination and luck, the cars had taken it all in their stride and our nervousness as to what lay ahead had gradually lifted. The worst of the road conditions seemed to be behind us, in any case. The vicious ruts had reduced in their depth and frequency, and our passage was further eased by a return to the harder, clay-red soil. Our confidence and self-belief rose as we proved ourselves to be equal to the toughest challenge of the trip so far. Such feelings are often the precursor to a fall and in this instance it was certainly the case.

I don't know where the feeling stemmed from. It was an odd sensation, which hinted at something untoward. Everything appeared fine; the engine was running normally, the car's gauges all gave the answers I was looking for. For some reason though, I couldn't shake my feeling of unease. Initially, I dismissed it as being caused by the rain, which had started thudding down again following a token hour of dry weather. However the apprehension refused to be dismissed so easily, and remained with me.

On a trip like this, it always makes sense to listen to such premonitions. When you spend every day relying unequivocally on the car – listening, feeling, hearing and smelling its every foible – you develop a kind of sixth sense as to whether everything is okay. I'm sure this sixth sense is what had finally allowed me to trust the scrap engine out of the donor car. After a while, its communications became reassuring and consistent, and hence my confidence in it built. This sort of acute understanding is also often the first thing to flag up that something is wrong. Unable to put my finger on the problem, I carried on driving, my senses on a heightened sense of alert for reasons I didn't yet know.

After about five minutes of this unease, I noticed the fuel gauge had moved by a millimetre or two. Obviously, this is a perfectly normal thing to happen when the engine is running; however I had been watching that fuel gauge every day for over a month and it didn't normally drop so suddenly from the half full point as it just did. I couldn't put my finger on why, but there was something not quite right about the way it moved.

I couldn't stand my feeling of unease any longer and I now had a shred of quantifiable evidence that maybe something wasn't quite right. I stopped the car for a look. The Shogun was ahead of us and carried on into the distance.

'What's wrong?' Laura asked.

'I think we've got a fuel leak,' I replied, feeling suddenly unconvinced.

I wandered around to the back of the car for a closer look. On the surface of the puddles we'd just passed over, a kaleidoscopic film glimmered on the water's surface. It was strangely beautiful, for something that confirmed the worst. We were leaking petrol.

While I began jacking up the car for a closer look, the Shogun had turned around and retraced its steps to see why we had stopped.

'Fuel leak,' I said to them, plainly.

'Oh no,' Louise replied.

In an attempt to keep myself vaguely clean as I crawled under the car, I laid down a groundsheet. Its hard, dry surface amplified the thudding noise of the raindrops. The Porsche's underside was filthy, caked with mud which dripped onto me continuously as I squirmed beneath it, but through the filth, the problem soon became apparent. The fuel tank was fine, but the fuel filter mounting had broken. In their wisdom, the designers at Porsche had positioned the fuel filter directly above one of the driveshafts, meaning that when it fell off, it came to rest on a spinning shaft, which had rapidly worn through the metal casing. Petrol was dripping into the mud from two freshly ground holes.

Predictably, in the frantic rush to get ready for our departure a month before, I'd forgotten to bring along a spare fuel filter.

I attempted to separate the filter from the fuel pipes, but in the cramped, squalid space under the car, I couldn't get it to budge. I would have to attempt a fiddly repair lying on my back in the muddy darkness, by the light of my head torch. First, I attempted to seal it by wrapping the cylindrical filter with gaffa tape. The mud, the damp, and the leaking petrol meant it was impossible to get the filter clean and dry, but I eventually got the tape to stick in a confidence-inspiring manner and emerged from beneath the car, caked in mud.

'Okay, someone look under the car while I try to start the engine and shout if there's a leak.'

I crossed my fingers that the bodge would hold and turned the key. After a few seconds, the shout came.

'It's pissing out again. Stop the engine,' said Brummy.

'Doh.'

The Porsche's fuel pump is located against the fuel tank, and all the fuel lines beneath the car – including the fuel filter – are highly pressurised. This meant that we didn't have to simply seal a leak – we had to seal it well enough to withstand a rather high pressure.

'Okay, so gaffa tape won't do it. What else have we got?'

'What about amalgamation tape?' Tom suggested. 'It's great stuff, bonds to itself to form a rubbery seal. We use it at work to seal hydraulic lines, so it should cope with the pressure. I've got a couple of rolls in the Shogun.'

'Yeah, sounds good. Let's give it a try,' I said. 'We could try to pressurise it into place with Jubilee Clips too.'

'Fair enough, but if it doesn't work, we really should get going. This isn't the safest place and I don't want to be out here after dark,' said Brummy.

'Point taken. We'll try the amalgamation tape, but if that doesn't work you guys are towing the Porsche to Marsabit.'

'How far is it to Marsabit?' Louise asked.

'Can't be much more than fifty miles now. We're well over half way.'

I shimmied back beneath the stricken Porsche. Once again, the mud and dampness was the biggest problem. Nothing was clean or dry. Even the rags I tried to clean things with were wet and muddy within seconds. Whenever I tried to wipe the fuel filter clean, petrol was smeared over it in place of the mud, giving a Teflon-like anti-stick coating. I wrapped the amalgamation tape around the filter with difficulty, as it stubbornly refused to stick to the metal surface. It was frustrating work, but eventually it was done. A couple of Jubilee Clips were tightened around the filter, clamping down to add extra strength to the bodge. I shimmied back out into the rain for a second time and turned the key. After a few seconds of building up the fuel pressure, the engine started.

'Yes! It's holding,' said Laura excitedly.

'Excellent.' The relief was immediate.

'Ah. No, now it isn't,' Laura added, deflated.

'Arse. Right, let's get the German on the tow rope,' Brummy said, springing into action.

'I'm really not convinced that's the best idea,' said Tom. 'The Shogun's chassis is cracking again and dragging a tonne of Porsche along isn't going to help things.'

'Well we don't really have any other choice,' replied Brummy.

I said nothing. I knew he was right. We had to get moving and we shouldn't linger in this lawless plain any more than we had to. However I was annoyed that I hadn't been able to fix the problem and felt humiliated that we would be finishing the toughest road of the trip on the end of a towrope. The Porsche had failed and so had I. Sure, with more time I may have been able to remove the offending component, get it clean and repair it properly, but that wasn't the point. We had still failed to get the Porsche along the road under its own steam. I helped to hook up the towrope to the front of the car and returned to the driver's seat. Tom inched the Shogun forward to take in the slack on the rope and we jolted onwards as it took the strain. We were moving again.

Fortunately, the conditions beneath our tyres had improved as we coasted along inertly behind the powerful four-wheel-drive. Inside the Porsche, however, everything felt wrong. For over a month, we had sat in its cabin as the engine brought it to live, purring and barking and pushing it forwards. The vibrations, smells and noises of progress had always accompanied us. Now, the car's lively energy had been replaced by a heavy, conclusive silence. All we could hear was the tinny rattle of stones spraying the wheel arches and the distant grumble of the Shogun. The car was inert. Dead. It was a depressing atmosphere, the polar opposite of the heady feelings of an hour before, when we had been getting to grips with the toughest challenge of the trip and confidently taking it in our stride.

Laura and I said little. We simply sat there, lost in our own worlds. I dwelled painfully on what I could have done differently in my attempt to fix the leak. Without being able to get the filter scrupulously clean, I was probably always doomed to failure, but it bothered me nonetheless. I had been put on the spot to make that one simple repair and I had failed. As a result, we had failed in our attempt to drive the Porsche along the toughest road of the trip. I knew that when I looked back on the journey it would always annoy me that in this moment of judgement, I had come up short. I tried to take my mind off the frustrations by concentrating on following the Shogun efficiently and avoiding the jagged rocks, which were becoming ever more frequent.

I had no control over the route we took along the road, but Tom did a good enough job of finding a smooth way through. More and more frequently however, a large unavoidable boulder would appear and clatter into the Porsche's vulnerable underside with a sickening thump. The silence in the car grew thicker with every impact. Once again, Africa was routing us.

After about half an hour of being towed, we encountered a little Suzuki four-wheel-drive, stuck in the mud. Its somewhat portly Kenyan owner was looking on as his driver attempted to dig it out with a stick. We stopped and helped to free them, our spade proving somewhat more effective than the stick. They were obviously nervous and explained with much gesturing and hand waving that they wished to continue to Marsabit in convoy with us.

229

Evidently the security issues were playing on their minds as well as ours.

The track continued dead straight, a streak of rocky mud slicing across a relentlessly flat plain. The boulders increased in size and the impacts on the underside of the Porsche became ever more frequent, and ever more violent. There was little I could do, as the rocks appeared with next to no warning from beneath the Shogun. Soon, our exhaust was knocked off, so we stopped, fished its mangled form out of the mud and strapped it to the roof. Other impacts were even worse, throwing the impotent sports car into the air. The engine's sump took a horrendous pounding, along with its suspension, fuel lines and brake lines – all of which ran vulnerably beneath the car. We said nothing, as there was nothing we could do. Our little convoy crept onwards as the Porsche was systematically shredded beneath us.

'Well, at least we're not overheating,' Laura said coldly.

I didn't reply. My mood was quickly returning to how it had been when the engine failed back in England, six weeks previously. I felt powerless. Northern Kenya was totally destroying the car, impact by sickening impact and there was nothing I could do about it. I knew this was the end. No way could the Porsche go on after this level of abuse. No car could survive it.

I thought about our failure. It wouldn't be so bad. We had made it to northern Kenya. It had been tough and I wouldn't be too disheartened to walk away from the expedition. I knew we'd given it our best shot and done amazingly well to make it this far. There would be no shame in calling it a day in Marsabit, the engine's sump cracked by a rocky impact, the underside of the car smashed away. With each impact, I retreated further into a dark corner of my psyche and willed the trip to be over.

The last of the daylight retreated behind a range of mountains which serrated the horizon, many miles distant but clearly visible thanks to the landscape's unrelenting flatness. In the sun's dying moments we passed about thirty camels, bathed luxuriously in the rich oblique light. Their nomadic herders stared as we passed and held their arms aloft in disbelief at the sight of the Porsche – the internationally accepted gesture for 'you idiots! What in god's name did you think you were doing trying to drive that stupid little car along this track?'

A little later, we arrived at a small stream, flowing across the road from an area of waterlogged ground. The Shogun made it through and as the Porsche bounced into the water I was sure we were stuck, but somehow Tom managed to keep moving and pulled us impressively onwards. Despite all the mocking I had directed at it, the Shogun was proving its mettle.

After dark, the atmosphere became even more malevolent. Lightning storms erupted on the horizon, forming a climatic backdrop to our situation. Their flashes were prolific, but too distant for the accompanying thunder to be heard. The rains of earlier in the day returned as a depressing drizzle. Forced to coast along without headlights, I could barely see the rocks which kept crunching into the car's underside, let alone avoid them. A few impacted directly beneath my feet. I felt the metal floorpan buckle terminally upwards as they did. One of the crashes made my seat move as the metal beneath it twisted. I thought about what they were doing to the vulnerable, unprotected components slung beneath the car – the fuel lines and brake lines, the engine, the driveshaft and the gearbox – and my last glimmers of hope evaporated. Behind us, the headlights of our friends in the Suzuki bobbed up and down, continuing reminders that we were limping wounded through a lawless night.

I was mentally destroyed when we finally reached the haven of Marsabit. The last sixty-odd miles of towing had taken nearly five hours. Five hours of dwelling on our inevitable failure, while trying to dodge rocks and obstacles in my impotent Porsche, failing, and weathering their pummelling impacts. I was sick of it. I wanted to go home.

'I'll go and see what the others want to do for accommodation,' a voice said. It was Laura. I'd forgotten she was even sat next to me in the darkness.

'Fine,' I grunted in vague acknowledgement.

Once the car's jolting movement had stopped, my senses gradually began to return to life. A strange, deep rumble in my mind slowly metamorphosed into a sound as an awareness of my surroundings returned. I sat for a minute, vaguely aware of it, but without the inclination to give it the attention required to figure out what it was.

'Just listen to those bull frogs chorusing away! It's incredible!' Laura said abruptly through the open window, jolting me to attention.

The dulled harmonics clarified into a deafening wall of song. The rains had clearly found favour with the amphibious population of Marsabit.

'Oh yeah, that's what it is. Frogs. Great.' Summoning up enthusiasm was not my strong point at the time.

'I've never heard anything like it. What an amazing sound!' Laura said. 'Anyway, apparently the best lodge in town is the JayJay centre, just over there. Brummy's gone to check it out. Are you okay?'

'I'm a bit down. I'll be better after a night's sleep,' I replied, without really believing it.

We checked into the JayJay centre, a clean and cheap place which was everything we needed and very little more. Muslim owned, the building was arranged around a central courtyard in the Arabic tradition and even boasted such unlikely luxuries as a conference room and taps labelled 'hot water'. By the front door, a scruffy guy dozed with a shotgun on his lap, dreaming of thieves.

While everyone else relaxed in the courtyard, preparing first popcorn then dinner on the stoves, I sat silently, my mental faculties effectively shut down by the deluge of negativity which had flooded my mind over the previous six hours. I wasn't even considering how to fix the car, or whether to sell it. My thoughts had dried up, being replaced by a cycle of depressed emptiness as I stared into space. I was dead to the world, dead even to my own attempts at rational thought. Finished.

The car and I had a lot in common.

TEN

DEJA VU

5th November 2008
Marsabit, Northern Kenya

It must have been light for hours. Brummy and Tom had already risen and left the room; mosquito nets hung over their vacated beds. I felt heavy and weary. When I finally got up, I knew my reward would be to see what could be done for the car, and the thought didn't appeal. A little longer lying in bed wouldn't hurt. I would stay there until my guilt got the better of me and forced me to get on with the day. It took less than an hour.

I opened the curtains. It had rained again during the night, but the morning had brought with it an overcast dryness. The sky looked uneasy, impatient to unleash its next volley. I wandered outside to get my toothbrush from the car. The swathe of mud where it was parked had flooded overnight and I had to tiptoe around the standing water to reach it with dry feet. As I was rummaging around behind the driver's seat, someone sidled over unseen and struck up a conversation.

'You hear! Obama?' the sudden voice startled me, unaware as I was of his presence.

'Yes, he's part Kenyan, isn't he?'

'Obama is the man. We are proud.'

'Well spotted.' It was too early in the morning for deciphering tentative conversations.

'He is the big man. Hero.'

'I'm sure he is.' I was in no mood for the conversation and my suitor must have realised this, as the small talk ended.

'This is your car?' he asked. I knew where this was leading.

'Yes…'

'I have a friend with a garage. You need a garage?'

'I thought you might know someone.'

And so went the conversation that seemed to take place every time we stopped. We agreed to speak later on, as there was no way I could pretend I didn't need a garage. Not as I ducked under the exhaust jutting from the car's roof and nearly tripped over the tow rope as I walked back to the hostel.

I found the rest of the team finishing breakfast and joined them quietly.

'Good morning,' said a chirpy Louise.

'Hi folks,' I replied.

'How are you this morning?' asked Laura.

'I'm okay I suppose. I'll survive. Not sure about the car though.'

'Have you looked at it yet?'

'No. It's currently sat in a big muddy puddle. I think we're going to be stuck here for a while though.'

'Well I went out to it this morning and a lady offered me two thousand dollars for it,' said Laura.

'Don't tempt me,' I replied.

'Hey, did you hear about Obama? He won the election,' said Laura smiling.

'Did he? Awesome. I'm so glad to hear that. A random Kenyan guy was just talking to me about him a minute ago actually, makes a lot more sense now.'

It was Wednesday, November 5th. Barack Obama had just made history by becoming the first African American president elect of the United States. I smiled for the first time that day.

'I'm just glad we won't have to put up with that Sarah Palin anymore,' said Tom, to much agreement.

Two cups of coffee overcame my inertia, so after breakfast I headed out to see what could be done for the Porsche. If we were going to continue, the exhaust and fuel filter would need fixing, as well as whatever else had been fatally smashed on the car's underside. Predictably, the Obama fan with the garage connections was still lingering outside. Naturally, the garage had an inspection pit where we could work beneath the car and yes, of course he could fix the fuel filter. Brummy towed the Porsche down the muddy main drag to the garage and we pushed it backwards over the inspection pit so we could work beneath it.

The garage was a very basic affair. Apart from a set of (empty) petrol pumps, the inspection pit appeared to be its only asset. Old tyres lay discarded on the concrete, while a few bored locals hung around, watching with bemused expressions as we dragged the impotent Porsche into position.

I set up the light from the Porsche's awning to illuminate the car's underside and we took a closer look. It was an awful mess. Mud caked every surface and dripped on us continuously. The metal floorpan had been brutally pounded upwards where rocks had hit it. The fuel and hydraulic lines were waved, bent and indented, while the vanes on the underside of the engine's sump were twisted and cracked away, as well as being covered in an ominous coating of oil.

With easy access, we were able to remove the fuel filter without too much hassle and our mechanic friend wandered off with it, adamant he could fix it. Another guy attacked the exhaust, bending its twisted, dented length back into vaguely the right shape. While they worked, we nipped off to have a look around the town. I was relieved at not having to spend the whole day under the car, as it would have been the last thing I needed.

The rains were the first to fall on Marsabit for two years and had engendered the place with an almost carnival atmosphere. People who'd previously had to buy water at hugely inflated prices from trucks coming up from the south could now collect it as it fell from the sky. Everyone was going about their day with a smile and a spring in their step, savouring the raindrops falling on their heads. Outside our lodge, children played in a flooded area of trees, splashing each other and laughing joyously. Even the area's toad population was rejoicing.

It didn't do much for the town's attractiveness, however. Small shacks of wood, plaster and corrugated iron lined the wide, muddy streets. Many of the thoroughfares held deep puddles, or were completely flooded for hundreds of metres. It looked as if the elements were trying to turn the place into a low-rent African version of Venice, with rundown properties opening onto canals of muddy water. The heavens opened as we wandered, so we sought shelter beneath the overhanging roof of a boarded-up shop. Across the flooded street, six disgruntled sheep sheltered beneath a similar overhang.

The showers soon forced us into a more long-term refuge in a café: 'the best in town' according to our new Kenyan best friend. In its dark – but thankfully dry – interior, cafeteria furniture huddled around televisions showing the aftermath of the American election. The rains weren't the only thing bringing a carnival atmosphere to town. The name Obama was on everyone's lips and even in this isolated corner of the country, everyone was inordinately proud of his election. Food arrived and I was relieved that the Kenyan take on spaghetti bolognese in front of me had little in common with the Ethiopian 'delicacies' of the previous week.

I spent the afternoon dodging the showers while doing what I could for the Porsche. An interested harem of folk had materialised around it, surrounding this strange car that had apparently made it through from Moyale. One of the guys was deaf and spent the afternoon trying to tell us in sign language how dangerous the road south was. He did this by repeatedly miming a beheading action or shooting an imaginary machine gun into our faces at point blank range. Suffice to say, this got rather tiring after a while. It would have been more worrying, were it not delivered with such theatrical over-exuberance, with comically bulging eyes and death feigned after the beheading action. Another member of our audience was evidently an alcoholic and was, even at two in the afternoon, blind drunk. Brummy and our Kenyan friend convinced him that the Porsche belonged to the man of the moment, Barack Obama, and we had to get it to Nairobi for the following day, as Obama was flying to Kenya for a surprise visit to his family and wanted to use it. Suffice to say, he got quite excited and drunkenly did his best to help us for the rest of the day.

By mid-afternoon, the fuel filter had been patched up with liquid metal in a surprisingly effective bodge. I was impressed, but such repairs are the bread and butter of frontier garages in places like Marsabit. We refitted it, but found that the fuel lines had sustained damage and were now leaking in several places. One step forward, one step back. We set to work cutting out the damaged sections and replacing them with lengths of garden hose, which were glued and Jubilee Clipped into place. I also gave the underside of the engine a good clean and was relieved to find that its coating of oil wasn't the result of a cracked sump, but rather a leak from somewhere on the front of the engine, probably the crankshaft seal. It didn't seem to be leaking too badly, so I left it be. Meanwhile, the girls returned from a stroll around town with a bag of Khat leaves and set to work seeing what the fuss was about.

Khat is a stimulant which, when chewed, apparently causes a degree of excitement or euphoria in the user. Despite their best efforts, neither Louise nor Laura seemed to get particularly euphoric, even though they consumed an impressive amount of the stuff. There must be something in it however. Several million addicts scattered across East Africa and Arabia can't be wrong.

It was soon clear we wouldn't be leaving Marsabit that day, given how fiddly and time consuming it was locating and patching up every leak on the fuel lines, so we booked another night in the JayJay centre and cooked dinner, before heading out for a night on the town. The frogs chorused their approval as we wandered into the darkness.

Marsabit, like so many small African towns, disappears after dark. Without ambient lighting, the world around us vanished into the blackness as we walked, doing our best to avoid the worst of the mud and water by the light of our head torches.

The bars followed a set pattern, all comprising a dimly lit room with the walls painted in some bright, vivid colour. The bar itself was normally in the corner, sealed off from the rest of the room by a wooden frame, which was made impenetrable with chicken wire. Drinks were served through a slot, well out of arm's reach of anything worth stealing. Faded old promotional posters for beer or Amarula hung from the walls, while a framed portrait of the president, Mwai Kibaki, usually watched paternally over the patrons. In the first of our impromptu pub crawl's venues, a young couple sat in the corner, chewing Khat. The Tusker beer lent a nice enough vibe to the evening, even if it tasted a bit too chemical-like to compete with the best of Europe. Still, it lifted spirits and lubricated the conversation nicely.

'So, a hundred and fifty miles of gravel tomorrow and then its tarmac all the way to Cape Town,' announced an uplifting Brummy.

'Don't take my word for it,' I said, sensing the abuse I might come in for if my previous prophecy turned out not to be true.

'That's what you said earlier.'

'I may have said that. I may be wrong.'

'I damn well hope tomorrow is the last tough bit. The Shogun is starting to crack in two again,' said Tom.

'I agree,' said Laura. 'Every day we spend on the rough stuff seems to cost us a day broken down somewhere, getting the cars fixed.'

'Well hopefully, this time tomorrow the worst roads of the trip will be behind us,' I said.

The nightlife of Marsabit had ground to a halt by ten, so sleep beckoned. The following day – a public holiday declared to honour man of the moment Barack Obama – dawned as rainy as usual and saw my Kenyan friend and I wandering the town, knocking on the doors of closed shops in an attempt to get hold of some Araldite glue to fix the last outstanding cracks in the fuel lines. We eventually succeeded and the car was up and running without any leaks by mid-morning. Team Shogun were eager to get underway after another day lost to repairs, so we headed south without any further ado.

The first obstacle was a steep hill, climbing directly out of town. Its uneven surface was partly mud and partly the polished granite bedrock which underpins the area. A lorry had attempted to make the climb and become stuck halfway up, unable to move forwards or back. Fortunately, we were now dab hands at negotiating such conditions and managed to make our vehicle's momentum last long enough to summit the hill.

Following this initial challenge, the difficulties eased. Less rain had fallen to the south of Marsabit and the road was fortunately not a repeat of the rutted, slippery horror show we had negotiated two days previously. However, an unwelcome feature of the dryness was the return of corrugations – the worst of the trip so far. We resigned ourselves to another day of crawling along at a frustratingly slow pace, as the roads pounded us relentlessly. Around us, sand once again began to predominate over mud and the grasses vanished, leaving an attractive yellow landscape of low-slung trees. Small monkeys played by the road and occasionally a regal bird of prey would swoop overhead.

We were soon halfway to Isiolo, the next town of any description, and the beginning of the tarmac. Silky smooth tarmac, all the way to Cape Town – or so we fantasised. We still had to make it out of the deserts of northern Kenya though and they weren't about to let us go without a fight.

First it was the exhaust. It was becoming almost routine. A day's driving on dirt roads wasn't complete unless the Porsche lost its exhaust. Spirits stayed high, and a few beers were cracked open as it was strapped to the roof.

Sadly, the next failure was also becoming routine and was a lot more of a hassle than the exhaust's spontaneous departure. An attempt to accelerate disdainfully past the Shogun was met with a hollow lack of power and I knew what the problem was immediately. Not enough power probably meant that not enough fuel was getting to the engine. I hoped it was a split in the fuel line reopening, rather than the fuel filter failing again. I was disappointed.

The repairs to the fuel filter mounting made by the garage in Marsabit hadn't been up to scratch and the continuous vibrations from the corrugated road had shaken it loose, dropping it onto the drive shaft, where another hole was worn into it. I cursed myself for not checking over the repairs more thoroughly before we left that morning.

'If you want something done properly, do it yourself,' I muttered to myself, under my breath.

'Ah, not again. Northern Kenya clearly doesn't like the German,' said Louise.

'I've got plenty of Araldite; I'll try to patch the hole with it,' I replied confidently. 'It'll take half an hour or so to dry, so best make yourselves at home.'

And so, for half an hour, home became a dusty plain somewhere in northern Kenya. Laura started to cook a snack of popcorn on the camping stove while I worked beneath the car. The dry, dusty conditions were considerably easier to attempt a repair in than the mud and rain of two days previously, though the petrol still meant it was difficult to get anything to stick to the filter.

As I applied the glue, I gradually became aware of clumps of mud landing around me, beneath the car.

'What's that?' I asked.

'It's Tom,' Brummy said.

'I'm getting the mud out of your wheel arches.'

'Why?'

'It'll wear your tyres down,' said Tom.

'You what?'

'They're choked with mud. You shouldn't drive it like that,' he replied.

'Don't be silly Tom. And stop throwing mud at me while I'm lying under the car.'

Tom always reacted to delays by trying to do something he considered constructive, even if to others it may appear to be a rather non-critical task. He always felt it was better to use the time to do *something*, rather than let it pass by unutilised.

Soon after we stopped, we found ourselves under the inquisitive gaze of two local women, from either the Rendille or Samburu tribe. I can't be sure which, as their lands meet near where we broke down, so we could have been in either tribe's sphere of influence. Whichever, they made an impressive sight, tall and thin, though with an aura of strength and a ready smile and laugh. Beads and jewellery decorated their bright yellow, sweeping robes, while their feet remained unshod. Despite the lack of a common language, we were able to communicate through gestures and they took great interest in what we were doing. They recoiled in surprise when Laura lit the camping stove and when they realised that the car was broken, they helped in the most effective way they knew. Laughing and smiling, they prayed for the Porsche in a most dedicated fashion.

'I bet this is the first Porsche ever to be prayed for by a Kenyan nomad,' I said.

'You should have brought a nice, reliable Shogun and saved them the trouble,' said Brummy.

Sadly, their prayers were in vain. Once the glue was dry, I started the engine. The repair held for about half a minute, before fuel started trickling out from beneath the glue. It hadn't bonded to the petrol-soaked metal well enough to withstand the pressure.

'Okay, we can either patch it up again and hope it works on the second attempt, or you guys can tow the Porsche again,' I said.

'We can't wait another half hour for a repair that might not work. Let's get it on tow,' Brummy suggested impatiently.

No one disagreed.

Once again the Porsche had made it two-thirds of the way through the day's journey before breaking down, and once again I had failed to make a successful repair. Depression didn't descend as it had two days previously, maybe because of the knowledge that we were nearing the tarmac, so Laura and I conversed in a muted fashion as we were dragged through the bleak, fading landscape.

With darkness came the weather. Boiling clouds unleashed a frenzy of rain upon the lush landscape from which Mt Kenya rises. This necessitated an emergency stop to close the Porsche's electric windows, which were now operated in a fiddly fashion, by touching together the bare wires which stuck out from the door. In the stormy darkness, Kenya seemed to close in around us. The bush at the sides of the road became closer, denser and more impenetrable; the sky above hung lower and angrier than ever, and the track beneath us became increasingly potholed and slippery. Unlit villages flashed briefly into vision as our headlights passed, before disappearing into the darkness behind us.

Nearing Isiolo, we arrived at an ominous line of lorries, asleep at the side of the road. Creeping past, we soon came to the reason for the queue. A usually dry creek had been brought to life by the rains and surged across our path. For about thirty metres, the road was a raging torrent. It looked deep. Just downstream of where the road once existed, the waters tumbled over a low waterfall. One lorry, which had attempted the crossing upstream of this, sat in the middle of the flood, tilted over at a crazy angle which belied the slanting terrain beneath the water's surface. We stopped at the torrent's edge, where Brummy engaged in a shouted conversation with a truck driver before donning his waterproof and wandering over to the Porsche.

'What do you think?' he asked.

'Looks deep.'

'Indeed it does. According to the guy over there, it's impassable and we'll have to wait for the waters to die down,' said Brummy.

'That could be days. I don't fancy waiting here for days.'

'We could give it a go. It looks shallowest on the lip of the waterfall. What do you think?'

'Well the Porsche will still run. I'm game,' I said positively, before adding: 'Just don't go too close to the lip in case it crumbles, and keep the revs up to make sure water doesn't get up the exhaust.'

'Fair enough, let's do it,' Brummy said, already striding back to the Shogun.

'Hold on!' I shouted back after him. 'Aren't we supposed to go for a walk in the water first, to check there are no big rocks or holes or anything? That's what proper off-roader types do.'

'Sod that!' Brummy barked back dismissively. We were doing it our way!

I fired up the Porsche's engine, accepting that we'd be leaking a little fuel while it was running, and took in some slack on the tow rope. The engine barked angrily from the stumpy remains of the exhaust, waking Laura.

'What's happening?' she asked drowsily.

'Erm, a bit of a river crossing,' I said sheepishly.

The Shogun crawled into the waters and promptly tilted over to the right at a jaunty angle, as the bow wave flooded over its bonnet and soaked up the light from its headlights. And then it was our turn. We plunged into the river like a thrown brick, the initial wave of water surging up the bonnet before engulfing the raindrops which were thudding into the windscreen. 'Oh crap,' I thought, as I fought the floodwaters. The car tilted over in the same crazy manner as the Shogun, water nearly reaching to the windows on my side of the car, while Laura rode higher and drier. This suited me just fine, as I knew the air intake for the engine was on Laura's side of the car and engines tend to run better on a diet of air than they do on Kenyan floodwaters.

Slipping the clutch, I revved the engine aggressively to make sure water didn't come up the stumpy remains of the exhaust, while fighting the current, staying well back from the Shogun and keeping a little slack in the towrope. As we passed the stricken lorry, the turbulence it was creating downstream shook the car. Unseen obstacles on the riverbed jolted us worryingly, but after what seemed like an age, the worst was behind us and we began the climb up the opposite bank. The water level dropped before first the Shogun, then the Porsche, scrabbled up the slippery track with difficulty and regained terra firma. Our audience of truck drivers, who had been watching our progress from the far bank, laughed and shook their heads at our stupidity.

I turned off the Porsche's engine and silence returned.

'How much fun was that!?' Brummy shouted back at us with a grin.

The last few miles to Isiolo were uneventful, the tarmac beginning soon after our river adventure. Following a frustrating half hour of looking for a hotel or campsite which wasn't horrifically overpriced, we found a place for the night which was merely painfully overpriced. Brummy and Tom got a room, while the rest of us slept in the cars. However tired we were, we resented being overcharged for a night's sleep.

Tarmac all the way to Cape Town, we told ourselves blissfully, as we drifted away.

ELEVEN

KOMOGI

7th November 2008
Nanyuki, Kenya

Thirty-four days. We had been on the road for thirty-four days. In just over a month, we had covered six and a half thousand miles, crossed sixteen countries on three continents, caught four ferries and negotiated nearly a thousand miles of dirt tracks. We had fallen ill, crossed deserts, broken down repeatedly and been chased past the pyramids by a policeman on a camel. Laura and I had learnt to trust our scrapyard engine and had gone from barely being on speaking terms, to being closer than ever. In short, we'd had quite an intense time of things.

What we needed was a holiday.

Fortunately, we knew just the place. Louise's sister Siobhan was living on a ranch about an hour's drive from Nanyuki, a small town which straddles the equator on the lush foothills of Mount Kenya. We towed the Porsche there, where it went into a garage recommended by Siobhan's Kenyan boyfriend, Julian, who was manager of the ranch on which they lived. The Shogun also went into the garage for some repairs, as its chassis was once again worryingly close to snapping in two, due to the poor quality of the repairs carried out in Ethiopia and the Sudan. It was Friday. We arranged to collect the cars on the Monday and set off to the ranch for a few days of much needed relaxation. The prospect of two whole days away from the faltering Porsche was beautiful, despite the slight residue of guilt I felt for not spending the weekend repairing it myself.

Predictably, the ranch was at the end of a dirt road, which crossed miles of rolling acacia scrub. It took us about an hour for us to reach it, bouncing along beneath a typically heavy sky. We were glad that for once, we weren't pounding our own vehicles along the road, especially when the Toyota pickup in which we were travelling suffered a puncture. It was changed quickly while we maintained a sharp lookout, as there were rumours of lions in the area.

The rainy season denied us views of the incomparable Mount Kenya and we didn't see any big cats either, but there was plenty of other wildlife on display. First, we spotted a few herds of zebra close to the road, apparently unconcerned by our passing. This was our first sighting of large game animals on the trip and it was all the more special for it. I dwelled on what we had achieved; with a little help and a lot of luck, we had driven the Porsche to a place where zebras roam. Brummy's take on the sighting wasn't quite so contemplative, however.

'What's the fuss? It's just a bunch of stripy old horses,' was his considered opinion.

Further on, as if we had moved from one enclosure to another in a safari park back home, we came across about fifteen buffalo. They stood majestically, chewing grasses with a grinding left-right jaw action, while completely ignoring the humans driving past – clearly, we weren't perceived as a threat. Given that the largest members of the herd weighed nearly a tonne and had sweeping horns over a metre across, their sense of invulnerability was understandable. If I weighed that much and fought off lions and crocodiles on a regular basis, I wouldn't worry too much about a few humans in a tiny pick-up truck. Taking in the herd from the safety of our vehicle, I braced myself for the inevitable 'mum' joke from Brummy. It wasn't long in coming.

We'd spent most of the day in Nanyuki, crawling around beneath the Shogun's chassis, writing emails and tucking into a blissful fry-up breakfast, so it was just getting dark when we finally arrived at Siobhan and Julian's house. They greeted us joyfully, like the welcoming hosts they proved to be and stories were swapped excitedly as we sat outside drinking tea, while the unfamiliar sounds of the bush chattered urgently all around.

Siobhan had enjoyed the same adventurous upbringing as her sister, travelling relentlessly from place to place and living in locations as diverse as Scotland, Tunisia and Cairo. She had come out to Kenya after finishing her A-levels, where she met Julian, a third generation descendent of colonial white settlers. This made him very much an ethnic minority within Kenya, as people of European descent accounted for only around sixty thousand people within Kenya's total population of thirty-eight million.

They made for an interesting couple. Siobhan, in her early twenties and very much of the same mould as Louise, was full of the mannerisms and phrases of young folk back in the UK and at first acquaintance seemed a strange person to be living out here in the middle of the African bush. I could imagine her partying the night away in some club back home much more easily than helping to run a ranch in Kenya. However, as I got to know her, everything began to make perfect sense and she clearly possessed the inner toughness and worldliness required to make the best of her uncertain life in Kenya.

No such question marks hung over Julian's eligibility to live out in the bush. Square of jaw, with a characterful dusting of stubble and permanently attired in his uniform of khaki shorts, shirt and knife, he projected the aura of someone completely comfortable in the wilds of Africa. He spoke slowly but decisively in a typically white-African accent and never wasted a word, or expanded in a flowery manner. You got the impression that whatever challenge Kenya threw at him, he would be its equal. Whether he was tracking lions, running a cattle ranch or summiting Mount Kenya, he'd feel right at home – which was just as well, as he did all of three on a regular basis.

Were he Australian, his name would surely have been Crocodile Dundee.

Our hosts lived in the manager's house on Komogi Lodge, a working ranch hidden deep in the wild scrubland of northern Laikipia, to the north west of Mt Kenya. Their house was a beautiful, open-plan take on the traditional circular huts which we'd been seeing for the previous few weeks. Exposed stone walls stood ten feet high, at which point a magnificent grass roof, held up by wooden rafters, sealed the space. The interior was about sixty feet long, twenty feet wide and felt charismatically colonial, sofas mingling with more rustic African fittings. A fire glowed comfortingly in the corner. Instead of a TV, there was a Scrabble board.

Siobhan and Julian shared the property with two dogs, Hector and Choca. Hector, the old man of the house, had lived there for as long as anyone could remember. A somewhat portly and arthritic black Labrador, his days seemed to involve an enviable amount of sleep, interspersed with the occasional stroll around his domain to check nothing had changed.

Choca, however, couldn't have been more different. About a foot long and as mad as the devil, the playful little three-month-old Labrador/terrier cross had been acquired by Siobhan a few months earlier and was brought to the ranch when Julian got the job managing the place. Full of precocious character and energy, Choca effortlessly stole everyone's hearts.

It seemed an idyllic existence, living out in the depths of the bush, farming cattle and entertaining guests from time to time. However it was also obvious just how isolated they were, stuck on the edge of the world with little company and no entertainment but what you make for yourself. It suited us just fine however, and we spent the weekend doing as little as we could. Revelling in lassitude, my sole achievement of most of Saturday was shaving off five weeks of beard growth, transforming me from a seasoned adventurer to a fresh-faced tourist in a few quick sweeps of the razor.

On the Saturday evening, Julian and Siobhan took us on a game drive. The wet and blustery weather did its best to keep any wildlife hidden from us, but we still saw a fair bit of life on the bleak grasslands. Warthogs ran for cover as Julian's Toyota crawled along, while antelope played among themselves, keeping a safe distance from us. Bird life was very much in evidence. An enormous bustard hastened away as we drove and we saw several examples of the hammerkop, a quirky little brown wading bird with a strangely distended head. Also starring in our little tour was a rare example of the Grévy's zebra, knowledgably identified for us by Julian. An endangered species, there are currently fewer than three thousand examples left in the wild. They are identified by their unusually large ears and densely packed stripes.

After an hour or so, we came upon a giraffe and parked the Toyota to continue on foot for a closer look. Julian took along his rifle, as if it were the most natural thing in the world to prepare oneself to repel a lion attack. The giraffe towered over the acacia trees which separated it from us and grazed away in an unconcerned manner. It looked a thoroughly improbable concept as animals go; all strong neck and stringy legs.

As the sun went down, we climbed a hill and took in a panoramic view of the area, while tucking into toffee apples and a few beers. I was disappointed that Mount Kenya still refused to emerge from the clouds, as I had spent the morning reading a fascinating book about it. *No picnic on Mount Kenya* by the Italian, Felice Benuzzi, describes his escape from the boredom of a British prisoner of war camp in Nanyuki with the sole intention of climbing the mountain, and his subsequent 'break in' to return to captivity. It was a touching story, full of spirit, which re-ignited my interest in the mountain, home to some of the finest mountaineering in Africa – as well as the celebrated 'Diamond Couloir', which was once the best ice climb on the continent, before global warming melted it away.

We drove back to the house through the darkness, scanning the bush by torchlight for any other wildlife sightings. Our lights picked out a hyena, which eyed us disapprovingly.

It would have been rude to visit a working cattle ranch, but not play cowboy by going for a horse ride and so on the Sunday we did just that. I'm not a horse person. Their unpredictability and flightiness has always made me shy away from horse riding. However, as the saying goes, 'when in Rome'. The horses walked around the ranch slowly with us perched inexpertly on their backs. My steed seemed intent on crashing into the back of Louise's horse for reasons known only to itself, while I solemnly hoped it wouldn't get spooked by something and run off into the undergrowth. Fortunately, it was far too bored to consider anything so energetic.

At dusk, we left the horses and walked slowly back to the ranch through the dense bush. Choca bounded along with us enthusiastically for a while, but her little legs soon tired. We picked her up, Laura and I taking it in turns to carry the adorable little puppy as we walked.

After dinner, we settled in for our final evening of relaxed chat with our hosts. Their stories, told over a cold Tusker beer, painted a grittier picture of the world outside, in the inky blackness of the Kenyan bush. Just as it is further north, cattle rustling is a problem for the ranch, and while the animals graze, armed farm workers guard them continuously. From time to time, the workers encounter other armed groups in the area – or their bodies. The ranch's grazing lands were located on the boundary between the terrotories of two different tribes – the Maasa and the Kikuyu. These two tribes weren't exactly on best terms and squabbles often arose, escalating to shootouts on a regular basis.

It's not only this remote pocket on the edge of the vast wilderness of northern Kenya which operates on such a tribal basis. Kenya is not so much a cohesive country as a vague amalgamation of tribes, which can splinter apart at any moment.

This splintering last happened shortly before our visit to Kenya, with disastrous effect. Rigged elections eight months previously had led to the unexpected defeat of the main opposition party, meaning power – and the corrupt spoils of power – would remain in the hands of the ruling Kikuyu elite. Supporters of the opposition leader cried foul and took to the streets, attacking members of the Kikuyu tribe and soon, the retaliatory attacks began. Roadblocks were set up by both sides and people were dragged from their cars and macheted for their ethnicity. The country momentarily ceased to exist as a unified whole, fracturing into a patchwork of bitter tribal areas. In all, one thousand five hundred Kenyans died in the upheaval, while over half a million were made homeless.

Suddenly, the dark world outside the windows seemed rather less innocent. The following day we would return to Nanyuki, and get back on the road. Next stop – Uganda.

We collected the cars from David, the likeable guy who ran the garage. They had done a sterling job with the repairs. The cross member on the Shogun's chassis to which the fuel tank attaches had come adrift, so they removed the tank and welded it back into place. They also changed the Shogun's oil and gave it a general service and tune up. The Porsche got a shiny new fuel filter, a reattached exhaust and new rear shock absorbers. They even cleaned it inside and out, so thoroughly that it was almost a shame to take it back onto the grubby African roads. It was nice to feel some confidence in the Porsche again, after the battering it had taken. We drove into town and went for one last coffee with Siobhan before recommencing our journey. We chatted about our plans as we waited to be served.

'So, how are we doing, time-wise?' Louise said.

'Not too bad,' I replied. 'We were a few days late getting to Mount Kenya because of all the car problems, but there were a few days' slack in the route plan to allow for that. Basically, if we leave today, we're back on track.'

'Oh good,' said Louise. 'So we can still go to Uganda and Rwanda like we talked about.'

'Well we can,' I said, with reservation. 'But if we do, we've got to loop back under Lake Victoria, through Tanzania. That's another five-hundred miles of nasty gravel tracks.'

'In the rainy season,' Laura added, as our coffees arrived.

'Oh, do we have to?' Brummy said.

'No. No we don't have to,' said Tom.

'Every time we go off road, we have to spend the whole of the next day fixing the cars,' said Laura.

'Yeah, I'm not overly keen on another five hundred miles of mud. We could just skip Uganda and Rwanda, and head directly south from here, into Tanzania,' I said, before scalding my mouth on the hot coffee.

'But I really want to raft the White Nile,' said Laura, 'and see Lake Victoria too.'

'Oh you're such a hippy traveller type,' teased Brummy, as Laura scowled back at him.

'Hmmm, well what we could do is pop over into Uganda for a day or two, before doubling back into Kenya. It wouldn't be much of a detour, as we wanted to visit the charity in Kisumu anyway and that's over near the Ugandan border. We could also see if we could get transit visas issued for our return to Kenya, to keep the costs down.'

'That would make sense. Let's do it,' said Louise and everyone agreed.

It was settled; we would visit Uganda, but miss out on Rwanda and the remote northwest corner of Tanzania out of deference to our fragile cars.

We had all settled into a state of inertia during our weekend off the road and it was afternoon before we finally said our goodbyes to Siobhan and got underway. Heading out of town, we stopped next to a sign proudly declaring:

THIS SIGN IS ON THE EQUATOR. NANYUKI, ALTITUDE 6,389FT

It was one of the trip's big milestones. The equator. Plymouth lay at fifty-two degrees north and we had driven to where north gave way to south. We were now in the same hemisphere as Cape Town and it was allegedly tarmac all the way there. As everyone who crosses the equator for the first time does, we watched water go through a hole in a bucket, its direction of rotation changing – whether because of the Coriolis Effect, or the way it had been poured into the bucket – with the hemisphere.

'Okay, perhaps it does change direction,' conceded Louise.

We stopped for the night just outside Nanyuki that evening, at the appealingly named 'Camel Camp.' No camels were in evidence, no other residents of any kind in fact, except for a few large, scary-looking dogs. It was nice to slot back into the routine of putting up the roof tent and cooking together beneath the stars. We all knocked back a few beers after dinner, but uncharacteristically, it was Brummy who was first to bed, followed by Louise and Laura. Tom and I sat up chatting – and polishing off the beer – well into the night. All was clearly not well in Team Shogun.

'It's like I'm the only one who cares if we actually do this. You say to Brummy 'I think there's a problem,' and he just dismisses it straight away. You can't discuss things with him, he just rants and that's that.'

'Yeah, you two are quite different characters,' I sympathised.

'You can say that again. Whenever anything goes wrong with the Shogun, it's always me that has to sort it out. He hasn't even checked the oil.'

'He does have his uses though, surely?'

'Probably, I'm not sure what they are though. He just jokes everything away. Trying to get a serious conversation out of him is a nightmare at times.'

The conversation had been brewing for weeks. As the most serious person in the relationship that is Team Shogun and the most prone to stress, it was perhaps inevitable that Tom would feel he was shouldering the bulk of the pressure. To make things worse, Brummy's habit of casually dismissing any ideas he didn't like had left Tom feeling ever more isolated as the trip went on. Brummy had similar issues and had complained of Tom's unconstructive seriousness to me the previous day. It was a shame Tom found it difficult to relax and fit in with the carefree approach the rest of us were taking to the trip, but it was in his nature to take things seriously. I couldn't see how things could change, provided the trip remained as pressured as it had been.

After doing what I could to help Tom get his problems off his chest, I climbed unsteadily into the roof tent and slept.

* * *

The road to Uganda took us through the rolling mountains of the Abadare range, a lushly vegetated series of summits which run along the east side of the Great Rift Valley. It rained continuously, the microclimate provided by Lake Victoria ensuring the area is seldom dry for long. Sickly terracotta mud flowed down from the saturated hillsides, forming a filthy paste on the road. The clouds came down low, or the road climbed up to meet them, so we were often driving through a fine hill mist, which condensed and soaked everything. It didn't take long until the cars were filthy once again.

The weather improved as we left the mountains, the road skirting dramatically along the edge of the Great Rift Valley for a few miles before dropping down to the town of

Nyahururu. We stopped to take some photos on the valley's rim, but were soon hounded away by the local hawkers, intent on selling us trinkets.

The roads in western Kenya were worse than we had anticipated and as the sun plummeted dramatically to the equator, we were still over a hundred miles from the border.

'What's the plan then? Shall we camp?' suggested Tom.

'There are people everywhere. We'll never find somewhere we'll be left alone,' Brummy pointed out.

'Well we could push on to the border. It's not too far away,' someone said.

'A good few hours probably,' I said. 'I'm cool to carry on if there's no other option.'

'Well there's bugger all around here in the guidebook,' Laura added.

'Excellent, more night driving,' said Brummy.

We were carrying on.

It took us three tense hours to reach the border. The roads were still thronged with people after dark and the Porsche's inadequate headlights struggled to pick them out. The lights of oncoming vehicles seemed to blind us on principle, while potholes and grooves worn in the road often made driving a dodgem-like experience. However, we got there eventually, pulling into the border town of Malaba with our nerves in tatters. I had no cause to complain about the day's drive though, as for the first time in a week, the Porsche had at least managed a whole day on the road without its exhaust and fuel filter falling off.

We made it out of Kenya fairly quickly, the border being dominated by a rotund middle-aged woman whose sharp voice and feisty temperament kept everyone in check. Even the soldiers manning the crossing were scared of her and it took great self-control on the parts of Brummy and I to retain straight faces during some of her more theatrical outbursts. Entering Uganda, we found we would not be able to obtain visas until the following morning and so we parked up in a muddy, uninspiring truck park between the two countries and slept. Once again, the roof tent proved its worth, Laura and I getting a much better night's sleep than Team Shogun, wedged in their steed with seats reclined as best they could.

* * *

Uganda turned out to be the Africa my mind's eye had imagined. The sun shone brightly upon a lush landscape, which rolled away from us in a playful manner, beckoning us on. All around was a thick, luxurious rainforest, densely packed with unfamiliar plants, with exotic birds fluttering through its canopy. Occasional troops of monkeys strode confidently at the side of the road, appraising us with quizzical faces as we passed. Lots of people walked or cycled along the road, always smiling and cheerful. The air was crystal clear and the temperature balmy, except inside the Porsche, of course, where the heater still blasted away like a furnace. All in all, it felt good after Kenya, where the rains and mud and bad roads and breakdowns had left us feeling somewhat embattled.

The destination for our brief visit to Uganda was Jinja, a small town which sits by Lake Victoria, a few miles from the source of the White Nile. Uganda is fairly small and the roads were far superior to those in Kenya, so we arrived at the day's destination in plenty of time for lunch. We made our way to a campsite at Bugajali and were soon drinking cold beers on a terrace, taking in the breathtaking views of the White Nile, churning powerfully over the rapids at the start of its four thousand mile odyssey to the sea.

It was a strangely sad, though satisfying moment. For weeks, the river had wound in and out of our lives and much of our route had been dictated by its stately progress. It had eased our passage through Egypt and the deserts of the Sudan and we had witnessed the marriage of its Blue and White tributaries in Khartoum. In Ethiopia we had passed near the source of the Blue Nile and now we were looking upon the birth of its white counterpart. Over the weeks, as our paths snaked across the map together, converging and diverging, we had grown strangely fond of its presence. The river had become a familiar companion, and a continuous yardstick of our progress. When we left Jinja, we would not see it again. We would quickly leave its drainage basin behind and push south to make our acquaintances with another great African river – the Zambezi.

Tom and Laura weren't quite ready to say goodbye to the Nile, however. Evidently they'd found the trip a bit too relaxing up to this point and had decided to make amends by getting up close and personal with the river, by spending the following day bobbing down the grade five rapids which were thundering away beneath us. Brummy, Louise and I opted for the somewhat more relaxing (and considerably cheaper) option of bimbling around town for the day, relaxing in cafés and seeing to a few odd jobs on the cars.

That commercial operations were offering rafting adventures at the source of the Nile was something of a miracle in itself, given Uganda's turbulent recent history, which parallels so many of the continent's young nations. First came the British colonisers, as confident in their purpose as they were naïve in the ways of the local populations. Independence from Britain in the early 1960s set free a fractious nation, ill-prepared for the challenges of unity. A succession of coups rapidly removed aspiring leaders of escalating ruthlessness, until only the most brutal remained. Uganda had found its 'Big Man'. Under Idi Amin, the 1970s became a decade of terror in which upwards of three hundred thousand Ugandans died, before an army from Tanzania drove him into exile. Unfortunately, the rejoicing was short-lived, as Obote, Uganda's first president, soon made his return to power and the cruel bloodshed resumed. This led to yet another coup in 1985, before the following year, the country fell to a rebel army, under the leadership of Yoweri Museveni, whose stable though autocratic rule continues to this day. The second half of the 1980s brought not only a welcome degree of stability to most of Uganda, but also a new brace of problems, which continue to the present day. AIDS swept through the country like wildfire, with over a quarter of the population becoming infected, before a spirited public information campaign brought it into check. Also, to the north, a rebel group calling themselves the Lord's Resistance Army (LRA) emerged. Despite their goal of establishing an uncompromising state governed by the Ten Commandments, the LRA seem quite willing to compromise on their lofty ideals when it suits their cause. After all, mutilation, rape, murder and the abduction of child soldiers sit rather uneasily with the bible's teachings.

Somehow, despite its past and current problems, Uganda is now moving forwards with a cautiously expanding economy and one of Africa's more benevolent autocrats at the helm. Watching the crimson sunset as it spread through a crystal sky, its soft reflection dancing on the fledgling Nile, it was easy to believe that the future would be brighter. Numbed by alcohol, I hoped my belief wasn't misplaced.

Now we were out of Kenya, the storm clouds dissipated and the sun became omnipresent once again. Laura rose with it for her day of simulated drowning on the Nile, while I slept in blissfully, until I was forced to commence my day when the sun heated up the tent like a furnace. We had a few jobs to perform. Firstly, we gave the Shogun's brakes the once over, as they had been crying out for some attention during the previous few hundred miles, squealing violently when applied and giving me some much needed ammunition to throw back when Team Shogun made jokes about the Porsche's reliability. It turned out the brake pads were worn through, so we headed into town to replace them. Fortunately this wasn't a problem, as the Shogun (or 'Pajero', as they are known outside the UK) population in

Uganda was reassuringly large. While Brummy saw to the brakes, Louise and I wandered around town.

Jinja was a pleasant place, all wide dusty avenues and characterful low-rise buildings. It was also the first place we'd been since Egypt with much of a tourist population; that is unless you count Nanyuki's omnipresent detachment of sunburnt British Army squaddies – I won't though, as they were generally much bigger than me and I doubt they'd take very kindly to being called tourists. It was nice to roam streets where Westerners were common once again, as their presence diluted the hassle we received from street traders and suchlike.

It was also nice to finally spend some time with Louise, away from the bravado of the group. Over the weeks I had come to respect her greatly for her positive, relaxed approach to life and her boldly adventurous streak. We chatted away about past exploits, of mutual experiences in Mongolia and of life back in Plymouth, where we had both lived for years before the trip made us first acquaintances, then friends. We wandered aimlessly among the cafés and tourist shops, looking for nothing in particular, before stopping for a cold beer in the sun. Halfway through our meanderings, Brummy reappeared.

'Well that was fun!'

'What was fun?' Louise asked.

'We got the new brake pads fitted and it was fine for the test drive around the block. Then I tried to drive here and it squeaked worse than ever. Turns out they'd forgotten to replace a catch holding one of the pads in position.'

'So you shouted at them?' I said.

'Of course. And they sorted it for free.'

'Marvellous. Sounds like you could use a beer. Grab a pew.'

'I think I will,' said Brummy, already heading for the bar.

Back at the campsite that afternoon, we reacquainted ourselves with Tom and Laura, who were looking somewhat weathered after their pummelling at the hands of the grade five rapids. Laura, in particular, had for some reason chosen to simulate the experience of being in a washing machine, by descending two of the rapids upside down in a kayak. My day of strolling around town and drinking beer in the sun seemed much more appealing. Maybe I'm getting old.

Louise and Laura then spent the early part of the evening having their hair braided. The rest of us mocked them as they winced with the pain of having their coiffures tugged at for two hours.

An overland truck had arrived that afternoon, with its cargo of adventure-\seeking young Westerners and that evening the bar filled with their lively banter, while videos of people descending rapids upside down in kayaks were shown on the television. It seemed certain that the bar's rowdy clientele would drink it dry before the end of the night. I wasn't in the mood and went to bed early, the hypnotic bass of the dance music shaking my tent as I tried to sleep.

A few hundred miles to our west lay the border with the Congo. Across it, yet another unthinkable refugee crisis was just beginning to unfold and around forty-five thousand people were still dying every month in the bleak aftermath of the Second Congo War, the bloodiest conflict since World War Two, which had taken the lives of over five million people in the previous decade. As the dance music kept me awake, drowning out the real sounds of Africa, I wondered just how much the youngsters, who are chauffeured around Africa in cosseting overland trucks, from plush bar to expensive campsite, know of what really happens on the continent.

We made an early start the following morning, but Uganda had already been awake for hours. As we drove, Laura and I promised each other that we would return in the future, to give this beautiful country the more thorough visit it deserved. Arriving at the border town of Busia before lunchtime, we crossed out of Uganda efficiently, sad to be leaving the country behind. The people, the good roads and the pleasant weather had all had conspired to relax us and make us feel welcome. We weren't savouring returning to the relative chaos of Kenya, but needs must.

Once stamped out of Uganda, I was beckoned through a gate into no-man's-land. Parking up, I joined Brummy for the border formalities. Brummy loved borders. He would strut from office to office, chest puffed out importantly, a bag of paperwork slung over his shoulder. He discussed and negotiated in a most authoritative manner and took great pride in getting things done. I was generally happy to simply leave him to take the lead and follow him around.

First stop was customs, to re-import the cars. We entered a building with a big customs sign over the door. 'Carnet? Triptique?' Looks of bemusement reigned and we were directed to the next building along. They had no idea either, waving us back to the first building. More blank looks. I could sense Brummy's agitation building beneath his calm exterior.

'Look, this is a customs document,' he said, holding up the carnet. 'This building is the customs building. It says so on a big sign above the door. Who must I speak to?'

Everyone looked on blankly.

'Fifty cars a day must cross this border! Don't tell me nobody's ever asked this question before!'

After another ten minutes of getting nowhere, we were gestured vaguely away in the direction of the immigration building. On the end of the nondescript structure, a door marked 'Hand Luggage' was slightly ajar. Inside, a man in uniform sat behind a tatty desk, upon which we spotted a carnet book and a few rubber stamps. We had found it.

Once the papers were complete, Brummy couldn't resist asking: 'Why is the carnet office in a room with a hand luggage sign on the door? Shouldn't it say 'customs'?'

The guy simply shrugged and said nothing. His shrug communicated much more to us than words possibly could. It said quite succinctly 'this is Africa, not Europe, and we do things our way here. Don't come here with your European ideas and expect everything to conform to them. Instead accept our institutions and traditions arc diffcrent to yours, and learn to adapt.'

We were adapting, but we still had a long way to go. We obtained our visas and headed back to the cars. Brummy ranted as we walked.

'Visas, customs, immigration and insurance. Why can't they just have four windows, or offices, or whatever, in a line. Then you could just go from one to the other getting the paperwork done. It's not rocket science!'

I agreed with him, of course. Half an hour to get a customs document stamped in a room marked 'Hand Luggage' seemed to reek of inefficiency. But as the guy had communicated to us, this was Africa. If we learnt to live with it, and to not get angry, it would begin to work for us.

Once the paperwork was done, the Porsche was officially back in Kenya. I turned the key. It took a while before the engine coughed into life and as I drove off I saw we had left a damp stain on the dusty ground. Evidently we had another fuel leak. 'Welcome back to Kenya,' I said to Laura, and more pertinently, to the Porsche.

We pulled over for a closer look once we were out of town. Joking and banter passed freely between Laura, Louise, Brummy and I, as I jacked up the car for a closer look. Tom was quiet, no doubt slightly annoyed that the Porsche was causing yet another delay, and not appreciating the lack of seriousness with which we were approaching it. As I jacked the car up, Laura lay down and had a look for the problem.

'Yep, it's leaking from just in front of the fuel tank,' she said, trying not to laugh as Brummy jokingly prodded her backside with a wooden stick.

I prepared for a similar treatment as I crawled beneath the now familiar underside of the car and checked out the problem. One of the fuel lines had been badly lacerated on the road to Marsabit, so we had cut out the damaged section and replaced it with a piece of hosepipe, glued in place and clamped with Jubilee Clips to prevent any leakage. This had worked for the past week or so, but our return to Kenya had caused it to begin leaking from one end of the hosepipe.

Brummy joined me beneath the car, while the girls continued to joke away in the background.

'What's happening?'

I showed him the problem.

'Typical. It's fine in Uganda, but the moment we cross back into Kenya, it breaks again,' ranted Brummy. 'Nothing works in Kenya; the roads, the borders, the weather, the Porsche – nothing. They should rename it Can't-ya.'

'It should be a fairly quick fix.' I replied, ignoring the anti-Kenya rant, however true it might have felt at the time. Meanwhile, Laura had begun to assault Brummy's backside in response for his earlier indiscretion.

'Ah! No, stop it. Don't do that. Or at least ask first!' he shouted back with a cheeky smile.

'You love it!' Laura laughed back.

Tom wasn't seeing any humour in our broken-down situation and our joking around was rapidly grating with him. He threw some glue to Louise.

'Fix the spotlights.'

'What?' came the bemused reply.

'They're wobbling, glue them in place,' he said. Brummy and I exchanged knowing glances, as we lay concealed beneath the car. Louise wouldn't stand for that. I continued to undo the Jubilee Clips and waited for the explosion to come. It came from Tom.

'If I tell you to do something, you do it!' he barked aggressively, before suddenly realising what he'd just said and leaving the conversation, stomping off to do something behind the car.

'You can't talk to her like that!' Laura shouted after him.

Brummy and I were shocked for a second, before a wave of silent laughter swept over us. Soon, tears rolled down our cheeks as we fought the urge to laugh out loud.

'Bloody hell, what was all that about?' Brummy whispered to me as we lay beneath the car.

'Oh, it's just Tom being Tom,' Louise chimed defiantly, loud enough for Tom to hear.

Just as a week earlier, when he had passed the time during one of our many breakdowns by picking the mud from my wheel arches, Tom had shown he didn't find it easy to idly sit around in a stressful situation while others worked. His mind told him the situation was serious and therefore he should be doing something – *anything* – to improve our chances of making it through. And just as he should be doing something, so should everyone else – rather than just wasting valuable time by joking about. This explained his outburst at Louise and his nervous fidgeting during previous breakdowns. His coarseness was also probably exaggerated by hunger. We hadn't eaten lunch that day; Tom had been unfortunately prone to becoming rather irritable when hungry.

While all this was going on, I slowly removed all the clips on the leaking joint and replaced them in a manner which I hoped would reseal the pipe.

'Okay Laura, make sure it's in neutral, then turn the key and let's see if it's fixed.'

I inched back from the pipe as she fired up the engine. The repair held.

'Right, we'll do a few miles then stop to see if it's still okay. See you in a bit,' I said to Brummy and Louise. Tom was already back in the Shogun, stewing out of earshot.

I returned to the Porsche and we pulled away.

'God, I'm glad I'm not in the Shogun right now,' Laura said.

'Yeah, for sure. I bet Tom is feeling pretty bad at the moment,' I replied.

'I hope so – he deserves to be after what he said. He can't go bossing Louise around like that.'

'He'll calm down. He's just hungry and stressed, that's all,' I said, as I swung the Porsche around an errant cyclist.

'I don't care,' Laura replied curtly, 'he can't go around treating people like that.'

'They'll get over it. And to think it was us not getting on at the start of the trip? Who'd have thought it?' I said.

Laura placed her hand in mine and our fingers intertwined as we drove along. We smiled knowingly at one another; no more words were needed. Kenya rolled kaleidoscopically past the Porsche's windows, like the backdrop to some far-fetched, over-emotional film.

'Right, we'd better pull over and check we're not leaking,' I said.

'Definitely, given the price of fuel around here,' Laura replied.

'Yeah, who'd have thought Africa would be so expensive?'

I glided to a halt in a lay-by, opened the door and bent over to look beneath the car. The repair hadn't held. Petrol dripped frustratingly from the join in the pipes. I glanced back at the Shogun and shook my head. Brummy and Louise jumped out, while a morose-looking Tom stayed put.

'So, how's life in the Shogun?' I asked.

'Oh, he's just hungry. He'll be fine once he's eaten,' said Brummy.

'Hopefully,' agreed Louise, trying to conceal the anger in her voice.

I jacked the Porsche up for a second time and made some adjustments to the Jubilee Clips. This time they held and we were able to drive to Kisumu, where we were due to meet members of the 'Kenyan Orphan Project', the charity we had been using the trip to raise money for. As we reached Kisumu's outskirts, the tense, bulging clouds finally exploded. Water and electricity were hurled all around the sky in a ferocious display of power. The road disappeared beneath the churning cascade which poured off a terracotta hillside to our left. Above, it was as if the sky itself was flooded, but even this failed to prevent a multitude of raw lightning bolts from strafing the boulder-strewn hillsides all around. Visibility was appalling, so we stopped while the worst of the storm dissipated, before inching cautiously into town.

'Good weather for ducks,' suggested Laura.

Perched on the dashboard, the two bath ducks Laura and I had brought along as mascots didn't hear her. They had turned to face one another and were too busy kissing.

Medical students from Nottingham University set up the Kenyan Orphan Project (KOP) charity in 2001. By the time of our visit to Kisumu – the city around which the majority of KOP's efforts are focused – the charity had grown to involve nine medical universities from around the UK, including Southampton, where Laura was studying medicine. During our visit, Sam, who worked for a Non-Governmental Organisation called the Omega Foundation, showed us around some of the rural projects which KOP funds and supports. Our first stop was Kochogo High School, located in the rural settlement of the same name, about ten miles out of Kisumu. The building had been completed by KOP and the Omega Foundation that year and provides schooling for around six hundred local youngsters. Being a Saturday, the place was fairly deserted, so we didn't stay long before heading off to the Kadinda Health Centre. The centre had been built and paid for by KOP and when opened should bring basic healthcare into the heart of the community for the first time. Unfortunately, the centre was built on the assumption that if KOP completed it, the government would provide the doctors. Only one side of this agreement kept their word and hence the centre was still awaiting its formal opening at the time of our visit. Despite this, KOP were planning to fund the provision of health workers and other staff in 2009, to ensure the centre becomes operational.

The last place on our whistle-stop itinerary was a facility set up to help rural AIDS orphans. Kochogo Feeding Centre (a name I found immediately distasteful, 'feeding centre' sounding to me like something you would find on a farm, rather than a place for human beings) provides meals, support, and a degree of education to the seventy-five children it catered for. Sadly, the problem of AIDS is so acute that a good few hundred more children could benefit from the centre's help if it were bigger. KOP were planning to double the centre's capacity shortly after our visit.

The centre was basic and functional. Smartly plastered walls held up joists of wood, which were topped off with a corrugated iron roof. Metal gratings across the windows provided security. Inside, wooden furniture was dotted around the spacious halls, while the walls were hung with posters about dealing with HIV/AIDS, diarrhoea, malaria and various other unpleasant issues. Outside, a selection of projects enabled the children to learn life skills for the future. A chicken coop was one of the projects, while a small patch of land behind the building was planted with a selection of crops. There were ten children drifting around at the time of our visit, aged from about seven upwards. They all looked healthy and happy.

We set off for Nairobi that afternoon, down predictably bumpy tarmac. Laura and I chatted about our visit to the charity as we drove. Our first impressions hadn't been good. Sam turned out to be of very much above average size for a Kenyan and his subordinate in the Omega Foundation was weightier still and drove the shiniest Toyota Land Cruiser we'd seen for quite a while. Were these people really putting everything into a non-profit organisation? Or was it one of those examples you hear about, where a selfish minority take advantage of good-willed donors and use ostensibly respectable projects to their own ends? In conversation, Sam had offset our first impressions by coming across as both knowledgeable and enthusiastic about the projects he was working on and my faith in his intentions gradually recovered. I have since learnt that the average salary for a manager of an NGO such as Omega Foundation was around two thousand pounds per month. Sam was simply a Kenyan lucky enough to be earning a Western wage.

I think the projects we saw around Kisumu are almost certainly doing a lot of good for the people they support and I don't doubt the motives of the folk around the world who make them possible. However, it is unfortunate how much aid is either misappropriated following its arrival in Africa, or is wholly ineffectual in concept.

As effective as small, grass roots projects like those undertaken by the good folk at KOP often are, many larger projects or donors find it harder to use their vast resources so efficiently. Often, aid agencies' and NGOs' best efforts can actually make things worse.

Aid agencies face many dilemmas. The biggest of these is how to meet their raison d'être most effectively – how to get food and medicine to those who need it the most. Often, the people who need help the most are weak, unarmed and living in warzones. Warzones are also by definition inhabited by strong, well-armed people, who need to eat too. How do you feed the weak without pacifying the strong by feeding them too? It's an impossible task and all too often, the aid agencies find themselves forced to feed armies to ensure some proportion of their food and medicine reaches an area's civilian population. While the moral justifications for such an action may be pure – and the argument that the soldier, if left unfed, will simply steal from the weakest to survive, is very valid – the messy reality is that aid can often actually prolong and worsen wars, by keeping the combatants fighting fit.

Governments sometimes also bully aid organisations, by dictating the terms of assistance to meet their own agendas. Often, aid workers are denied access to starving or needy people because corrupt governments want to avoid negative publicity or, as during the famines in Ethiopia in the 1980s, because starvation is actively being used as a weapon. Sometimes, governments are even more blatant and simply steal some of the aid for themselves.

As an example, in the early 1990s, any aid organisations wishing to operate in northern Sudan were forced to deposit the funds they allocated to the country into one of two Islamic banks. These funds were then converted into Sudanese pounds at half the going exchange rate before they could be used in the Sudan, meaning half the money was effectively siphoned directly into the government coffers. It was a daylight robbery which, at its peak, was netting the Sudanese government four million US dollars a week and effectively paying for them to wage war against the south.

Meanwhile, the southern Sudanese were able to fight back, thanks partly to the aid being poured into the south – up to two million US dollars a week, which as well as keeping civilians alive, kept the rebel armies fed for battle. Just to make sure the moral bankruptcy of those waging the wars was complete, both sides then used food and aid as weapons, by trying to deny it to those who supported their opponents.

Without the money and resources provided by aid agencies and foreign governments, it is doubtful that either side in Sudan's long civil wars would have been able to keep fighting so long. Sadly, however, the conflicts have smouldered on for most of the past half century. Even the best intentions can sometimes have disastrous results.

These thoughts wandered idly through my mind as we ploughed on towards Nairobi, two hundred and fifty miles south east of Kisumu. Somewhere along that road, the car's odometer decided to die. It probably felt overworked, as it had clocked up eight thousand, two hundred and seventy-eight miles since leaving the UK. The distance chart in our road atlas told us it was possible to travel from Nairobi to Cape Town in under four thousand miles. We were getting there.

The second breakage of the day was the roof rack. Both of the rear legs, which dropped down onto the roof, fractured and were lost to the roadside. The roof rack itself clung on until Nairobi, where I jammed a metal bar between the roof and the rack's aluminium frame to keep it tight against its mounting bars.

Most of the day's driving had been on gravel, as the government had ripped up the old road with every intention of replacing it with fresh new tarmac, but had not quite got around to laying said new tarmac yet. Wherever we went in Kenya, things didn't seem to change.

The weather stayed the same too. Heavy showers were an hourly occurrence, forcing Laura and I to repeatedly close the windows by touching together the bare wires poking out from the door. This required two hands and hence wasn't the safest thing to do while driving. As one shower started, I pulled alongside the Shogun and gave them the thumbs up. Laura was lying in my lap, head down, fumbling with the wires for my window. It must have looked pretty strange as, through the open window, I heard Louise let out a rather blokeish 'Oi oi!' while Tom, in the driver's seat, looked down somewhat disapprovingly at our childish exploits. For some reason, Laura felt slightly embarrassed by the incident and was very cautious about putting up the driver's side window for the rest of the trip.

We entered Nairobi in the dark and Team Shogun's navigation had a day of form, taking us quickly and efficiently to the campsite. Sadly however, the guidebook was having one of its regular off days, as the campsite had moved, a map on a gate directing us to its new setting a few miles away. I turned the key to start the Porsche up for this last stint of the day. Nothing. Everything was dead. Not even the dashboard lights came on.

'That's not good,' I said sheepishly to Laura, before climbing reluctantly out of the car to investigate.

'What's the problem?' Brummy had appeared.

'Don't know. Something electrical probably,' I replied, as I opened the bonnet and took the cover off the fuse box.

'This has got to count as a breakdown!' Brummy said as I pulled out the relays one by one and shook them before putting them back into place. I then opened the boot and checked the battery connections were okay.

Everything seemed fine, so I tried again. Evidently, I'd fluked a repair, as second time lucky, the car fired up as if nothing had happened. Relieved, we set off to the campsite's new location.

'Well, it's never done that before!' I said to Laura.

'I think it just wants to see the back of Kenya,' She suggested.

'Wake up, you lazy bastards!'

It was Tom, with a tongue-in-cheek alarm call. I looked at my watch. A quarter past six. Clearly at least another hour of slumber was in order and it seemed Laura agreed, as she rolled over in her sleep and shouted: 'Sod off.'

Back on the road, Kenya never seemed to change. The highway south out of Nairobi wasn't quite finished yet. It was only about four hours' driving to the Tanzanian border, but over half of it was on gravel. Often, we would be forced to drive through the bush as machinery worked on a shiny new superhighway where the old road once was. If all the various infrastructure projects come to fruition in a few years' time, Kenya will have a fantastic road network. Unfortunately however, they hadn't quite got there in time for our visit, and from what I'd seen so far, I doubted much would change for quite a while. With Nairobi behind us, we crossed into the territory of the most famous tribe of them all – the Maasai. Occasionally we glimpsed them in the bare bush, their traditional clothes looking at home among the acacias. As in northern Kenya, we were apparently crossing a desert, but just before our visit the rains had spurred the landscape into adopting a deep green colour.

Bad roads and epic rains, that's what our abiding memories of Kenya would be.

Laura and I chatted as we drove.

'So you're thinking of coming back with KOP for your placement in September?' I asked her. She'd mentioned that it was on the cards, given her medical school's links with the charity.

'Yeah maybe. We'll see, I might just stay in the UK and work towards the final year exams. I was just thinking about what to do when I graduate actually. I'll have about a month off in summer 2010.'

'Funnily enough, I had a thought about that the other day.'

'Go on?'

'Well, you know those auto-rickshaws they have in Egypt?'

'They're all around here too, but yeah. Go on?'

'We could buy one in Egypt and drive it back to the UK. It'd be awesome,' I enthused, as I changed gear. Laura's hand was resting on the centre console as I did and our arms brushed. She took my hand and held it as we talked.

'That would be great. How long do you reckon it'd take?'

'Well in India we managed two thousand miles in eleven days. If we went from Egypt, across Libya, took the ferry from Tunisia to Italy, then home from there, it couldn't be more than four thousand miles. I'm sure we could do it in a month easily, with plenty of time to relax.'

'Imagine that! Tearing across Libya in a rickshaw! How much fun would that be?' Laura said with a smile.

'Imagine the paperwork trying to get the thing out of Egypt, more like,' I replied.

'Yeah, that would be interesting,' she said sarcastically, before adding, 'God, listen to us, holding hands and making plans for the future. Like a right married couple, we are!'

'Brummy keeps saying we're like a married couple…'

'It's not right,' she said, her tone changing as she took her hand from mine.

'No, it's not,' I agreed. We drove the last ten minutes to the border lost in our own thoughts, aware of the conspicuous silence within the Porsche's cramped cabin.

At the border, the usual selection of touts, money changers, hawkers and randoms who always stalk such places were present, but were overshadowed in both spectacle and boldness by the three Maasai women who immediately approached us when we parked. They looked dazzling, their bright robes, beaded jewellery, headgear and jutting teeth making a powerful statement of identity. They eagerly offered us bracelets and charms and implored us to take their photo – for a fee, of course. Laura escaped the ambush to go and phone her boyfriend. I didn't envy her, as I could sense just how confused she was feeling inside.

Meanwhile the Masaai ladies focused their attentions on Brummy and I. Fortunately, over the years we'd both become old hands at avoiding such advances, and knew the tricks to defuse their sales drive. Don't make eye contact, don't show an immediate interest in anything and definitely don't accept anything they suggest you hold, as they won't take it back, and will hold out for money instead. Their persistence was rather impressive, but also somehow sad, given what a proud, traditional tribe the Maasai are. Even telling them: 'Look, I don't want your bracelets, your trinkets or your photo. Goodbye.' served only to encourage them. I suppose any level of communication is a start.

Brummy's patience started to fade after about five minutes of the aggressive hard-sell and five minutes of polite refusal.

'Look, please just go away. Leave us alone. We don't want any of your stuff,' repeatedly gleaned no response.

Often, when faced with such determination, the only way to escape the attentions of your suitors is to be as direct with them as they are to you.

'Do you understand English?' I asked one lady bluntly.

'Yes,' came the reply.

'Then you understand the word 'NO' then?' I suggested.

'Yes. Photo?' she replied. I gave up and tried to ignore them, busying myself with tidying the car.

Meanwhile Brummy had lost patience with trying to escape politely. After ten minutes of unwelcome, non-stop hassling, his temper had left him completely.

'Look! I'll only buy it if I can shove it up your arse!' I heard him bark at one of the more persistent women.

This mention of possible sales terms seemed only to encourage them. At least Brummy saw the funny side, adding with a cheeky glint in his eye, 'How much for you? You, yes you. How much for you?'

Thank goodness they didn't understand.

We eventually escaped, slipping off to find a much needed cold drink. Returning a few minutes later, we found the ladies' attentions had turned to Tom. They had managed to surround him by cornering him against the Shogun, with nowhere to run. Sensing weakness, they went for the kill mercilessly, strapping bracelets onto his arms and thrusting trinkets into his hands like there was no tomorrow. He was wearing no less than five bracelets and holding several more. He looked panicked and his eyes darted around nervously, like a rabbit caught in three unavoidable headlights.

Tom escaped by buying a bracelet for his sister, and claiming he'd intended to do so all along. He probably had, but we chose not to believe him.

'You should have just threatened to shove it up her arse. It worked for me.' Brummy suggested constructively.

Soon Laura returned from her telephone call, and Kenya became a memory. We slipped across the border into the land of Kilimanjaro, the Serengeti and Freddie Mercury.

We savoured the change of scenery, but would be happy if Tanzania merely proved to have better roads than Kenya.

TWELVE

COPS AND ROBBERS

16th November 2008
Kenya/Tanzania Border

'You need to change money? I can give you good rate.'

I had anticipated the question. It was a sales pitch that took place at every border. Usually, unofficial moneychangers offered a better exchange rate than the banks, so we made full use of their services. It was generally illegal of course, but everyone seemed to turn a blind eye.

'Come with me. I can't change your money on this side of the border, it's illegal and the guards won't let me. We must do it over there, out of Kenya.'

The guy gestured to a dusty area just past the border post, a no-man's-land populated by resting lorries and a few shacks. He wore a T-shirt which was once bright yellow, but had been faded to a dull lemon colour by the equatorial sun. His trousers were tattered, while his serious, angular face was that of someone you wouldn't follow down a dark alley.

We walked about thirty feet and then began discussing the exchange.

'Okay, I have about two and a half thousand Kenyan shillings to change. The official rate at the bank is nineteen. What can you give me?'

'Twenty.'

'Come off it, I may be a 'mzungu' but I'm not stupid. At that rate, I'm better off changing it at the bank so I at least get a receipt. Give me twenty-three.'

'Okay, I can do twenty-three,' he said quickly, his lack of bartering being somewhat unusual. He began tapping away quickly on his calculator, before counting out some well-worn Tanzanian shillings and thrusting them into my hand.

'Here. Forty-six thousand shillings,' he said, holding up his pocket calculator.

I did the mental arithmetic as I turned the notes over in my hand. Two thousand five hundred, multiplied by twenty-something. It should be over fifty thousand.

'Hang on a minute,' I said, trying to sound stern. 'It's more than that. It should be over fifty thousand.'

He held his calculator up where I could see it and typed in the numbers correctly. The answer came out at forty-six thousand. He hit the keys quickly, but not quickly enough to prevent me from seeing that he completed the sum by hitting the memory recall key, rather than the equals. He was trying to rip us off.

'Hey, you hit the memory key,' I said, before thrusting the notes back into his hand. 'Give me fifty-five thousand shillings, or no deal.'

He agreed and started counting out the cash. I turned to where Brummy was having the same problems with one of the moneychanger's accomplices.

'Watch them. This guy just tried to rip me off by hitting the memory key on his calculator.'

'I know. They just tried the same trick with me.'

'You're changing about four thousand Kenyan, aren't you? It should be nearly ninety thousand I'd reckon,' I said to him, doing the maths quickly in my head.

'Yeah, don't worry; I'm getting through to them.'

I turned back to my guy. He was gone. While I chatted to Brummy he'd run off into the parked lorries and scattered shacks of no-man's-land. With my money.

'Brummy! He's just done a runner. Don't give any of them any cash,' I said urgently.

We ran in the direction our robber had disappeared in, but he had gone, melting away into the scenery. Somewhat chastened, we completed our money changing in the bank which formed part of the Kenyan border post, then entered Tanzania.

The robbery was insignificant – only about eighteen pounds – but it sat heavily on my mind. I was immediately angry with myself for letting it happen and for not reading the warning signs. I kept telling myself that it was only eighteen pounds, but the fact I had been outwitted really grated with me, disproportionately to the loss. It reminded me that despite wanting to imagine myself a worldly and experienced traveller, I still had so much to learn. The robbery stayed with me for most of the short drive to Arusha, as I analysed it over and over again. *What could I have done differently?* Not handed over any money until I was happy with the deal, of course. Another lesson learnt the hard way, and filed away. It wouldn't happen again. *Trust nobody, and keep your guard up whenever money is involved,* I kept telling myself.

One of the few facts we knew about Tanzania was that it was the birthplace of the great Freddie Mercury, lead singer of the rock group 'Queen'. In recognition of this fact, we listened to their Greatest Hits compilation as we cruised across the Masaai. Soon, a familiar song came beating out of the speakers. I recognised it immediately. Freddie's powerful lyrics spoke of empty spaces, abandoned places, and questioned what we are living for, before the chorus began – *the show must go on.*

It was that song again. It had first become part of the trip on that day in South Wales when, with the expedition in tatters before it had even started, I had begun to remove the unknown engine from the donor car. Exactly seven weeks had passed since that day. I felt like I had lived a lifetime in those seven weeks.

Written by the lyrical genius during his slow, painful struggle with AIDS, the song had travelled with us throughout our trip. We had listened to it in northern Kenya, as our broken sports car was dragged through the rutted, washed-out desert; and in England as, barely speaking, Laura and I had edged uncertainly through the drizzle towards Dover. It had become our rallying anthem for the trip and never failed to move us.

The tarmac seemed pretty good in Tanzania, perhaps because our memories of Kenya's appalling roads were still so fresh. Ninety minutes of pleasant cruising, encouraged onwards by Freddie, had us passing Mount Meru, an active volcano whose conical bulk lofts skyward to a height of over four thousand metres. As we passed, thin cotton-wool clouds wisped playfully around its summit – the fifth highest in Africa. Further away, converging slopes rose into the low cloud base. Somewhere above the overcast floated the receding snowfields which crown Kilimanjaro; Africa's highest mountain. Typically, we never saw it. I was resigned to the weather hiding all of Africa's famous mountains from us on this trip. First Mount Kenya, and now Mount Kilimanjaro had concealed themselves as we passed. This always seems to happen to me. The year before I had managed to travel the entire length of the Indian and Nepalese Himalayas without seeing a single snowy mountain, such was my bad luck. If the whole of the Himalayas can hide themselves from me, Africa's more modest mountains should have no problem repeating the feat.

Following an unusually short day on the road, with only one further repair to the fuel lines beneath the Porsche being needed, we arrived in Arusha. A coffee was called for, followed by a spot of wandering around town and a look into the possibility of a Serengeti safari the following day. Shocked by just how much it would cost to visit a national park for a day, we headed over to a campsite on Arusha's eastern outskirts. Brummy opted to fork out for a room, while the rest of us pitched our tents, saving a little money. We cooked dinner together, coming up with a fine risotto which went down very well. Predictably, the campsite had a well-stocked bar, which offered the perfect backdrop to our first night in Tanzania. The beer seemed to be improving as we headed south, Kilimanjaro lager being a nicer way to end the day than the Tusker beer found in Kenya. For once on the trip, we were well rested and therefore in the mood to give the new lager an extensive trial. A few bottles of the stuff soon washed away my lingering annoyance over the robbery at the border.

It was one of those evenings when everyone was in the same mood and we contributed many shillings to Tanzania's economy that night. Brummy and Tom retired first, leaving Louise, Laura and I partying on, blurring our senses and inhibitions into a distant memory. Two in the morning saw us drunkenly debating whether to cautiously inch the Shogun over to the other side of the campsite, where it would be hidden from view. It certainly seemed like a good idea at the time and we had the keys, but I couldn't do it. Even hammered by beer, my mind was clear enough to know that Tom really wouldn't see the funny side.

Eventually, we retired to the roof tent. Laura still had half a beer left, so we sat up and finished it, the drunken conversation flowing mellifluously between us. Ambient light from the campsite meant I could just make out Laura's braided hair and familiar smile. We chatted about our surprise at making it to Tanzania, about how nice it was that we were finally enjoying each other's company and probably about many other things, the memory of which was quickly purged from our minds by the alcohol. Laura apologised for our differences before the trip and I returned the apology, insisting it was as much my fault as hers. Sitting up in the tent, we hugged in a beer-fuelled apology, full of the understanding of two people who had barely been apart during the previous six weeks. Drunkenly balanced in the tent, I was pleased for the momentary support. As we parted, she caught my eye with a surprisingly focused stare for a few seconds, as if suddenly regaining her senses from the alcohol. I sat there, trying to get my drunken mind to think of something to say, to break the sudden heavy silence.

Before I could, she leaned over decisively and kissed me. She then rocked back away from me for a second, as if analysing her actions, before springing forward again and kissing me twice more. It was so sudden and unexpected, that I didn't register what had happened immediately. I just sat there as my heavy mind tried to ponder what had just happened. Laura's face swam with a mix of emotions, ranging from satisfaction to regret.

Eventually the events of those few seconds fell into place and I attempted to conjure up a witty comment to break the silence. I failed, eventually blurting out: 'Well, I wasn't expecting that.'

'I know. I'm sorry,' she said, looking rather sheepish.

'Don't apologise. I don't remember complaining.'

'True,' she said, pausing to think for a while. 'I shouldn't have done it though. It was wrong'

'No, you're right,' I agreed solemnly.

Sleep came quickly after we lay down, my mind brimming with confusion over what had just happened. The alarm was set for half past five, bright and early to take the Shogun on a do-it-yourself safari drive to the Ngorongoro crater the following morning.

'Wake up you lazy bastard!' Laura shouted, shaking Tom's tent in an unsubtle response to our wake-up call in Nairobi the previous morning. It was six in the morning and we were still comically drunk. Tom grunted a response. He had been rather insistent that everyone should be awake by half past five.

I felt heavy. My tiredness, hangover and dehydration sat like weights on my shoulders, while the lingering traces of beer in my system turned both co-ordination and rational thought into abstract concepts. As I tried to get on with the day, even simple tasks seemed to take twice as long as usual. I told myself that getting more than two hours' sleep would probably have helped, but didn't have much conviction that I wouldn't make the same mistake again. I got together what I needed for a day's Shogun safari and collapsed on a nearby picnic bench, dozing with my forehead resting uncomfortably on the table, next to a cup of strong coffee.

Soon everyone was ready except for Laura, who was drifting around the place with little direction, looking very distant. I could sympathise completely. Summoning the energy to stand, I wandered over to the car, where she was rummaging through the boot.

'Dude, don't worry. You were drunk, okay?'

'It's not that,' she said.

'Well why are you looking so worried?'

'It's my handbag,' she replied apologetically. 'I can't find my handbag.'

'Well it must be here somewhere?'

'I've looked everywhere. It's not here. Everything's in it. My phone, my passport, my money. Everything.'

Soon everyone joined in the hunt. We turned everything upside down; the Porsche, the tent, the Shogun that we had so drunkenly debated moving a few hours before. We asked if it had been found in the bar, but to no avail. After twenty frantic minutes we admitted defeat. It was gone for good. Laura had put it down by her chair in the bar the previous night and it had disappeared by the time we returned to the tents. It must have been stolen while we were talking. We gave up on the day's game drive and discussed what to do over breakfast.

'Right, so what exactly was in the bag?' Brummy said.

'My passport, phone, wallet, everything,' replied Laura, sobbing slightly.

'Can we ring the phone?'

'Ben's already tried that,' Laura said

'Yeah, it's turned off. I lent my phone to Laura to cancel the bank cards, so at least that's one less thing to worry about,' I added.

'Right, so it's just the passport then,' said Tom.

'Yep.'

'How far is it to the embassy?' he asked.

'You don't want to know,' I said fatalistically. 'It's in Dar es Salaam, about three hundred miles away according to the map. At least the roads are rumoured to be okay though.'

'Are we sure we can get a new passport there?' Louise asked.

'Erm, no,' I replied. 'We've just got to hope for the best.'

'What if they don't do replacements?'

No one answered.

'Right, let's get going then,' Brummy said decisively, breaking the silence.

'Not just yet,' replied Laura. 'I'll need a police report for the robbery so I can claim on my travel insurance.'

'Town it is then,' said Brummy, already reaching for the guidebook to find the location of the police station.

The police station consisted of about half a dozen uncared-for storeys stacked unattractively in a compound on the north side of town. I parked nervously outside, well aware of the corruption which pervades in so many African police forces. If they wanted to find a problem with the Porsche – and make us pay for it – no doubt they could. We locked it and went inside, trying to look as inconspicuous as possible.

'Whatever happens, no bribes,' I said to Laura as we walked in. 'Let's not even go there.'

Laura agreed.

The reception area was, as expected, a bit of a scrum. A stiflingly hot room about twenty feet wide was divided by a well-worn wooden counter, which served as both a partition and a desk. Even at half past eight in the morning, there were about twenty people in there, jostling for attention, holding aloft official-looking bits of paper and attempting to catch the eye of the aloof policemen behind the counter. Their hustling presence made the oppressive humidity in the room feel even more crushing. As 'mzungus' – the ubiquitous Swahili word for whites – we were more conspicuous than most and soon had the attention of a young officer, immaculately kempt and handsome, who radiated a deep sense of pride in his job.

Once Laura had filled out two forms detailing what was stolen, along with the location and circumstances of the theft, I had to pay for a statement. For this, I was sent upstairs to queue outside a small office on the first floor. Around me, a somewhat dishevelled cross-section of Tanzanian society queued with me to pay for minor offences or favours. I wondered what they were here for. I guessed most were paying petty fines or the like, but none of them looked particularly untrustworthy. The queue terminated at an intimidating middle-aged woman in spectacles and a floral dress. She steadfastly refused to rush, sending one guy to the back of the queue when he expressed the smallest hint of dissatisfaction about how long things were taking. I made a mental note not to make the same mistake. After ten minutes, I reached the head of the queue. My shillings were exchanged for a stamp on the paperwork, which I took downstairs and gave to the young officer, who then gave Laura the police report. We were free to go.

After an early lunch and a spot of Internet, we hit the road. I was relieved that everything had gone smoothly in the police station, as the police forces of Africa come second only to the military and political groups for their power-abusing reputation. Laura, however, wasn't really thinking in terms of relief and had collapsed in the passenger seat, feeling ill from the previous night's beer.

After so much time together, we could often tell what each other was thinking without a word being spoken, as if by telepathy. As Laura sat silently next to me, I knew that she was painfully overanalysing the robbery, just as I had done after being ripped off at the border the previous day. We cruised along in silence, listening to music by someone other than Queen for once. To our left, the drama of Kilimanjaro continued to elude us, hidden by the bubbling clouds.

After a while, I broke the silence: 'Laura, don't worry about it. It's not your fault. I don't blame you for this and neither does anyone else.'

'I'm sorry, but I blame myself. I just let my guard down. I'd never normally take my bag into the bar like that, but we were camping right by it so I took it without thinking. It was so stupid of me! I don't know why I did it.'

'Come on dude, you couldn't have foreseen this. And anyway, it's not the end of the world. We'll get you a new passport in no time and be back on the road before you know it; and everything else you lost is covered by insurance,' I said.

'I can't get my old passport back though, can I?' she replied. 'I've had that passport for years. It's got all the stamps from my previous trips in there; South America, Australia, New Zealand. It meant a lot to me and now it's gone.'

'Well think of the new one. At least it'll have a story behind it.'

'It's not the same though. And we don't even know if I can get a new one here. I could be on a plane home tomorrow.'

'I'm sure you'll get one. When I washed my passport in Uzbekistan the other year…'

'Stop showing off,' she interrupted, 'namedropping exotic places into the conversation.'

'Yeah okay,' I said, backtracking. 'But anyway, it took half a day in the embassy and we were on our way with a new passport. I don't see why it should be any different for you here.'

'I hope so.'

'Come on, we've overcome worse problems than this on the trip so far. It'll be fine!'

Laura said nothing, silently staring out of the side window as Tanzania rolled past. After a minute or so, she spoke again.

'I'm sorry about what happened last night.'

'You apologised last night. And I said not to worry, so please don't,' I replied briskly.

'Yeah, but I was so drunk. I'm sorry I crossed the line. I'm still so confused about what I want.'

'I understand. Don't worry; I won't put any pressure on you. You've got to make that decision yourself, without my input. This is one thing I can't help you with, I'm afraid.'

'I know. Thanks for understanding.'

'And Laura…' I added.

'Yes?'

'You're banned from apologising for things until the end of the trip.'

'What?' she said, looking confused.

'You keep blaming yourself for things which aren't your fault. I don't like seeing you running yourself down like this.'

'Erm, okay,' she said, unconvinced.

'Anyway, you look drained. Don't feel like you've got to stay awake chatting. Get some sleep if you want.'

'Fair enough, I think I will. Thanks for driving, Ben. I really don't feel up to it today. I don't feel up to anything today.'

'No worries. Get some sleep, you'll feel better for it. I'll wake you up in Dar,' I joked.

No further encouragement was needed and Laura was soon drifting off into an afternoon's slumber as we made a beeline for the embassy. The sparsely populated farmland made for easy, uneventful driving and soon I was lost in my own thoughts, oblivious to the orderly landscape of palm groves and foreshortened mountains.

I hadn't anticipated the previous night's drunken indiscretion and I was unsure as to whether I welcomed it or not. Laura and I had, from barely being on speaking terms to start with, drawn rapidly closer as the trip went on. I really didn't relish the possibility that we could continue becoming closer over the last few weeks of the trip. And yet I was attracted to her and evidently her feelings reciprocated mine. Ever since Ethiopia, we had been getting on brilliantly, with seldom a quiet moment passing when we were in the car together. We had got to know each other better than ever and from that mutual understanding had grown a genuine closeness and respect.

But she was already in a relationship. She and Alan had been together for about three months before we left on the trip. They had only spoken a handful of times since and she hadn't been overly positive about the relationship, but that wasn't the point. They were still together and that had to be respected. If any further indiscretions happened between us during the remainder of the trip, it would be wrong. If none happened it would be surprising, however, given the gradual increase in the waves of attraction between us.

'Ah well,' I mused to myself with a smile. 'At least we're on speaking terms now!'

As the afternoon wore on, the clouds boiled ever higher. Dainty cumulous rose to become daunting, anvil-shaped thunderheads, their tops smeared off like a plume of spindrift as they reached into the jet stream. The humidity in the air skyrocketed as we neared the Indian Ocean and a few light showers began, threatening to break into full-blown storms. I turned on the wipers, but the one on my side of the car ceased to work, smearing to a halt pointing skyward, directly in front of me. Not wanting to hold up our progress just because of a bit of rain, I leaned forward and operated it occasionally by hand, reaching out of the open window to swipe raindrops from the screen. As I did so, a rainbow swept down ahead of us, appearing to alight directly on the portly Shogun's roof. I couldn't think of anything less like a pot of gold for it to touch down on.

Soon, the bulging thunderheads filling the sky started to take on a salmon hue as the sun set behind us. With the faulty windscreen wipers and only one working headlight, I wanted to push on for as long as possible, making the most of the remaining light before we stopped for dinner. However Team Shogun had other ideas, pulling into a restaurant a hundred miles short of our destination for a leisurely evening meal.

I accosted them as they opened the doors. 'Do we have to stop? There's nearly an hour of daylight left, shouldn't we push on and make the most of it?'

'But we're hungry and it's dinner time,' said Tom.

'So because you're hungry, I've got to do another hour of driving in the dark, getting blinded by headlights, as this storm breaks?'

'We all agreed to stop,' he said, walking off briskly in search of a toilet.

'Brummy! Why aren't we pushing on? What happened to not driving at night?' I asked.

'We're lucky to get this far. He's wanted us to stop for the last hour,' said Brummy.

It always felt dangerous driving the Porsche in the dark in Africa. Even with both lights working, animals, livestock, and potholes would appear just in front of us without warning. As the Porsche was so low, any oncoming traffic would dazzle us so completely that all we could do was aim to just miss the other vehicle, and hope there was nothing on our side of the road in the darkness. And, of course, there are the security concerns inherent in driving through the wilderness at night. It took me a good few hours to stop being angry over the dinner stop, as I felt my concerns about driving at night were more important than going without dinner for another hour.

On the plus side, the food was rather good. Peppercorn steak, Pepsi and coffee brought a bit of life back into the group. Outside, however, the clouds were flexing their muscles ever more, their crimson bulk building ominously in the humid air.

It was completely dark when we got back on the road, but luckily the expected storms didn't break and we were able to drive to Dar without getting too wet. My sole remaining headlight was woefully poor however, and my fatigue total thanks to minimal sleep and a full day of driving through searing temperatures and oppressive humidity. The Porsche also seemed to be feeling the strain that day, and had acquired a new trick for us to worry about. At certain speeds, it would vibrate violently, the steering wheel bucking roughly in our hands. We had begun to notice these bumpy intrusions to our comfort in Kenya, where they had been minimal. However, by the time we were nearing Dar es Salaam they had worsened so much that the car was almost undriveable at certain speeds. Any attempt to cruise between forty and fifty miles per hour was painful, as were speeds around fifty-eight.

This made it rather difficult to convoy with the Shogun, which seemed to favour these speeds. With their better headlights, visibility and comfort, the Shogun disappeared off down the road as we crawled towards the day's goal. Laura was wiped out by the combination of huge humidity and an even huger hangover, while my sleep deprivation made every mile a struggle. Quite a few trucks were still on the road out of Dar and every time their headlights shone in my eyes, I wanted to close them and just fall asleep. I continuously had to shake my head and drink water to keep my concentration, while loud rock music did it's best to drive away the beckoning tiredness. This went on for hours. It felt like the day's drive would never end.

A few of the trucks had broken down and sat silently in the darkness, invisible until we were nearly on top of them. The practice in these areas is to rip off tree branches and lay them in the road to force oncoming cars around the obstacle, much as cones are used in the UK to guide motorists around road works. Obviously, cones are a lot more visible than a few bits of tree lying in the night and it wasn't long until we ploughed through some fairly hefty branches while blinded by oncoming traffic. I felt them pounding the bottom of the car, while some branches flew up the bonnet and over the windscreen. Fortunately, we just made it around the stranded lorry, but by the time we reached the deserted streets of Dar es Salaam, the continuous concentration had left me tired beyond measure.

'Right, we're going to head for the Jambo Inn. It's in the guidebook,' Brummy suggested through my open window, when I caught them up.

'Fair enough. Do what you want. I'll follow.'

I was too tired to even consider playing an active part in navigating into Dar. Laura, asleep beside me, obviously felt the same.

The hotel was basic, but welcome. They only had a few rooms left, so Laura and I ended up sharing a double bed. It was in a bland room, with whitewashed walls and windows with mosquito netting permanently stapled in place. I expected no more. We collapsed on the bed, destroyed. Overhead, an enormous ceiling fan wafted air around the room. Its heavy blades shook and made a coarse grinding noise as they rotated directly above us, bringing to mind the spinning helicopter rotors so beloved of Vietnam War movies.

'What if it falls?' said Laura.

'Then your passport will be the least of our worries,' I replied.

We tried turning off the fan, but the heat and humidity instantly became unbearable. Despite our reservations, we elected to sleep beneath its spinning blades. It was pretty easy to do so. I'd been fighting off my overwhelming tiredness all day.

Even at eight in the morning, Dar es Salaam was baking in the thick, suffocating air. Laura was finding it unbearable and suffered next to me as we overheated our way through the packed, dusty streets. As well as the stifling heat, she was clearly nervous about the uncertainty of getting a new passport, but at least she retained her sense of humour.

'I just want a gin and tonic. It's an embassy. Surely they serve gin and tonic on the lawn with the ambassador?'

We parked the Porsche beneath a shady tree and progressed through the airport-style security. It was unsurprisingly tight, with metal detectors and plenty of armed guards; ever since the American Embassy here was bombed in 1998, security has been taken seriously.

The embassy building was uncompromisingly modern. A wave-shaped roof capped its modern lines, which rose six storeys above us. Stylised slats covered the windows, preventing direct sunlight from taxing the building's occupants. Various European flags flew outside, as the building also housed the embassies of Holland and Germany and the EU consulate.

Once through security, our hopes of high tea on the lawn were quickly dashed. We entered the waiting room, a typically bland but efficient space fitted out with wooden chairs and posters from various European tourist boards. Blissfully, the space was air-conditioned. Laura filled in an application for a replacement passport, but was told to her dismay that it could take anything up to ten working days for it to be processed.

We really didn't want to spend ten days waiting in the sweltering heat of Dar es Salaam.

Back at the hotel, Team Shogun were just finishing breakfast when we arrived and told them the news.

'Well we can't wait that long. I've got a flight booked from Cape Town in less than three weeks,' Brummy said, as he eyed his toast suspiciously.

'Yeah, we're not sticking around that long,' agreed Tom.

'No, of course you can't. You guys should go on ahead,' I suggested.

Laura added: 'The passport could take one day or it could take ten. We'll stay here until we have it, and then try to catch you up. How does that sound?'

'Sounds like a plan,' agreed Brummy. 'When shall we hit the road?'

'Tomorrow?' suggested Louise. 'We've got to get some food and stuff sorted first, and I for one fancy a day out of the Shogun for once.'

'How about then,' I said, 'we all stay tonight and tomorrow morning you guys hit the road. Me and Laura will go to the embassy first thing and if the passport's ready, we'll get going and catch you up tomorrow. If it's not, hopefully we'll see you in Malawi, or Zambia.'

'Yeah, that's a plan,' said Brummy. 'But I want to be on the road first thing tomorrow. I don't want to end up driving into the night again, after another late start.'

'No worries,' I said. 'So, we've got a day in Dar. Where are we staying this evening? Another night here?'

'Noooo!' Louise said. 'Let's go to Zanzibar. It's just north of here and is supposed to be really nice.'

'It's an hour and a half ferry ride away though. Not really ideal for us to pop into the embassy every day,' said Laura.

'Well we're not staying here another night,' said Louise.

'Apparently there are some nice beaches down the coast. We could head there?' Laura suggested.

'Marvellous,' I said.

No one argued with spending the afternoon on a beach.

The glistening white sand was perfectly soft underfoot, so soft it squeaked between our toes as we walked. Palm trees dotted the beach, punctuating the azure blue sky with explosions of broad green leaves. One of the campsite's staff shimmied skilfully to the top of the tallest tree and freed a coconut for each of us.

'Looks about VS 4b,' I said to Laura, referring to the grading system we used to measure the difficulty of rock climbs back home.

The coconut milk tasted sour and I wasn't really a fan, so I stuck to beer for the rest of the evening. Dinner was a particularly fine curry, the quality of which wasn't unexpected, given the large number of people from the subcontinent living on Africa's east coast.

After eating I spent a few hours making repairs to the Porsche. The headlight that had fallen apart in Kenya had its bulb replaced and the lens glued back on. Brummy got the screen wash system working again. The air filter was cleaned out and a few other general checks made. Laura sidled over as I worked.

'Shall we get the handbrake working again?' she said.

'I looked at that earlier. The workshop manual made me laugh.'

'How on earth can a workshop manual be funny?'

'Well, you know how on the Mini, pretty much all you have to do is tighten a nut and it's done?'

'Yes.'

'Well on the Porsche, there are about twelve different steps to adjusting the handbrake. I gave up reading when I got to number seven, where they tell you to remove the driver's seat.'

'Stupid piece of German rubbish!' Brummy shouted, from the bar.

'What! Why would you have to do that?' said Laura.

'Goodness knows. Stupid car to take to Africa, this Porsche,' I agreed, adding: 'We've driven from Ethiopia to here with no handbrake, I'm sure we can manage for the rest of the trip.'

'Yeah, beats having to take the seats out,' agreed Laura.

We camped on the beach, the Indian Ocean lapping peacefully against the sand a few yards from our tent. The almost full moon arced its way overhead through a sky thick with stars, painting the sands and waves a haunting shade of white. 'Very *Pirates of the Caribbean*,' suggested Laura. It was hard to believe that only five miles away, over two million people were living in Tanzania's commercial capital.

Laura and I stayed up for an hour or so after Team Shogun retired, saying little. We simply sat on the beach and gazed out across the shimmering, moonlit bay, content with where our lives had led us.

Team Shogun was long gone when I awoke. Laura had already been awake for some time and welcomed me back to consciousness with a cup of tea. I drank it lying in the tent, looking out over the bay. Despite the problems we faced, life felt good. It wasn't perfect, however, as I awoke with the lines from some banal Monty Python song running through my head, an irritatingly catchy number which refused to go away.

'I like Chinese. They only come up to your knees,' I hummed to Laura.

'Why are you singing that extremely annoying song?' she said.

'They're wry and they're witty and they're ready to please,' I continued.

'Oh shut up. You've got me humming it now!'

'Yeah, annoying, isn't it?' I said.

'I like Chinese food,' said Laura.

'The waiters never are rude,' I replied.

Laura stopped: 'Oh, don't tell me I'm now stuck here all alone with you? You've gone mad.'

'Yep. And the madness must be contagious, because you're humming it too.'

'Leave me alone,' she replied.

It was fortunate that Laura had waited until Tanzania to get her passport stolen. Previously in the trip, the prospect of the Shogun going on ahead would have been most unappealing. However, since Kenya we had been enjoying each other's company so much more. Our chat on that stormy night in Ethiopia had cleared the air, but it had taken another few weeks for us to settle into being completely comfortable with one other.

The news from the embassy was unexpectedly good. The passport would be ready that afternoon. I was almost disappointed at the good turn of fortune, as I rather fancied a few more days relaxing on the beach. We were told to come back and collect it in an hour's time, so we went off for some lunch while we waited. Two days before, as we left Arusha on the mad dash to the embassy, I had promised Laura I'd take her out for dinner in Dar es Salaam, as consolation for being robbed. So I did, to a rather Western-style pizza joint located in the capital's diplomatic heartland. If I was taking Laura out for dinner back in the UK, it would have been a rather poor choice, but after so long on the road, we were both strangely drawn to the bland fast food, a taste of back home.

'So, we pick up the passport at half one, that gives us an hour and a half to get to the Tanzanian immigration department and get a replacement visa before they close at three,' Laura said, as we waited for the horrendously expensive pizzas and Pepsis to arrive.

'You sound very confident in your timings,' I said.

'Yeah, who am I kidding? This is Africa. We'll never get the visa that quickly.'

'Aye, it all sounds rather tight,' I replied. And so it was.

We had the new passport by two in the afternoon, but it took us an age to negotiate the choking streets to the immigration building, a nondescript grey government structure completely lacking in flair. We parked hurriedly and rushed in to get the replacement visa. Predictably, our rush was stopped by a scrum of people jostling for the attentions of a number of bored civil servants, whose demeanour was that of people counting down the minutes until they could leave the office at three. The heat in the room was unbearable and it smelt heavily of sweat. We

298

were able to get the attention of the ubiquitously portly, though authoritative lady behind one of the counters and were told that we needed photocopies of the passport to get the visa. We rushed off to another part of the building and got the copies, only just making it back into the visa office before the doors were shut. Another humid wait led us back to the desk, where we filled out forms, handed over cash and gained a visa. It had taken forty-five minutes. We were as surprised as we were impressed.

While we were sorting out the visa, I received a text message from Brummy. They would be spending the evening under canvas at a place called Iringa, about two hundred and fifty miles down the road. We could catch them up that day if we hit the road straight away. Begrudgingly, I gave up on spending another night on the beach and resigned myself to driving into the night once again.

We stopped for petrol on the way out of Dar es Salaam, only to find the fuel leak had started again. It took three attempts to stop the hose from leaking, but eventually we were fixed and on the road out of the city. Unfortunately, so was everyone else. For over an hour, we sat in the traffic with the engine turned off, until frustratingly, the queue moved onwards with no sign as to what had caused it, finally allowing us out of the city. Although we'd enjoyed relaxing on the beach, we wouldn't miss Dar. Its unthinkable humidity had overwhelmed us and the uncertainty of our situation had made it difficult to relax. It felt good to be putting the miles under our belts again, and to really be making progress into southern Africa. 'Only another four countries, then we're in South Africa,' we repeatedly told each other.

For once we weren't in any rush, so we plodded slowly into the night. We'd changed one of the front wheels and the vibrations now prevented us from cruising between about fifty and sixty miles per hour, so we just chugged along at around forty-five, glimpses of Africa flickering in the periphery of our headlights. We saw our first elephants as we drove, a family of them feeding next to the road. We stopped and spent a few minutes watching their slow, languid movements bring the darkness to life. They seemed completely at peace.

About an hour later, another familiar shape flashed by, lying by the side of the road. My tired brain slowly started to process what it had seen and determine a response. Laura got there first.

'Stop! That was a body!' she shouted.

I had recognised the shape for what it was and had slowed down as we passed, but for some reason – possibly shock – I didn't instantly stop. We pulled over a little way up the road.

'What should we do?' I asked nervously. 'Do you think he's been hit and just left there?'

'Well we've got to see if we can help.'

A part of me didn't want to. I knew we had to try to help, but I was scared of getting involved with some dead body by the side of the road and also nervous of what we could do for him were he still alive. And what if he was actually fine and it was, in reality, a trap? Fortunately Laura was less inhibited and jolted me out of my selfish reluctance. I backed up and directed the car's spotlights onto the body. From its shape, I could see it was a man. He didn't move and looked completely lifeless. While I stayed in the car, keeping the engine running ready for us to make a quick getaway if we had to, Doctor Laura cautiously went over and put her ear near his mouth.

'He's breathing!' came her relieved response.

She shook the inanimate body vigorously, while shouting, 'Hello, can you hear me?'

He didn't react.

'He reeks of alcohol,' she said quietly, as she drove her knuckles first into the inside of his elbow joint, then into his chest, in an attempt to trigger consciousness. After a fashion, he moved uneasily, beginning a slow return from his drunken oblivion.

'You can't lie here,' Laura shouted clearly into his vacant face. 'This is a road. You have to go home.'

He mumbled something unintelligible and rolled over. We could see him better now. His face was hollow and vacant, his eyes unfocused. His clothes were dusty from the ground, his fly was open and his trousers were stained to a darker colour where he had wet himself. Next to him, a half empty plastic bottle contained some vile looking homebrew. The foot-long knife tied to his belt caught our attention the most however. After about five minutes of coaxing, we got him to his feet and set him staggering uneasily into the undergrowth towards his village. I felt selfishly relieved that my worst fears hadn't been realised.

As we neared where Team Shogun was camping, the road wound up into some hills. We passed a lorry which had snapped in two trying to climb one of the hills, its broken back reminding us of how lucky we had been to make it this far. And then we were in the town. Milky-coloured buildings appeared a little way back from the road, punctuating the night and signalling that our turn off was near. The directions Brummy had sent led us into a campsite, where the sounds of happy banter were rising from around a flickering campfire.

'Beer me!' I shouted in greeting as I parked.

A gusty wind buffeted our tent, as the threatening clouds melted together overhead. We got everything packed away just in time, before the first wall of rain advanced over the boulder-strewn hillsides, raking us as we pulled out of the campsite. We were three hundred miles from our day's goal, the Malawian border. We'd been on the road for so long that three hundred miles no longer qualified as a long drive, especially as the roads in southern Tanzania weren't supposed to be too bad.

It was good to be reunited with Team Shogun. Driving through the previous night all alone had felt strange after so many weeks together, but now normal service was resumed. Even the weather was back to normal, the brooding clouds mixing laser sunlight with tropical deluges. It reminded me of the washed out summer we had just endured back in the UK, shower after shower rolling in from the horizon. However, the difference was that here in Africa, it was considerably hotter and the equatorial air contained much more energy and menace than the temperate systems which were no doubt washing over the UK as we drove. Back home it rained. Here, it deluged.

We stopped for a drink in a sunlit village halfway to the border. As Laura purchased some Cokes, the Shogun carried on into the distance, before eventually coming back and joining us. Tom looked unamused and I could guess what was coming.

'I wish you wouldn't do that.'

'Do what?' I asked.

'Just stop like that.'

'Like what? We told you we wanted to stop for a drink a while back.'

'Well you could have flashed us, or something, to let us know you wanted to stop.'

Laura ambled back with the much needed ice cold drinks and overheard our conversation as she walked.

'Look,' she said, 'I've been flashing you for the last four villages. I can't help it if you don't look in the mirrors. And anyway, we told you we wanted to stop when we chatted at the junction back there.'

'Well you could have made a bit more of an effort,' Tom replied, his statement trailing off as he returned to the Shogun, where Louise had just returned with drinks.

'Oh sod off Tom,' Laura shouted after him as he went, before turning to me and saying, 'It's all very well when he's hungry and wants to stop, but it's a different matter for anyone else.'

'I know, Laura. I know,' I replied, before wandering back to join a discussion about the day's progress with Team Shogun, who were poring over a map spread out on the bonnet. Laura stayed sitting in the Porsche, stewing over her differences with Tom. After agreeing to drive all the way to the border before getting a late lunch, I returned to the Porsche, where Laura now found herself in an argument with the guy she had bought the Cokes from. Evidently, it just wasn't her day.

Sounding exasperated, she said sternly: 'Look. You said five hundred shillings. I gave you five hundred shillings. You can't just change your mind and ask for two thousand after I've already bought them.'

The guy wouldn't budge and insisted on the higher price, arguing that his boss had insisted on charging us extra. I was already fired up from our chat with Tom, and didn't hold back, shouting straight into the salesman's face.

'Look. You said five hundred. She gave you five hundred. Finish. We only paid eight hundred in a posh restaurant in Dar, for fuck's sake. Your little hut isn't a posh restaurant. You're not getting another shilling out of us, now fuck off!'

He looked rather shocked, having suddenly gone from trying to intimidate some extra money out of a petite lady to having an angry mzungu shouting expletives into his face. The rest of the folk in earshot looked shocked too, turning to watch the spectacle.

'Right, fire up the engine, we'd better leave,' I said to Laura urgently, before shouting, 'Let's roll!' back to the Shogun. They needed no further invitation, speeding past us as we went to make our urgent exit and in the process kicking up a dust cloud so thick that we couldn't even see the end of our bonnet. Instead of quickly putting some distance between the angry vendors and ourselves, we were forced to crawl away, feeling vulnerable as we slowly felt our way through the dust. Fortunately, they didn't feel the need to enforce their opportunistic change of price by coming after us.

'Thanks for that, Ben,' Laura said, once we finally made it out of the dust cloud.

'I'm sorry. I don't know what came over me. I guess I'm just a bit stressed by Tanzania, I mean we've both been robbed in this sodding country – haven't they got enough out of us already without trying to rip us off like that?'

I tried to explain my actions and in doing so justify them in my own mind, but I was cross with myself for my outburst, as it meant my self-control had failed me. I hoped I wouldn't end up having a similar disagreement with Tom before the end of the trip, but given the way that tensions had slowly been increasing within the group as the continuous pressures wore people's patience down, I wasn't too confident I could refrain. I told myself I'd be back to my usual self once I was out of Tanzania. Fortunately, Malawi was only a few hours of rolling hills and a couple of tropical deluges away.

THIRTEEN

AGAINST THE LAW

20th November 2008
Lake Nyasa, Malawi

Malawi is one of the poorest countries on the planet. The average income for each of the twelve million people who live on this lush slither of land next to Lake Nyasa is about three hundred dollars per year. When new, the Porsche cost seventy-seven times that amount – and the gap is even greater if inflation is considered. Over half of the population is below the age of fifteen and the vast majority of people lead a gruelling rural existence, eking out a precarious survival from the land, the productivity of which is completely dependent on the fickle rains.

We couldn't have guessed this from our first acquaintances with Malawi, however. During our time in Africa, we had become accustomed to the poverty, and the straw huts and pitiful shops we passed seemed no worse than those in Kenya or Tanzania, or anywhere else for that matter. In some ways Malawi seemed gifted – the land was lush and beautiful, while the lake never seemed far away, stretching out of sight like a molten mirror.

On our first night in the country, we stayed on the lake's shore, in a campground that proved most effective at insulating its residents from the harsh realities of Africa. A well stocked bar provided as many cold beers as we could handle while the latest Western music pumped out across the sandy beach and the million dollar view beyond. Several beefy overland trucks were parked up and their cargos of young travellers had already found their way to the bar by the time we arrived. European and South African accents competed to be heard above the overwhelming music. We pitched our tents on the beach and joined them for the evening. However, our minds were already further ahead, dreaming of Cape Town.

'So how far is it exactly?' asked Louise.

Our progress was gradually turning into an obsession as the finish line drew closer. Earlier in the trip, reaching Cape Town had seemed so unfeasible as to be an irrelevance, but now we'd made it into southern Africa, we were finally allowing ourselves the luxury of dreaming.

'The road atlas reckons it's about four thousand kilometres by the quickest route. Call it about two and a half thousand miles,' Tom said.

'What day is it?' I asked. They had all been blurring into one since the trip had started.

'It's Thursday. We've got just over two weeks until me and Brummy's flights,' said Tom.

'Plenty of time!' I responded enthusiastically, taking another swig of my beer, which had cost the same as two days' income for the average Malawian.

'I'm not so sure,' said Tom. 'I don't want to cut it too close getting to Cape Town. We're going to have to push on and not waste any time.'

'But it's only a bit over two thousand miles; call it three thousand to include a bit of sightseeing in Namibia. That's nothing. We can do that in less than a week if we want,' said Brummy.

'I just don't think we should be wasting time sightseeing, that's all. I really don't want to risk missing my flight,' Tom replied.

'You won't miss the flight,' I chimed in. 'We've got ages and the roads are good all the way now. I'm not going to miss seeing Namibia. It sounds stunning.'

'It is stunning,' Laura added, thinking back to her time there years before.

'Okay, so we've got about three thousand miles to go,' Brummy summarised. 'That's a week or so of driving, which leaves another week for the fun stuff. Okavango Delta, the cool bits of Namibia...'

'Yeah, we can easily see Spitzkoppe, the Skeleton Coast and Sossusvlei in that time,' Laura said, adding nostalgically, 'Sossusvlei is lovely.'

'I don't think we should be tempting fate by going sightseeing. The whole point of this trip is to make it to Cape Town,' Tom said, unconvinced. 'I don't want to put the Shogun's chassis through any more punishment than we have to.'

'Dude, it's been fine since Kenya and we're on good roads now,' I said, trying to be diplomatic.

'I'm really not convinced. The quickest route is down through Zimbabwe. You guys feel free to take the Porsche to Namibia, but I'd rather just go the quickest route.'

'Tom. We're not going through Zimbabwe,' Brummy said.

'Why not?'

'Does the name Mugabe mean anything to you?' Brummy said, adding, 'He's not the most level-headed of characters, you know. And anyhow, there are three of us in the Shogun.'

'And we're not going through Zimbabwe,' said Louise.

The debate trailed off into the night, with everyone gradually becoming resigned to covering a few more miles in Namibia before getting to Cape Town.

The Malawian Highlands were just as stunning as the lake to which their verdant slopes fell. Densely vegetated hills undulated around us, the road picking the line of least resistance as it contoured towards Lilongwe, the nation's capital. Bald granite domes often stood proud of the tree line, peering aloofly down to the sweeps of unruly life below, while guinea fowl darted into the undergrowth as we approached. The air was pleasantly fresh and cool, while the ominous storm clouds of the previous days gave way to a harmless dappling of cotton wool.

Laura and I chatted away happily as the miles rolled effortlessly under our wheels. It was a great feeling, the two of us working together perfectly as the Porsche purred away positively around us. We reflected on how, together with the car, we'd come together to form a unique combination, an exquisite triumph of teamwork which no one else would ever experience. We had been moulded into a team in the cramped cabin, as Africa aged the Porsche into a unique companion. To anyone else, it had just become a smashed up old car, with dozens of shortcomings which would make it impossible to live with. To us, however, the shortcomings were like a living record of what the car had taken us through and we worked around them, neutralising and overcoming them through our experience. We knew we couldn't cruise at fifty miles per hour because of the vibrations, or crawl along slowly for very long without the car overheating, so we didn't. Only we knew the trick of how to open the windows, or had mastered hill starts without a working handbrake. No one else could ever know this unique car as we did at that moment, or ever work with it as efficiently. From not trusting it an inch at the start of the trip, our successes over the previous six weeks had engendered the Porsche with a feeling of inevitability – as we powered across the Malawian Highlands that day, we just knew that whatever happened, we would be driving it into Cape Town one day soon. That we had come together to think like this was achievement enough, given the huge reservations Laura and I initially had about spending time together. That we had learnt to trust the car – and its scrapyard engine – was just as remarkable. Together as a three, bounding across the hills of Malawi that day, we felt blissfully unstoppable.

Days like that made any of our trials worth enduring.

We reached Lilongwe after nightfall and slept at St Peter's guesthouse. A power cut meant we dozed off beneath our mosquito nets as a sole candle threw dancing patterns across the walls around us. The next day, we would be in Zambia.

From Lilongwe, the Zambian border was only a few pretty hours' drive away. The miles passed uneventfully until we were almost within sight of the border, when a policeman flagged down the Shogun ahead of us. I parked the laughably conspicuous Porsche behind it and watched as documents passed backwards and forwards from the car. The policeman, like most young policemen in Africa, had a cocky, arrogant demeanour about him. I didn't like him and could sense Brummy getting frustrated with his self-righteous manner. Meanwhile, another member of the Malawian constabulary had wandered over to my window and barked to Laura – who was driving – that he wanted to see our insurance documents. Then, I understood the problem.

We didn't have any insurance documents for Malawi. Neither did the Shogun. There hadn't been any signs on the border insisting that we buy insurance and as a result we'd forgotten to get any.

After having our driving licenses confiscated, we were escorted into the dusty compound of the Mchinji Police station, and then on into the building. It wasn't a particularly well-loved structure. The peeling cream-coloured walls desperately needed a repaint, while the ancient wooden furniture that failed to fill the room was in need of a lot of varnish. The five of us were marched into a small office, lit by a dim desk light and a thin shaft of light slicing through the small window, which was split into five by the iron bars which prevented escape. We perched on a bench to one side of an old desk, which was littered with forms and documents. Behind the desk sat the young policeman who Brummy had already met and an older colleague of his, waited to start proceedings. They held themselves in a confident manner, like sportsmen empowered by the certainty of their coming victory.

'Why do you not have insurance?' he asked pointedly. 'Every vehicle in Malawi must have insurance by law.'

Evidently there was to be no small talk. And there wasn't much we could say to escape. Brummy replied, throwing the question back.

'We have just driven the whole length of your country. Your border guards did nothing to tell us we needed insurance. We have been stopped at five other police checkpoints in the last two days. None of them said we needed insurance. What makes *you* any different?'

'I am doing my job. You are driving illegally in Malawi. According to the Road Traffic Act of 1926, all vehicles must be insured. You thought you could just drive around our country illegally?' he challenged.

Everyone started talking at once. As it became clear that an orderly conversation wasn't going to happen with seven people in the room, the older policeman took charge.

'Right, everyone except the owners of the cars leave the room and wait outside,' he ordered. Tom, Laura and Louise retreated back to the cars. It was up to Brummy and I now and we would have to think pretty quickly to talk our way out of this one. I decided to go on the offensive.

'This is ridiculous!' I barked at the younger officer. 'There were no signs at the border saying we need insurance. Give me your name, number and the name of this police station. I'm calling the embassy.'

The young officer took off his I.D. badge and hid it from sight, before saying, 'Calm down. There's no need to call the embassy.'

He was right, of course. The embassy was irrelevant to our situation, but for us to extract ourselves from our predicament without having to pay an extortionate bribe or fine, or even having the cars confiscated, we had to rattle their authority somehow.

I stood my ground: 'I'm not speaking to you anymore unless you tell me your name and number. If you're not willing to do this, get your superior officer in here and I will speak to him.'

He was beginning to get angry and ignored my requests.

'None of that is important. You are in violation of the Road Traffic Act of 1926. You are breaking the law. That's what is important,' he shouted, slamming a copy of said road traffic act down on the table. A few beads of sweat rolled down his forehead as he did so.

'I'm sorry, I haven't had a chance to read your road traffic act of 1926. It's not like they were giving out copies at the border,' said Brummy.

The posturing continued from both sides for several minutes, with neither the police nor us willing to concede anything. The more Brummy and I stood our ground, the more angry the police got, and the more we had to lose if we couldn't find a way out of the accusations levelled against us. As our predicament got more serious by the minute, I sensed a weakness through the raised voices, heavy threats and stern accusations:

'How are we supposed to know we need insurance if nobody tells us?' I asked.

'Of course you need insurance,' the older policeman replied.

'No you don't,' I replied. 'We didn't need it by law in Ethiopia. Many other countries around the world don't require it by law. How were we supposed to know Malawi is any different?'

This may have been stretching reality slightly, but the point was made.

'This is not Ethiopia. This is Malawi.'

I changed tack a bit: 'Okay, so according to this road traffic act of yours, what does the law say about warning triangles?'

'Every car must carry two at all times,' came the reply, the younger officer looking slightly confused by my question.

'Why weren't we told this at the border? We've only got one per car. How are we supposed to know every little law in your Road Traffic Act of 1926 if no one tells us?' I

311

replied. 'It makes it impossible for us to abide by all your laws.'

Brummy saw what I was doing and joined in.

'Egypt, for instance. Every car needs a fire extinguisher. There are signs telling you this at the border so people know. How would we know whether we need one in Malawi? It's not like we can carry the regulations for every country we're going through in the glovebox.'

The policemen were now on the back foot, but still arguing defiantly: 'You are still breaking the law.'

'So why didn't your border guards tell us this? It's not like we want to break your laws,' I said.

'Because it's not their job.'

'So whose job is it?'

'The police,' he replied.

'The Malawian police have stopped us five times to check our papers, and not one of them has said we needed insurance,' said Brummy. 'Are you telling us that your own police force is incompetent?'

'Well, they are not doing their jobs properly,' he said, somewhat taken aback.

'So if your police force was doing its job properly, you shouldn't even have had to pull us over?' Brummy suggested.

The policeman smiled as he realised he had been outmanoeuvred. By pointing out that no watertight system existed for making overlanders aware of the various laws in Malawi, he couldn't coerce a bribe or fine without us taking things higher up in the police force – and he couldn't charge us directly without getting a dozen of his fellow officers across the country into trouble for not noticing our lack of insurance.

'My name and number are written here,' he said to me, pointing at a form on his desk. 'Are you going directly to Zambia from here?'

'Yes. Don't worry, we'll not be on your roads any longer.'

'In that case you are free to go. Have a nice day.'

Brummy and I strode out of the police station into the sunshine with a spring in our step.

'Fire up the beasts,' Brummy announced. 'We're off to Zambia.'

'How much did you have to pay?' asked Louise.

'Nothing. We got them to admit that their police force was incompetent and their borders didn't work instead,' Brummy joked, with a glint in his eye.

Laura and I returned to the Porsche and set off for Zambia.

'Thank goodness for that,' she said.

'Yeah, Brummy and I have got quite a bit of practice in dealing with officialdom over the years,' I replied.

'I would have rather been in there with you,' she said, 'Tom's spent the last five minutes lecturing us on how we were in the wrong and should have just admitted it and paid up. I know he's right, but still. He's really getting on my nerves now.'

Of course, Tom was right. We were in the wrong, and Brummy and I had taken quite a risk by taking on the police in a straight confrontation – a risk that would have bordered on foolhardy in much of Africa. However we also had a point – that the mechanisms for informing travellers of a country's laws on entry were often woefully inadequate. We had been lucky to have been able to talk our way out of the predicament and took no chances as we entered Zambia, buying insurance and paying the somewhat opportunistic 'Carbon Tax' which the government was extracting from folk passing through the country. With petrol prices running a ridiculous twenty-five percent higher than back home in England, the Zambian government could rest assured that our carbon emissions would be kept to a minimum.

Despite our scepticism, the 'Carbon Tax' was one of the more defensible and least damaging policies of the cash-strapped Zambian government. Thanks to poor leadership Zambia had, from promising beginnings, managed to get considerably poorer since independence.

In 1964, the country seemed poised for success. As the Zambian nation came into existence, its citizens celebrated the departure of the British colonists and looked forward to the better future which seemed within their grasp. Zambia's seemingly bottomless copper mines had already made it one of the wealthiest nations in Africa and, following independence, their revenue was supplemented by a considerable amount of donor money. It seemed nothing could go wrong. Sadly, however, the bright future that Zambians were hoping for was denied to them.

One of the first acts of the incoming president, Kenneth Kaunda, was to declare himself 'president for life' and embrace socialism, by nationalising much of the nation's private business and shutting the country to investors. It didn't work, and sectors like agriculture suffered. Corruption was rife and little investment flowed in, while officials systematically looted the budgets of state-owned companies – including the copper mines – over the decades. When the price of copper crashed in the 1970s, suddenly the government couldn't pay its bills and so yet more aid money had to flow in. Nothing was learnt, however, and at the turn of the millennium the country remained a basket case, picked apart by scavenging politicians. Meanwhile, the income of the average Zambian has nearly halved in the forty years since independence, dropping to around three hundred dollars per year.

Zambia may only be one country in Africa, but the theme of corruption and mismanagement holding back economic growth, and aid failing to provide a kick start, is a common one on the continent. By the year 2000, Western donors had pumped around 2.3 trillion dollars into the continent, yet Africa finished the century poorer than it was in the 1960s – the only continent to do so. Sadly, it takes a lot of poor leadership and corruption to produce such a statistic.

By way of comparison, Malaysia achieved independence from the British at roughly the same time as Zambia, and received less aid. However, it has been able to build itself up into a strong manufacturing economy, with its own stock market and now even hosts a round of the FIA Formula One World Championship. From a similar starting point, the average Malaysian is now twenty times richer than his Zambian counterpart.

Malaysia's neighbour Singapore has progressed even more dramatically and from humble beginnings on gaining independence, it has risen to become the fifth wealthiest country in the world, based on GDP per capita. Good, trustworthy governance and sound policies are the main things which set these 'Asian Tigers' apart from their African counterparts. However, this is no consolation to the average Zambian, and neither is the fact that a few Zambians are indeed getting sickeningly rich, at the expense of the general population.

As we cruised on into Zambia, it struck me that I was beginning to find Africa's open vistas a bit samey. Undulating swathes of tree-studded grasslands. Well defined skies of cloud and blue. Dust, children, villages. All accompanied by the drone of the exhaust, the hum of the big slant-four engine and the vibrations from the front wheel. It felt like my life had always been the same, sitting in the Porsche as Africa scrolled by. My existence back in the UK before the trip had become a blurred and remote memory, softened by distance to the point where it could just as easily have happened to someone else. It just didn't matter anymore. All that mattered was that there were still another three hundred and eighty miles of reasonable tarmac to go to Lusaka, Zambia's capital and the day's destination. A minor obstacle in the grand scheme of things.

Lusaka was just another overnight stop, entered in the evening darkness and left early the next morning for Livingstone, another three hundred miles away. Most of the distance passed in a monotonous blur, until the road decided to disappear about fifty miles from the day's destination. Early in the trip we might have been fazed by the change in conditions, but we were old hands now and simply took it in our stride. Thick red mud foamed beneath our wheels as we drove through the building weather, until we were brought to a halt by a few stationary trucks and 4x4s. Ahead, bulldozers worked indifferently on a mound of earth, patiently flattening it to facilitate our progress.

Evidently the road wasn't quite finished yet.

Our fellow road users had been parked for about ten minutes, waiting for the Chinese workers to level the soils sufficiently to let them through. This was too much for one Zambian truck driver, who continuously unleashed clichéd outbursts about the Chinese to anyone in earshot.

'They come over here, don't mix with us, take our jobs and what for?' – went his slurred challenge. 'Their roads are terrible and quickly fall apart. They don't care about Africa. They should just go home.'

He absolutely stank of booze.

The Chinese are not about to go home. They are in Africa for the long haul, guaranteeing their share of the continent's boundless natural resources and in return sweetening their presence with aid projects, such as the unfinished road that was delaying our progress. Unlike Western businesses in Africa, they make no bones about the fact that they are there to make money and to meet the demand for raw materials back home. And unlike the West, they make little effort to reform governance, improve human rights or protect the environment, instead preaching non-interference and hiding behind the mantra of 'business only'. In 2008, trade between Africa and China was valued at nearly one hundred billion dollars per year and was increasing rapidly. Is this the constructive relationship that exists between doctor and patient, or a return to colonial exploitation? Only time will tell. However for nations like Zambia, the relationship must seem too good to be true. As the West's patience with the continent fades, Chinese investment is bringing an improving infrastructure, new trade partners and even the dollars and expertise to breathe new life into Zambia's ruined copper mines.

After fifteen minutes, the track ahead was smooth enough to be attempted. One by one, the lorries, the 4x4s and the Porsche took their chances, bouncing their way through. On the other side, the acute need for the new road became clear. A depressing streak of potholed tarmac stretched away towards Livingstone, its grey dampness aping the now brooding sky. Keeping the Porsche moving forward required extreme caution, so deep and tightly packed were the craters. Negotiating this mess of a road, the abused car flexed pitifully, creaking and groaning, crying out for some sympathy. Accelerating between the obstacles, the gearbox had lost its famed precision and selecting fourth gear was almost impossible. The imprecision of the other gears hinted that the whole drive train was slowly being destroyed. The overheating engine flooded the cabin with heat, but cooked itself all the same. It felt as if it was only our willpower that was going to get the decomposing Porsche past the remaining obstacles to Cape Town. We knew beyond doubt that we had enough willpower, however.

As the car creaked through one hole, its exhaust note suddenly deepened, the loud rasp telling us that yet another crack had opened up in the fragile piping. Once again we donned home-made earplugs and willed our way through the rain to Livingstone, the Zambian home of the Victoria Falls, and the country's tourist capital. It was late in the afternoon when we got there, the heavens opening violently in recognition of our arrival. Chuckling to myself, I parked the Porsche next to a very well-equipped Land Rover which proudly displayed the slogan 'Just done it 4x4' on its front wing in bright red letters, before ducking into a café for a much needed coffee.

Typically, Livingstone's banking system didn't allow any of us to obtain money, so we scraped our funds together and checked into one of the many travellers' lodges in town. Like Africa, they were beginning to feel samey. The snappy name, sanitised African appearance, exorbitant bar and gap-year Western clientele of Jolly Boys Backpackers felt completely interchangeable with the trendier places we'd stayed in throughout southern Africa. We could have been in Uganda, or Kenya, or Malawi. After setting up the roof tent in the courtyard, I bought a bland bottle of beer. It cost over two dollars; or more than two days' income for the everyday Zambians, who live in a very different world to the sterile one hidden within the high walls of the hostel. Jaded by the continuous contradictions and with little desire to drink the overpriced beer, Laura and I went to bed. Heavy rain played on the taut fabric of the tent, drowning out the noises from the nearby bar. We lay in each other's arms, holding back from one another as we drifted off to sleep. I pondered my strange state of affairs as consciousness drifted away. 'Only *I* would end up in such a ridiculous situation,' I thought to myself as I lay there.

In southern Zambia, straddling the Zimbabwean border, there is a cleft in the basalt bedrock, over a hundred metres deep. As the Zambezi approaches the cleft, an ominous cloud of spray and vapour fills the sky, hinting at the violence ahead. The river slows nervously, as if appraising the inevitability of its fate, before widening to over a mile across as it prepares to take centre stage in one of nature's greatest spectacles. With a serene finality, it idles up to the brink, before accelerating sickeningly, churning violently into the void with a barbaric roar.

The local Lozi people call it Mosi-oa-Tunya, meaning 'the smoke that thunders'. When David Livingstone 'discovered' the falls for Europe in the nineteenth century, he was sufficiently moved to name them in honour of Queen Victoria, as great an accolade as a colonial explorer could bestow. 'No one can imagine the beauty of the view from anything witnessed in England,' he wrote, theatrically adding: 'Scenes so lovely must have been gazed upon by angels in their flight.'

Just like the African skies, Victoria Falls have their own wet and not-so-wet seasons. Our visit coincided with the dry season in the Zambezi basin, upriver of the falls, meaning flow rates were only a tenth of their flood season peak.

It was still a deeply impressive sight however. For over a mile, the dramatic sweep of cliffs was dotted with huge torrents of water, arcing down to pummel the brown water below with a roar which was felt as much as heard. Water droplets crowded the air, thrown up from the chaos to cool us pleasantly from the white heat of the morning sun. Rainbows floated delicately in the spray, contrasting with the raw power surging all around them.

Victoria Falls is a miraculous point on the earth's surface, at once both frighteningly primeval and beautifully sublime; an incredible juxtaposition of opposites, which depend upon one another for their existence. Without the thunder of hundreds of tonnes of water, no rainbow would curve weightlessly through the air. The churning dynamics of the torrent would not exist were it not for the solid permanence of the rocks. The fine droplets of water which float over to touch your skin and the cool breeze which rises from the gorge provide a physical link to the raging falls, a delicate connection through which to comprehend their power.

Following a morning of strolling around the falls we returned to the cars. One of the area's many monkeys had taken up residence on the roof of the Shogun, and peered down at us in a superior manner. 'Watch this,' declared a confident Brummy as he strode up to the back of the off roader, where the monkey's tail hung down temptingly. Reaching up slowly with a childish grin on his face,

Brummy managed to get his hand within a few inches of pulling the monkey's tail before it jolted to life, leaping towards its taunter and bearing its teeth with an angry snarl.

A startled Brummy retreated about ten feet in an instant, his face losing several shades of colour in the process, while the rest of us burst into unsympathetic laughter. Fortunately the monkey abandoned its claim to the Shogun's roof soon afterwards and we were able to hit the road to Botswana, Laura and I sporting our fashionable loo roll earplugs in deference to the exhaust. Soon, we arrived at the border. Yet another border. We were becoming fairly well practiced at such formalities. Once cleared out of Zambia, we boarded the sturdy old pontoon barge that would carry us the few hundred metres across the Zambezi to Botswana. Those few hundred metres took us from one of modern Africa's most underachieving nations into one of its few real success stories.

When they achieved independence in the 1960s, Zambia was considerably richer than Botswana. Four decades on, as our ragtag expedition crossed the Zambezi from Zambia into Botswana, it crossed into a nation where the average citizen was seven times richer than in the country we were leaving. Botswana achieved its economic miracle not through bulging aid packages and radical policies, but by simply embracing good leadership – an apparent rarity in African nations. By shunning corruption, employing sound policies and investing in long-term planning, Botswana was able to stand on its own two feet and grow. There are certainly still problems – the AIDS epidemic being foremost among them – but even so, it was good to be entering a successful nation after crossing so many which have been stunted by poor governance.

Botswana is proof that Africa holds its destiny in its own hands. With the right leadership, it can forge a better future. Sadly, such good leadership has been a rare commodity on the continent.

We droned our way to Kasane, the nearest town to the border and made home at the Chobe Safari lodge's campsite, before heading to the bar. As the sky darkened, an electrical storm drifted lethargically across the plains to our west, too far away for us to hear thunder, but close enough to captivate us as its strobing flashes shot out through the humid air. As we sat out on the fine decking, sipping beers and scanning the murky river for crocodiles, the lodge's well heeled clientele gave us a wide berth. It must have been the smell. Crossing Africa in a car with the heater stuck on full has that effect.

We had been pushing ourselves fairly hard for days, without a break in our progress since Dar es Salaam. Thanks to this, we now had some time in hand to relax, so we elected to cash in one of our free days by piling into the Shogun and heading out for a safari drive in Chobe National Park. This huge swathe of scrubland is less famous than its prestigious neighbour, the Okavango Delta, and considerably cheaper to visit as a result, which suited us perfectly. Smooth dirt roads led us to the river Chobe's flood plain, where we crawled along slowly, scouring our surroundings for wildlife. Tom drove carefully while Brummy, still recovering from a cold he'd picked up in Zambia, sat alongside him in the front passenger seat, navigating. On the back seat, a kind of carnival atmosphere reigned. Laura and I were happy to have a day away from the temperamental, oven-like Porsche and, along with Louise, we laughed and joked our way through the day as we scoured our respective sides of the track for any signs of wildlife. Initially the park seemed deserted, but it didn't matter. For once on the trip, we actually felt like we were on holiday. Tom, concerned at taking the Shogun off road once again, kept imploring us to keep a sharp lookout. I couldn't resist mocking him back.

'Well there's a tree over there,' I joked. 'Some dead branches. Oh my! That's a fine piece of petrified wood!'

'If there's a lion over there, you'll be glad you kept a lookout,' said Laura, taking the safari slightly more seriously than me.

'If there's a lion over there, I'm getting on your side of the car!' I countered.

'Oh look!' Brummy shouted, coming alive, 'Another hamster. How lucky, we've seen two hamsters on this safari. The lions must have eaten everything else and just left the hamsters because they don't do appetisers.'

Laura laughed at his irreverence, adding, 'Look, they're not hamsters, okay?'

As the only member of the team to have been on a safari before, she had become the self-appointed knowledgeable expert of the group.

'Ah well, at least there are ducks as well.' Louise said, as some waddled across the path ahead of us.

'Yeah, but that's only because the lions can't catch the ducks,' I said, in mock seriousness. 'After all, lions can't fly.'

'And there's not a lot of meat on a duck,' said Laura.

'Yeah, but these ducks are the size of flamingos,' I pointed out, 'Look at the size of them. That'd be a good snack for a cheetah. There's no way a duck can outrun a cheetah.'

'It could fly away, Ben,' came the deflated reply from an annoyed-sounding Brummy, before he was interrupted by Laura.

'There's something over there. An antelope or springbok or something.'

'Wow, I've still got bushes on my side,' I replied. 'Oh, look, a cabbage. And a beetle.'

There were indeed impalas grazing on the flood plain next to the river. They appeared relaxed, but at least one member of the herd was always alert for the smallest hint of danger. Impalas are elegant creatures, about the size of a goat, but considerably more lithe and slender. Their taunt lines hint at the athleticism that enables them to escape the lions, leopards and cheetahs which provide the danger in their outwardly idyllic lives.

As we drove, a few warthogs came into view. Compact and muscular, with outsize teeth jutting randomly from their pugnacious heads, they were gloriously ugly. Dropping onto their front knees to graze, they exuded an arrogant confidence and completely ignored us. I remembered how in Kenya, Julian had told us how it was dangerous to approach their burrows head on, as people had been seriously hurt as they rush out in defence.

'Excellent. Something other than vermin,' commented Brummy.

'Yep, and check out all the bacon on it,' I said.

'I bet it tastes shit,' was Brummy's response.

'No, I ate one yesterday actually, at the lodge. It was quite nice.'

'Oh yes. Warthog tastes good,' Laura said, 'I might have it again this evening.'

'Look, guinea fowl,' said Louise.

'Turkeys, you mean?' Brummy said.

'Well they are a bit like turkeys.'

'If I wanted to see a turkey, I would have gone to Norfolk,' I said.

The hours rolled past in a hail of banter, interspersed with wildlife sightings. Bands of mongooses prowled through the grass, inquisitively sniffing the air as they went. Impalas roamed among the bushes, alert and proud. Once, we stopped for a while as three feet of uninterested monitor lizard crossed the road just in front of us, flicking the air with its tongue as it ambled along. Further away, hippos stayed close to the river, their bulky, rounded frames dotting the middle distance like granite boulders, dwarfing even the buffalo with which they shared the plain.

Obviously, almost all of these sightings took place on the right side of the car. To my side, there was generally nothing. I continued to take the turn of luck light-heartedly.

'Oh look, some twigs. And some funny, tussocky grassy stuff.'

'I feel like I'm in a car full of chavs!' Louise said, stuck in the back between Laura and I.

'You're the only one that looks like a chav,' I fired back.

'Oh look, another impala on this side. Just here,' Laura said, pointing.

'Isn't it pretty,' said Louise. Laura agreed. I was growing bored of the constant impalas, however.

'How can elephants hide in this sort of bush?' I enquired, half serious for once. The vegetation was all less than ten feet tall – certainly shorter than a five-tonne elephant.

'They're around somewhere. They destroyed all of this,' said Laura, pointing at the swathes of damaged acacias.

'Yeah, and then they just ran off and hid?' I said.

'They fly away. Like Dumbo,' said Louise authoritatively.

'They migrate,' said Laura, our resident animal expert. 'Everything must have migrated to the other side of the park, where it's wetter.'

We drove onwards, through a landscape choked by thickets of trees, until we reached a clearing, which contained a bowl-shaped depression. In the middle of the depression was a small pool, a quintessential African watering hole. Next to the pool stood a dead tree, its bleak branches curving down artistically over the water. We timed our arrival in the clearing perfectly. As we stopped, movement in the vegetation signalled the slow, ambling arrival of some of the watering hole's locals. Elephants. There were five of them, three adults and two calves. They made calm progress down to the water and began to drink, while behind, two giraffes appeared in the trees, towering up to reach the highest leaves. The elephants stole the show however and we watched them in near silence for about ten minutes, as their dextrous trunks sucked up gallons of water. They appeared relaxed and playful, though their hard leather skin must have been baking in the sun. Such a combination of power and elegance; graceful in spite of their bulk.

'Beautiful,' Laura whispered, breaking the silence.

Nothing could top those peaceful ten minutes. We decided to head back into town and set off towards the park entrance, past kudus, monkeys, warthogs, hippos and dozens of the ubiquitous impalas. Unseen by the others, Laura and I held hands as we were chauffeured back to the campsite, where a pair of monkeys were sharing a noisy, intimate moment in the tree next to our tent.

That evening, Louise and Tom went on a river safari, while Brummy stayed in the bar. Laura and I returned to the Porsche, intent on getting the cracked exhaust welded back together.

I climbed into the dark, cramped cabin and turned the key. After turning over a few times, the engine spluttered into life and idled roughly, a far cry from the purring sophistication one expects of a Porsche. The exhaust rasped away unpleasantly, assaulting our hearing. I always found it slightly depressing returning to the Porsche after snatching a few carefree hours out of its presence. As Tom had done about ten days previously, I'd reached a point where I just wanted to get to Cape Town and return to a life that wasn't dictated by the unpredictable foibles of a tattered car.

Tucked away on the side of the hill overlooking Kasane, we found a shack of corrugated steel, little bigger than a phone box, advertising 'flat tyre mending and welding'. It had begun to rain and even getting the Porsche up the muddy slope to the shack was tricky, but it was worth the effort as the shack's young proprietor was confident he could fix both the exhaust and a slow puncture we'd picked up a few countries before. I helped him to remove the exhaust and we left him to it, returning to the lodge for a beer, having been told to come back in an hour – which we did. Back at the lodge's bar, wealthy tourists eyed our matted hair and muddy clothes disapprovingly.

'I don't know what they're being all posh and superior about,' I whispered to Laura. 'We're the only ones with a Porsche outside.'

Taking the direct route, the tourist hub of Maun is only a few hundred miles away from Kasane. However, the direct route went via the rutted sandy tracks of Chobe National Park and would have resulted in yet another pummelling for what was left of the Porsche. Because of this, we travelled in a long dogleg which doubled the distance, but at least kept us on tarmac. With only one junction in four hundred miles, we couldn't get lost, so we travelled separately; the Shogun at its trademark fifty-eight mph, while we cruised at seventy in the Porsche. Most speeds below this had become unbearable due to the worsening vibrations coming from the front wheel.

Botswana is a huge, sparsely populated wilderness; a swathe of desert and scrub the size of France. From the low vantage point of the Porsche's cabin, it felt empty. Mile after mile of savannah. The only interest for hundreds of miles occurred when a huge bull elephant wandered across the road directly in front of us. Fortunately our brakes worked, but the gentle giant didn't even bat an eyelid as we slowed for it.

Approaching Maun, Laura's mood began to deepen, her relaxed chirpiness being replaced by a withdrawn trepidation. She had been to Maun before, during her previous travels in Africa and the town had played host to the darkest weeks of her life. At the time she was dating a South African called Cliff, an ambitious pilot who worked flying wealthy tourists into the safari resorts of the Okavango Delta. Cliff had dumped her uncaringly while they were there and she had spent weeks alone on a tourist camp just out of town, feeling dejected and abandoned, spiralling into depression. Laura had sworn that she would never return, but there was no easy way to avoid the place so we pulled into town that afternoon, Laura directing us to a bar near the airport which apparently served the best steaks in town. I suppose if you're going to put your ghosts to rest, you may as well do so over a good piece of medium-rare.

As we sat eating, Laura said little. I could tell just how hard she was finding it being back, returning to a place that had come to represent darkness and loneliness to her. I tried to be supportive but knew I couldn't do much. She sat on the verge of tears, wanting only to be left alone and to get away from the town. We finished our meals quickly and headed into town. Once we were back in the Porsche, just the two of us, she felt able to show her emotions once again, tears on her cheeks.

'I just want to get away from here. I can't stand it, all the memories coming back.'

'Don't worry,' I replied emptily, trying to sound reassuring. 'We will. We'll have a nice braai this evening, you can lay your ghosts to rest and by tomorrow you'll feel so much more positive about everything.'

I knew my reassurances were falling on deaf ears but at least they went said. Just like her previous visit to Maun, this was something she would have to get through on her own.

Back in town, I went to the bank to get some cash, while the others headed into a pleasantly air-conditioned shop to get food and firewood for the evening's braai, a traditional South African barbeque. I waited for my turn at the cash point, before inserting my bankcard. It vanished, without any acknowledgement from the machine.

'Oh crap,' I uttered aloud.

This would be enough of an inconvenience in the UK, but as I was in Africa my mind immediately assumed the worst. It would be a long time before I saw it again and the chances of money going missing from my account were high. Also, since Laura's bag was stolen, my bankcard had become Team Porsche's only source of cash.

The bank was already closed for the day, but fortunately a security guard was lingering by the front door. He called the bank manager for me, who within minutes came back to work and liberated my card, returning it with an apology. There was no hint that a bribe was wanted and no attempt was made to profit from my situation. I couldn't imagine such businesslike efficiency in the other African countries we'd travelled through and to me it summed up the reasons for Botswana's economic success. The atmosphere of trust and clarity, and the oppression of corruption, made the country an easier place to make honest money than places governed without these principles.

I wandered back to the cars, expecting the others to already be there, waiting for me. Only Laura was. She was leaning against the locked door of the Porsche, crying dejectedly into her hand.

'Are you okay?' I asked limply, already knowing the answer.

'Tom's being such a bastard to me,' came the reply.

'What's he done now?'

'We were getting the stuff for dinner and he ripped into me. He was being all self-important about what we should have on the braai, but when I said I fancied something other than beef, he just turned around and said, 'Laura, it's not always about what you want' in a really nasty way.'

'Oh, that's just Tom being irritable. He was probably just hungry...' I replied before being cut off by Laura.

'I shouldn't have to put up with it. Why has he always got to be such a bastard?'

'He's just finding the constant stress of the trip really difficult, that's all...'

'Well I don't even want to speak to him,' she said.

The character clash between Tom and Laura had been brewing for weeks, but it was a terrible shame for Laura that it boiled over in Maun. As the others approached she got into the Porsche, ready to leave.

'Where have you been?' Brummy asked.

'The bank. Cash machine ate my card,' I replied.

'Oh dear.'

'It's fine, I got it back. Come on, let's go to the campsite.'

We headed to the strangely named Audi camp, just out of town. 'Shouldn't there be a Porsche camp?' I mused. It was the usual, samey fare; space for overland trucks, a self-consciously African looking bar, a swimming pool and a mildly preposterous price tag on everything. In reception, there was a large wall map of the African continent. It gave us immense cheer to see, laid out in front of us, just how far we'd come. Brummy and I traced our fingers down the route, even then barely believing what we'd achieved so far. Compared to what was already behind us, Cape Town was a mere stone's throw away.

As we got the braai going, Laura left us for a swim in the pool and some time alone with her thoughts helped her to recompose herself. Ever since she'd arrived in Maun emotions had been crushing her and now more than ever, all she wanted was to hit the road away from the place as early as possible the following morning.

The braai's embers were soon hot enough to cook our dinner and we ate without ceremony, the tension in the air being clear to all. After dinner Brummy and I took Laura over to the bar, to cheer her up over a Windhoek beer. We didn't have to in the end, as a somewhat uninhibited dung beetle did the job for us. It came rasping into the bar, wings blurring as they lifted its bulky, shot-like body.

'Good god! What is that?' came the predictable recoil from Brummy, triggering Laura's first laughter in hours.

It landed on the floor a few metres from us, and tucked away its intricate wings beneath their protective outer shell. After a spot of ambling around, it came to the conclusion that there was no dung in the bar and decided to move on.

The wings unfolded and clunked into place like some tiny machine and it rose vertically, hovering momentarily before accelerating rapidly forwards, straight at Brummy.

'Oh piss!' was his alarmed response as he dived out of the way. It thudded heavily into the terracotta wall of the bar, directly behind him. Laura and I burst out in uncontrollable laughter.

Once again, the wings folded efficiently away as the beetle regained its bearings, then unfolded once more and it levitated before whizzing across the room straight at Brummy, who narrowly dodged it, allowing it to shoot out of the bar, into the night.

'Why does Africa hate me so much?' Brummy protested, as we continued to laugh at his misfortune.

* * *

For four hundred miles the road sliced defiantly through the sandy ground towards the Namibian border. Whole days spent cooking under the sun, nursing the Porsche along such roads, were now the most natural thing in the world to us. Today's drive took in the northern reaches of the Kalahari Desert, which had become disappointingly green after the recent rains; I prefer my deserts to be more desert coloured. We cruised along, glad that Cape Town was getting noticeably closer by the day.

Botswana is so unpopulated that, in four hundred miles, there were only two road junctions to negotiate. Predictably, we went the wrong way at the first, signless junction, heading north back towards the Okavango delta. Realising our mistake, we looked at the map and reasoned that we could cut down to the south fairly easily, regaining the main road via a few miles of dirt tracks. I led in the Porsche, monitoring our progress on the GPS, while the Shogun followed, with Tom driving. The track consisted of two sandy ruts, formed by the passage of tyres, with a slightly raised strip of grass between them. Trees crowded closely around us as we drove. Despite the remote location of the track, we could maintain a respectable speed, as the bottoms of the tyre ruts were smooth and dry.

'I don't think this track is going to get us back to the main road,' said Laura. 'We're not heading south enough.'

'It might curve round to the south,' I replied hopefully. 'The map seemed to think it would.'

We continued for another few fruitless miles in the wrong direction before Laura was proven right and I admitted defeat. We slowed to a halt, so we could tell Team Shogun what they probably knew already.

I somehow sensed it was coming. Months of driving together in close proximity had sharpened my senses. Looking up at the rear view mirror, the Shogun appeared silently from the within the blankness of our dust cloud like a charging elephant. I knew at once that there was no way they could stop in time. Everything happened in slow motion. Still fixated on the apparition in the mirror and bracing myself hard, I took my foot off the brake, floored the accelerator hard and sidestepped the clutch as quickly as I could, attempting to get moving again before the Shogun reached us.

It was too late.

Just as the clutch bit and began to pump power to the rear wheels, the Shogun hit us, hard.

Metal ruptured and crumpled behind us as the Porsche's rear end yielded to over two tonnes of charging four-wheel-drive. A startlingly loud bang assaulted our ears, the twisting body of the Porsche cried out in shock as the Shogun bulldozed it towards the scenery. The impact slammed us back violently in our seats, snapping our heads back as a cloud of dust flew through the cabin. And then, it was over. It had taken less than a second from seeing the Shogun to the moment it smashed into us, but it had seemed like so much longer as I concentrated on attempting to minimise the impact. I applied the brakes to stop us rolling on down the track and turned off the engine. Silence. A sudden headache throbbed violently through my head.

'Are you okay, Laura?' I asked shakily.

'I think so. I've cut my lip.' Blood dripped heavily from the side of her mouth where the impact had caused her to bite it. 'What about you?'

'I think so too,' I replied. 'But I've got a headache and I can feel my neck stiffening up already.'

We got out to survey the damage. Tom was already out of his precious Shogun, inspecting its front end in a concerned manner. I was amazed. I had expected its radiator to be damaged at the very least, but the 4x4 was practically unscathed. Only a pair of cracked spotlights betrayed the fact that it had just ploughed into the back of another car at thirty mph. Evidently four-wheel-drives are designed to be crashed through other road users at unfeasible speeds without even sustaining a scratch.

The Porsche was a complete mess. The smooth lines at the back of the car had ruptured forward, metal waving and buckling under the load. All the rear lights were shattered, while the bumper had been twisted upwards by the impact. I glanced along the side of the car. The impact had caused the rear wings to pant outwards, ripples reaching forwards as far as the doors, almost half way along the car. The boot wouldn't close, the roof box had been shunted forward in the impact and the hinges holding its lid in place were broken. However all in all, the damage still wasn't nearly as bad as I expected. The Germans certainly knew how to build tough cars!

'Thanks Tom,' I said, as he continued to inspect his beloved Shogun.

'I couldn't see you through all that dust,' he replied.

'Well why didn't you slow down then?'

'I'd sped up because I wanted to catch you up and tell you we were going the wrong way.'

I said nothing, as any reply would have been harsh and undiplomatic, to say the least. I wandered around to the

Shogun's passenger window. Brummy and Louise were still in their seats, looking a little confused.

'How are you guys?' I asked.

'I've smashed my knee on the dashboard,' replied Brummy, 'and Louise banged her head.'

'I told him he was going too fast, but he wouldn't listen,' she said, sighing with defeatism.

The cars still both still seemed to work, so we retraced our steps back to the road and headed towards the grandly titled Trans-Kalahari Border Crossing – our gateway into Namibia. With every mile my anger at Tom grew deeper and more irrational. I knew he hadn't wrecked my Porsche on purpose, but through my red mist, I still blamed him for it. I hadn't owned and cherished the car for six years, and nursed it most of the way across Africa, only for him to smash it up in a moment of idiocy. Laura, sat holding a tissue to her bleeding lip, was going through a similar escalation of anger. 'He didn't even apologise,' she kept saying.

It wasn't only the back end of the Porsche that was destroyed in the impact. Temporarily, so too was our group's already fragile friendship.

FOURTEEN

BEGINNING TO BELIEVE

27th November 2008
Near Windhoek, Namibia

Our view differed little from that of the previous days. The Porsche's expansive bonnet swept down to an arrow straight blur of mottled grey tarmac. Yellow lines at the road's edges hemmed it in, separating the smooth road from the uninviting wilderness to either side. Yet somehow, my interpretation of the view had changed. For the first time in the trip, the road had a definite end. For most of the preceding two months, the prospect of reaching Cape Town had seemed so distant and unlikely that I seldom let the concept linger in my mind – such were the obstacles that had stood between us and our ultimate destination. Now, however, things were different. Cape Town was in the next country, less than a thousand miles away. We could be there in a couple of days if we chose to. I was beginning to believe even more strongly than ever that we could go the distance. It was a nice thought to dwell on and certainly beat thinking about the sorry state of the back of the car. I silently indulged myself in glorious thoughts of our imminent achievement. *England to Cape Town in an old Porsche!* Now that the finish was close enough to comprehend, I knew nothing would stop us.

'Shall we pull over and wait for the Shogun?' Laura suggested.

We'd been driving alone for hours and quite a gap had built up.

'Yeah, I'll stop in the next lay-by. I hope they see us this time.'

We coasted to a halt by the side of the road and climbed out of the car. Despite the late hour, it was still well over thirty degrees and the playful gusts of wind that whistled in our ears did little to cool us. Ahead, the sun came into view, dropping down from behind a heavy black cloud. Its glorious explosion of red was contained within a narrow slither of sky, pinned between the horizon and the smothering cloud base. All around us, crisp shadows stretched back into the Kalahari, while the landscape crystallised into a sharper focus, made somehow more real by the rich oblique light. Laura and I stood in silence, taking in our vivid surroundings. I still couldn't believe we'd made it so far.

'Fancy a sundowner?' Laura said, breaking the silence.

'Sorry?'

'A sundowner. We've still got a few small cans of Windhoek beer in the fridge.'

'Laura, I think that's a splendid idea.'

We exchanged cheeky smiles and Laura got us each a beer. In spite of being stored in the fridge, a day on the road with the car's heater on full meant they were rather hot and badly shaken up to boot. Still, we both enjoyed our drink, as much for its symbolism as for its taste. *We were going to do this.*

While we waited for the Shogun, we set about improvising some rear lighting for the car. The crash had left only the indicator lights functioning and if we were to drive at night some form of additional rear lighting would be necessary. This problem was easily solved by slotting the light which hung in the awning each evening into the orange fabric bag in which my inflatable camping mattress lived. This was positioned in the rear window, and shone out into the night most effectively. We also closed the boot lid with a ratchet strap, as it had refused to shut properly since the accident.

Eventually, the Shogun pulled up.

'Cheers!' Laura and I said in synchrony, holding up our beers.

'Right, give me one of those,' was Brummy's predictable reply. The rest of the Shogun's occupants shared the sentiment. Still angry over the state of the Porsche, I tried to avoid eye contact with Tom.

It was completely dark when we arrived in Windhoek and the air had a strange energy about it, charged and ready for a storm. We found a cheap hostel with secure parking and made the place our home for the night. I was too tired to set up the roof tent platform and so we pitched the tent on the dusty ground before joining the others in the bar.

'What are you drinking?' asked Tom, seeking to break the obvious tension between us.

'Well, we're in Windhoek, so obviously I'll have a Hansa please.'

'Of course you will. One Windhoek coming right up.'

'Cheers.'

After a few drinks the need for sleep overwhelmed us all, so we retired to our tents. It had been quite a day, with both Laura and I trying to keep the peace and conceal our anger with Tom. It was difficult, as our isolation from him following the accident had led to a huge build up of pent up resentment, which didn't seem to dissipate.

'Has he apologised yet?' Laura whispered as we lay in the tent.

'Nope.'

I awoke gradually, aware of the rain drumming on the tent's flysheet. It was still dark, but the hostel's lighting lent a dim illumination to my surroundings. The rain was torrential, the pounding droplets falling so densely that the noises from their individual impacts blurred into one, like the deep rumble of a passing freight train. Every few minutes, a flash of lightning would light up the tent like day. I wasn't concerned. I'd owned the tent for years and it had weathered much worse assaults than this. Lying there, I thought back to a climbing trip to the Alps many years previously, when the tent was nearly new. I had pitched it

337

on a glacier over three thousand metres up, in the shadow of Mt Blanc. An Alpine storm had raged all night and winds of over eighty mph drove rain and snow and hail before them, pummelling my fabric shelter. Lightning had strobed into the hard granite ridge, less than a hundred metres away, while a nearby snow slope threatened to avalanche in the maelstrom. The tent had survived then – this little Namibian shower would be no problem.

'Ben.' Laura was obviously awake.

'Yes.'

'I'm lying in a puddle. I think it's coming in through the bottom of the tent.'

'Really? I don't believe you.'

'Yes, I really am.'

I fumbled for a torch and shone it around. Water was seeping through the bottom of the tent and pooling beneath our camping mattresses. Laura unzipped the porch.

'Ben, you're an idiot!'

'What have I done now?'

'You've gone and pitched the tent in the middle of a stream, that's what!'

Water was pouring down the slight slope from the hostel, forming a small stream that flowed right under our tent. We were camping in our own miniature wadi.

'Well it was dry when I pitched it,' I pointed out, lamely.

'Yeah, well it's not now. I'm getting soaked.'

We stayed in the tent for a little longer, before Laura could take no more and made a dash for the hostel at about seven AM. By this time, my camping mattress had become an island in the flooded tent and I tried to remain on it, not touching the expanse of wetness surrounding it. The desire to sleep still outweighed the discomfort of staying put.

During a lull in the deluge, Laura stuck her head into the tent.

'Come to the bar. Free pancakes for breakfast.'

'Not like the ones in Ethiopia I hope?'

'Nope, you're safe there. Oh, also, terrorists have taken over the Taj Mahal. It's on the television.'

'That's rubbish news,' was my tired reply.

Eventually, the dampness drove me out of the tent and I joined the others for breakfast. It was the 28th November. Terrorists had taken over the Taj Mahal hotel in Mumbai, not the *actual* Taj Mahal. I breathed a selfish sigh of relief that the beautiful building which had captivated me the previous year was safe, and tucked into the pancakes as I watched the news in a detached manner. As I did so, Tom turned to me.

'Ben.'

'Yes Tom.'

'If you want to get the back of the Porsche repaired in Cape Town, I'll pay for it.'

'Cheers, but don't worry. The car's a write off, it would cost a fortune to straighten that mess out.'

'Okay, well if you change your mind, let me know.'

While I appreciated the offer, I was still too angry with Tom to discuss what had happened in a rational manner. A lot of my anger was selfish. I was saddened that I'd driven my Porsche all this way, but the triumphant photo of it parked beneath Table Mountain would now be of a battered carcass of a car. I was angry too that my plans to sell it in Mozambique for a tidy sum were now dead in the water and that we might even have trouble getting it across the border into South Africa in its battered, apparently unroadworthy state. I knew Tom hadn't caused the accident on purpose, but I couldn't separate his occasional overconfidence behind the wheel from the collision. Rightly or wrongly, if someone else was driving the Shogun, I felt sure the collision wouldn't have happened. It took quite a while for Laura and I to forgive Tom for his mistake.

'Come on, it's stopped raining. Let's stop faffing and head into town,' said Brummy.

'We'll be ready in a minute.'

Central Windhoek is, by day, a pleasant, though somewhat soulless place. Aspirational, not-quite-high-rise buildings nestle closely together, though you're never more than a few hundred metres from a decidedly low-rise township. Everything looked a few years old; almost new, but already starting to develop a patina of age before its time. We went to a shopping centre, which felt positively advanced after the previous month's more modest offerings. Internet, department stores, Pick and Pay, Wimpy, all the conveniences we'd been missing were there. There was even a Christmas tree in the centre's atrium, giving us a rare reminder of what time of year it was. I went into a burger joint for lunch, something I rarely do in the UK, but I felt I could justify on novelty grounds, as it was my first opportunity to do so for many weeks. After a few hours drifting aimlessly around the decadent building, we hit the road once again.

On the way out of town, we passed a familiar sight. Another Porsche 944. Its beautiful grey bodywork served as a sharp reminder of what a mess our example had become. It was the first one we'd seen since Slovenia and offered yet another sign that we were gradually returning to a world similar to the one we knew from back home. Since leaving England, our journey had gradually peeled back the layers of what we refer to as 'Western civilisation', as we left our wealthy world behind to venture through ever poorer, more challenging lands. Now the process had reversed. The closer we got to Cape Town, the more things seemed to run in a manner similar to our lives back in the UK. Shopping centres, fast food, flash cars, Visa cards; all were gradually reappearing as we approached our goal. This whetted our desire to get to Cape Town even more, filling our minds with images of some utopian home from home.

Windhoek was left behind quickly, its northern extremity marked by an unusually attractive power station. The landscape soon reverted to the African norm and was considerably greener than I had expected Namibia to be, no doubt a product of the unexpected rains.

As we neared the point where a gravel track left the main road and headed towards Spitzkoppe – our day's destination – a huge mushroom cloud towered high above our path. Billowing high into the atmosphere, its rounded plume was completely symmetrical, like a nuclear nightmare. Connecting the bottom of the cloud with the ground was an apparently solid column of steel-grey rain, swamping the parched earth with both moisture and electricity.

'That looks worryingly like a huge tornado,' I said.

'Well the cars coming towards us made it through okay,' rationalised Laura.

There was no way around it. Beneath the mushrooming cloud, a moody gloom tinted the landscape, before our world darkened yet again as we thrust into the turmoil. Visibility dropped to a few metres as the rain exploded all around us, forcing us to crawl along, barely able to see the edge of the road. We crossed our fingers that the unreliable windscreen wipers would outlast the storm. With the windows up, the car's cabin became uncomfortably hot as we crept the few miles through the downpour. And then, the rain eased and it was over. We crossed the threshold from a world where apocalyptic rains had turned the landscape green, to a bleached vista of sand and gravel. The storm continued to churn in our rear-view mirrors, but ahead a sky of the most tranquil blueness, dotted with cotton wool clouds, welcomed us.

With only an hour or so of driving left to reach Spitzkoppe, we pulled into the next town for a drink and fuel stop. As I filled the Porsche, a bystander wandered over. He wore a loose checked shirt and slack baggy trousers. His left eye wandered disinterestedly around the petrol station, while the right one appraised me in pin-sharp focus. The conversation was familiar.

'What is this car?'

'It's a Porsche. They're German.'

341

'Ah, German. Very good, expensive. You are German too?'

'No, we've travelled from England.'

'No, it is too far!'

'We have, look.' I pointed to the map, displayed conveniently in the car's back window for moments such as this. 'Here, through Europe, the Middle East, down to Cairo. Then Sudan, Ethiopia, Kenya, Uganda, Tanzania, then across to here. We're heading for Cape Town.'

I had listed the countries on our route so many times over the previous few months that they had became like a chant, recited on demand many times a day.

'That's amazing,' came the reply. 'Can I come with you? To Cape Town?'

'I'm sorry, I'm afraid there's no space. The car is small enough with only the two of us in it.' I gestured over to Laura, who was buying some water.

'She is your wife?'

'No. It's a long story.'

'Will you be coming back here again?'

'Not in this trip. Maybe one day in the future.'

Suddenly, his wandering eye ceased its journey and locked onto my face. 'I can come with you then?'

'Maybe.'

'You promise?'

'I don't know,' I said evasively, somewhat uneasy about where the conversation was going.

'When you come back to Usakos, you find me and we will go to Cape Town, okay?'

'Yes, okay. If I come back here I'll take you on a road trip to Cape Town,' I said, making a mental note never to return.

This seemed to pacify the guy's advances and he wandered off to talk to Tom, who was still trying to get diesel for the Shogun. I paid for the gas and climbed back into the Porsche. Laura joined me, clutching an impressive stock of food and water and even a bottle of red wine. Once

Team Shogun was ready, we completed the last few miles of tarmac before taking a gravel track off into the desert.

The first spectacle of our little tour of Namibia's sights floated into view, hovering ghost-like on the horizon as we approached. Its shark's tooth outline, and the row of giant molars which make up its satellite peaks, seemed to hover statically on the rim of our vision as we approached, before exploding suddenly in size as proximity brought us beneath them.

Spitzkoppe is a mountain of golden granite whose jagged silhouette has led to it being popularly known as the 'Matterhorn of Africa.' This lofty accolade is somewhat optimistic, however, as other than the vague similarity of the mountains' outlines, the two mountains have almost nothing in common. The Matterhorn is a monolith of snow, ice and granite, approached through the craggy greenness of the European Alps and is but one summit in a vast sea of snow-capped peaks. In comparison, Spitzkoppe is located on a flat plain of sand and gravel and as you approach it, it towers two-dimensionally on the rim of your world for many minutes, growing imperceptibly, before the drama escalates suddenly with your arrival at its flanks. Instead of the fashionable Swiss town of Zermatt, at its base there is a nondescript township. Instead of chill snow and crisp air, there is only a dry heat, as granite bakes beneath a dominating sun.

We arrived between the main peak of Spitzkoppe and its satellite peaks late in the afternoon. The heat was still intense and most of us elected to lounge around in what shade we could find, drinking water or beer. Tom, however, chose to climb up the craggy outcrop behind our campsite, in search of the view and probably more importantly, some time alone. It was clear just how tough he was finding the continuous stresses of the trip and how all he wanted was to get it over with – to get to Cape Town,

343

put the trip behind him and relax for the first time in months.

The rest of us delayed any attempts at rock climbing until the heat of the day had eased off a bit, but the handholds on the brittle boulders around our camp area were very friable and had a disconcerting habit of breaking off, so we soon gave up and retired to our chairs once again. After the setting sun had cycled the granite around us through a full spectrum of vivid colours, we got a campfire going and cooked dinner, before the wine-fuelled banter stretched well into the night.

The following morning we set course for the Skeleton Coast. Sixty miles of pleasantly uncorrugated gravel led us westwards, before we entered a thin mist, a welcome drop in temperature signalling the sea was near.

The gravel became a road of packed salt, and the Atlantic loomed into view through the mist. Initially a false horizon in the salty air, it soon gained form as we approached, breakers rolling in to end their long journeys on the sands.

The place had a strange atmosphere, as if the usual rules of the natural world had been put on hold. Despite the mists and the pounding of the waves, the coast was uncompromisingly dry. Bleached bones dotted the high water line; remnants of whales or seals. Randomly patterned salt lakes were scattered across the landscape, while the ground beneath our feet felt like it had never seen rain. Nothing grew, not even the occasional spurt of green or thorny brown which lends relief to the eye in other deserts. The forbidding nature of the landscape was total.

I thought of the countless shipwrecks which had occurred on the shores and shivered. Even if you escaped the initial fury as your vessel ran aground in the mists, there was no hope of survival once ashore; no water or shelter or food. Until recently, the only way off the Skeleton Coast was a slow departure through thirst, heatstroke and delirium.

We detoured north through the lingering mist, passing salt lakes and mirages and crossing featureless vistas, until we arrived at Cape Cross. Here, in 1486, Portuguese explorer Diego Cao reached the southernmost point of his voyage down Africa's west coast and planted a cross to mark the fact, providing the bleak headland with its somewhat unimaginative name. Today, Cape Cross is more famous for its huge colony of brown fur seals. Up to a hundred thousand of them inhabit the rocky headland, making it the largest such colony in the world. We smelt them before we saw them, a pungent combination of rotting fish, shit and death which combines to produce a stench that cuts straight through you. Lesser smells come and go on the wind, catching you intermittently by surprise, but the smell at Cape Cross is so heavy that it sits permanently at the forefront of your senses, impossible to ignore. Still, at least its consistency meant we began to get used to it after a while.

The colony was an impressive sight. Thousands upon thousands of mammals living crammed together on a rocky bluff, hemmed in between sea and sands. In the surf, hundreds more seals floated effortlessly, while those jammed together on the land lounged lazily, or hobbled ungracefully about on their flippers. During the breeding season, seals become very territorial and confrontations between neighbours were a common occurrence, with survival of the fittest appearing to be the sole law governing the colony. Adults moved with no concern for the welfare of the young, often crushing them through their carelessness. The injured were ignored, left for the gulls to pick apart. Orphans often took refuge just outside the colony, awaiting their inevitable fate in relative peace. The sound of their tortured barks rang out in the air as the big adults challenged or warned each other and lost babies cried out for their parents.

'What a disgusting species,' was Brummy's take on the world of seals.

'I would pay good money to see a couple of killer whales come half way up the beach and smudge out a load of them,' I replied half seriously, as I imagined the spectacle.

'I wouldn't shed a tear,' he replied.

Following twenty minutes at the colony, we'd all had enough of seals. We headed to Cape Cross lodge, where a rather upmarket dinner was served by a pristine waiter who made us all feel a little self-conscious about our unwashed state. Once our appetites were satisfied and the free coffee service had been thoroughly abused, we hit the salt road south. I was pleased to be heading south, and I was sure Tom would be too, as leaving Cape Cross represented the beginning of the end. From that moment, we would be following a fairly direct route to Cape Town. Every mile we covered was a mile less between us and the finish line. The Porsche vibrated away worse than ever as we cruised down the Skeleton Coast, but I wasn't overly concerned. We had less than a thousand miles to go. The car had come so far over the previous few months that the remaining distance seemed like nothing. It was going to get to Cape Town, even if we had to push it there ourselves.

Following a few hours vibrating through the mist that tends to envelop the Skeleton Coast each afternoon, we arrived at Swapokmund. It had been an uneventful drive through a surreal wilderness, with the sea drifting in and out of view to our right. Occasionally, we'd passed a shipwreck, some stricken vessel sitting abandoned on the sands. At least these days, it didn't represent a death sentence for the crew. A hundred years ago, they wouldn't have been so lucky.

Swakopmund became our home that evening, at yet another lodge with secure parking facilities. We headed into town and soon found ourselves enjoying mojitos in El Cubana, the local Cuban theme bar and our first such experience since we left Bar Cuba in Plymouth almost two months earlier. Mojitos led to Windhoek beers as day led to night, the air staying warm and clear way after sunset.

Eventually evening became morning and El Cubana's bar closed apologetically. Tom and Louise sensibly returned to their tents outside the hostel; however Brummy, Laura and I set off across town in search of a bar which was still serving. Brummy led the search, adopting an important air as he asked anyone still awake where the nearest open bar was. Laura and I followed on behind, our fingers intertwined subtly behind our backs, hidden in the darkness. Team Shogun knew nothing of how close we had become.

Everywhere seemed closed, but our hazy quest for just one more Windhoek resulted in us staggering towards the only bright lights left switched on – the Mermaid Casino. Despite a few strange looks from the exquisitely turned out staff, we were able to get a much-desired last beer – a Hansa from Swakopmund's own brewery. The evening slid ever further into oblivion and Brummy soon slurred his excuses and left, abandoning his drink half-finished on the table. I finished it for him as Laura sipped her Hansa at a somewhat more civilised pace, before we zig-zagged back through the clean cut buildings to the hostel, arms draped over each other's shoulders as if it were the most natural thing in the world. Back in the tent our whispered conversation drifted further into the night, attraction and tension charging the atmosphere between us. Fatigue took Laura first and then it was my turn to sleep.

It felt strange to awake in the clean desert air when so close to the Atlantic Ocean. Camping outside had kept hangovers to a minimum, but preparing for the day on the road was still a struggle with lethargy. While I packed away the tent, Laura popped into town and found the ingredients for a fry-up, which gave a kick-start to the day. While she cooked it, I checked the car over, beginning by topping up the oil, a daily task now the leak from the crankshaft had worsened and we were losing over a litre a day. The other fluid levels were fine and my inexperienced eyes couldn't see any other potential problems beneath the bonnet. I tightened the roof rack mounts and jacked the car up to give the vibrating wheel the once over. When I grabbed it and tried to rock it back and forth, it moved slightly, indicating the ball joint was worn, but the movement was almost imperceptible, so I figured it couldn't be too bad. While the car was jacked up, I bodged the fuel line once again, where the garden hose had begun to leak petrol again slightly. I wandered around to the back of the car. It was a sorry sight. The rear suspension was sagging from the pounding it was receiving and the lights and bodywork looked terrible following their close encounter with the flying Shogun. There was nothing that could be done about either issue, so I tried to ignore them. They wouldn't stop us getting to Cape Town.

Once everything was ready, we went into town to use the Internet, full of confidence and sure of our imminent arrival in Cape Town. Laura sent out an update on our progress:

'All is well here other than the passport palaver and the lack of money. Ben is pretty much bailing me out until next week when I am hopefully having a card sent to Cape Town. We are having a lovely time and are only 20 hours by road from the finish! Can't believe we've nearly done it. Going to spend the next few days enjoying Namibia, which is a beautiful country and get down to Cape Town on Tuesday.'

The feeling that we had the trip in the bag was total. Nothing could stop us.

Eventually, we dragged ourselves away from the computers and hit the road south to Walvis Bay, Namibia's primary port. As the view across the bay opened up, a sprinkling of cargo vessels could be seen at anchor, dotting the natural harbour as they awaited their turn in port. The view reminded me of the life I'd put on hold back in the UK. I turned to Laura.

'That one there with the four cranes is a handy-size bulk carrier. It can carry about thirty thousand tonnes of cargo,' I said, while Laura listened politely, though no doubt

348

disinterestedly. 'I survey similar ships back in Bristol. And those two smaller ones, they're coasters. I often do Draft Surveys on them when they're carrying grain or fertiliser.'

'Fair enough,' said Laura. Evidently enthusiasm isn't always contagious.

We stopped in Walvis Bay and had a fine seafood lunch at the yacht club, watching as the Atlantic swells stroked the rocky coast. Sadly the flamingos for which the bay is famous didn't materialise. Laura had seen thousands here on her previous visit to Namibia, but it appeared only two of them were polite enough to hang around for my arrival.

It was mid-afternoon and time for the trip's final adventure. With barely a thousand miles remaining to Cape Town, we set off east, into the Namib Desert.

FIFTEEN

DESERT STORMS

30ᵗʰ November 2008
Namib Desert, Namibia

Already we had visited the parched sands of Syria and
Jordan, crossed the Sinai and traversed the Sahara. The
Dida Galgalu Desert in northern Kenya had nearly ended
our journey, while only a week before the Kalahari passed
by us almost unnoticed. I was losing count of all the deserts
we had driven across so far, but there was only one more to
go. The Namib, whose curvaceous dunes and rough plains
built around us as we drove. With the miles, the Atlantic
Coast receded from the Porsche's rear view mirrors, finding
a home in our memories instead.

'Last one,' I said as the tarmac ended abruptly. The roar
of the tyres increased suddenly when they found themselves
on gravel once more, but the vibrations stopped as if we
were in a plane at the moment of take off.

'Yep. Cape Town on Tuesday!' came Laura's upbeat
reply.

The gravel track was little more than a line swept through
the rocky desert, cleared of the worst of the rocks. It ran
straight for mile after mile, rising and dropping slightly with
the terrain, never detouring too much from its course. There
was no need for it to, as the landscape was empty. A flat
expanse of sand, gravel and small dunes stretched out to the
rim of our vision, where the equally featureless sky began.
Often, it was only the Shogun that provided any relief from
the nothingness, its dust plume rising far in the distance.
Occasionally the arid ground would erode away to reveal
apologetic extrusions of granite, jutting forth like bones
from beneath the parched skin of some ancient corpse. But

mostly there was nothing. Only us, the gravel, the sky and the Shogun in the distance.

'Why can't the rest of the tracks in Africa be like this?' I asked, as we flew along at about fifty miles an hour, unbothered by ruts or corrugations.

'The Namibians certainly know how to look after them.'

'It must be because of all the tourists,' I said.

'Like us?'

'Well we are on the way to Sossusvlei. I guess that makes us tourists.'

'Cool tourists. We'll have driven there. In a Porsche.'

'That is true. They've got to be less than a few hundred miles away now. I can't wait to see the dunes, they sound awesome.'

'They're even more stunning than you can imagine,' Laura replied.

The sun began to drop behind us, a pleasant change after weeks of drifting west across Africa, towards the setting sun. Given our laziness in the mornings, the fact it had tended to rise behind us had been of scant consolation. We drove on towards the outpost of Solitare in comfortable silence, both anticipating our arrival in Cape Town. *The day after tomorrow*, I thought. I couldn't help but smile at how close we were. I glanced at Laura and she smiled back. Nothing needed to be said, such was the telepathy between us after so many hundreds of hours together in close proximity. I tried to imagine what it would be like to finally see Table Mountain shimmering on the horizon, after all we'd been through; but I couldn't.

After a while, a change came over the desert. Instead of parched nothingness, the ground all around became carpeted with wild grasses, shooting a few inches clear of the dry soil. Their yellow hue was unheard of even during the longest droughts back in England, but this was as good as it got here, slap bang in the centre of one of the world's oldest and driest deserts. In an average year, less than a centimetre of rain falls upon the hard ground. I was glad of the

352

grasses, as they made the wilderness seem less unfriendly. As if to prove the point, we passed a pair of gemsbok trotting contentedly to the side of the road, gracing the desert majestically.   Uncompromisingly straight horns swept back from their heads like a pair of javelins.

The road rose playfully over a crest and we could see the sky ahead slowly taking on a milky hue as storm clouds grew. I guessed they were building where the air began to rise against the great escarpment, many miles to the east. They shouldn't affect us out here in the desert. Everything seemed tranquil; the silent bulk of the storms rising so far away, the shadows lengthening all around, Laura dozing by my side, the lack of vibrations and the peaceful blooming of the desert. Even the air in the Porsche's cabin felt cooler than usual. It was a beautifully serene moment, but the most vivid feelings of serenity came from the knowledge that we were nearly there.

We coasted gently over the crest, which grew in size as it stretched away to our left, becoming a rare edge of rock disappearing into the unknown desert. I was cruising at forty-five miles per hour, feeling no need to rush off towards the horizon like the Shogun was doing. It was enough just to be there and enjoy the moment. As the road left the rise and dropped back into another open, shallow valley, it turned to the right, before shooting off towards the next low ripple of hills. I turned the wheel and the nose of the Porsche began to come around as instructed. But then there was a rubbing noise and the car began to choose its direction in a somewhat eccentric manner, trying to dart left and right and largely ignoring my inputs.   The steering wheel bucked indecisively in my hands.

I slowed to a halt and wandered round to look at the front wheel on the car's passenger side.

'Is everything okay?' Laura asked, the unexpected stop having returned her from a shallow sleep.

'Erm,' I replied, looking at the car. 'Well the wheel's fallen off.'

It was still connected to the car, but instead of sitting in its normal position, it had somehow come adrift and wedged itself against the back of the wheel arch.

Laura joined me standing there, staring at the wheel. The Shogun had disappeared into the distance and was nowhere to be seen.

'I'd better get the jack.' I said after a while.

'I'll find some rocks and chock the wheels,' offered Laura.

'Good idea.'

The Shogun had returned before I'd loosened the Porsche's wheel nuts and got it jacked up. They parked just in front of us. Tom was driving.

'Fuel filter again?' he asked, looking down at me as I worked the jack.

'Not this time. The front wheel's fallen off.'

'That's not good, is it?'

'Not really.'

Once the car was jacked up sufficiently for the wheel to be removed, I undid the nuts and slid it off the hub, placing it beneath the car for safety. I then checked the ground carefully for any scary-looking beasties, before crawling beneath the front of the car. The problem quickly became apparent.

The suspension's spring, which had been absorbing the impacts across Africa, sits vertically, connecting the hub – onto which the wheel was attached – to the car's body. On the bottom of the hub there is a ball joint, which is slotted into the wishbone-like slab of aluminium that forms the bottom of the suspension. This arrangement means the wheels can turn left and right when the steering wheel is turned and can bounce up and down with the suspension, but can't move in any other direction.

At least that's how it works when the suspension is intact.

The ball joint had popped out of its socket in the wishbone, enabling the wheel to bounce around,

354

unrestrained in the wheel arch. Once I saw this, I knew immediately what had been causing the car to vibrate at certain speeds. The ball joint must have been badly worn. I felt around the socket into which it slotted. Part of the rim, which makes the joint tight and holds it in place, was missing. It must have cracked and fallen away, letting the ball joint pop out.

I crawled out from beneath the car. All eyes looked at me expectantly.

'The ball joint on the bottom of the suspension has gone.'

'We can fix that, right?' Brummy said.

'Yeah, I reckon it's bodge-able.'

'How?'

'I don't know yet, let me have a think. Feel free to crawl under there yourself and see if you can come up with anything.'

Laura was already shimmying under the front of the car, while Tom squatted by the wheel arch, looking quizzical.

I've always found myself to be rather slow at coming up with solutions to problems when they suddenly put me on the spot like this. My mind goes into overdrive and ideas arise and are discarded irrationally, rather than slowly and methodically working out a solution. Often, I will find myself rushing in with an ill thought out plan rather than refining it into a better solution. Conscious of this, I wandered a few metres away from the rest of the group and tried to get my thoughts together. Slowly, I turned the problem over in my mind.

Come on. You had the suspension collapse on the Mini in Kazakhstan and you fixed that. You can fix this too. Right, the ball joint is popping out of the socket. Basically, you've got to hold it in. It's popping out where the rim of the socket is cracked, which is on the side furthest away from the car. So you've got to make sure the wheel hub can't move in that direction. And you've got to make sure the bottom wishbone can't move down and let it pop out that way. You can fix this.

I played the geometries over in my mind, trying to analyse the forces and their directions, as if I was back at university, working out some piece of coursework for my engineering degree.

Okay, so we need to hold the hub tight towards the centre of the car. A ratchet strap should do it. It worked on the Mini. So we ratchet the hub onto something inboard of it. The mounting for the anti-roll bar could work. Then when we load the suspension, the geometry should move the two points further apart, increasing the tension and locking everything in place. Yeah, that's good. That'll work!

I glanced over to the rest of the group. Louise was taking photos in the fading light. Everyone else was crowded around the broken corner of the car, filling the desert air with urgent chatter. I wandered back and joined the chatter.

'Any ideas?'

'If we just pop it back in, won't it stay there?' Brummy suggested.

'Don't think so. Not with the cracked rim.'

'Did you bring along a spare ball joint?'

'Don't be silly!' I replied. 'If this was an earlier model 944 we could have, but on this model the ball joint socket is part of the aluminium billet which makes the wishbone. We'd need a whole new suspension arm. They're about four hundred quid back in the UK. And they only fit one side or the other.'

'Yeah, we actually discussed that,' said Laura. 'Ben reckoned there's no point bringing any suspension parts because you can always temporarily bodge suspension back together.'

'I hope Ben was right,' I said, feeling suddenly put on the spot.

'So, what are we doing?' asked Tom.

'Well, I reckon this'll all go back together with ratchet straps,' I replied. 'We can use them to clamp the ball joint together so tightly it can't come apart again.'

'Fair enough, let's do it,' said Tom.

I lay down again – careful not to move beneath the wheel hub in case the car came off the jack – and took another look at the problem. I had an idea in my mind, but hadn't considered how I was going to make it work in practice. As I lay there, a procedure formed in my mind.

'Okay, we're going to need the spare ratchet straps out of the boot of the Porsche, the grease – I think it's behind the driver's seat – the bag of cable ties, and the scaffolding pole out of the Shogun.'

'And there was me thinking we dragged that great big pole across Africa for no reason,' said Tom.

'Nope, I got you to bring it along for exactly this eventuality,' I replied smugly. 'Anyway, before we do anything, we've got to reassemble the joint. Tom, if you use the scaffolding pole to push the wishbone down, I'll try to lever the wheel hub into position so the ball joint slots back together when you let go.'

'Okay.'

Tom pushed down while I attempted to manoeuvre the hub, but I couldn't see the ball joint well enough to align them.

'I'll lie at the front of the car and direct you,' suggested Laura.

'A fine plan.'

It took a few attempts, but with Laura's guidance we managed to get the ball joint to sit over the socket.

'Brummy, can you get the jack out of the Shogun, so we can use it to push the ball back into the socket? I'm just going to grease the ball a bit.'

'Cheeky!' was Brummy's predictable response.

Tom jacked up the wishbone while Laura watched.

'It's not going in,' she said.

'Doh. Let's try again, but this time I'll hold the hub in place using the scaffolding pole as a lever,' I suggested.

'Okay.'

The second time didn't go to plan either, but on our third attempt we managed to get the ball to slot back into the socket.

'Right, jack it up some more and then I'll thread the ratchet strap around it.'

Tom did so, with Laura still looking to make sure the assembly didn't come apart.

'Excellent, nearly there,' I announced, eyeing the reassembled suspension confidently, before taking a swig of water and crawling back beneath the Porsche.

I wrapped the sling around the components as planned and threaded the end of it back through the ratchet. I then tightened the ratchet as much as my arms would allow, before adding some heavy duty cable ties around the broken parts for good measure.

'Right, that ought to do it,' I said, returning from beneath the car.

As I did, I noticed how dark it had become for the first time. The sun had just dipped below the horizon, but its rays were still painting the clouds artistically. Away to the east the cumulonimbus storm clouds were bubbling up dramatically, appearing closer than ever in the sharp light.

We removed the Shogun's jack from beneath the Porsche's suspension and reattached the wheel. I lowered it to the ground, tightened the wheel nuts, and climbed in.

'Fingers crossed!' I shouted at Team Shogun, before starting the tired engine and popping up the headlights. Very cautiously, with both Laura and I holding our breath, I moved the car forwards, first at walking pace, then slightly faster. I could feel the wheel being bucked around by the gravel. The Porsche's legendarily precise steering had become more like a rudder. I didn't want to turn the steering wheel in case it caused the wheel to fall off.

The Shogun sat behind us. Its headlights burnt bright in the Porsche's wing mirrors, dazzling me. Ten miles per hour, fifteen miles per hour. The bodge held. After a few minutes, we had the confidence to push on up to twenty-five mph. A coarse vibration started to transmit through the car, so I slowed down, limping along at around twenty.

At least we were moving.

'How far to the next outpost of civilisation?' I asked.

'Hold on, I'll just take a look.' Laura turned on her head torch and shone it on the map. 'Solitare. There's petrol and a lodge there. I'm not sure exactly where we are, but it's probably about fifty miles away.'

'And tarmac is another hundred miles beyond that?'

'Depends if we go to Sossusvlei or not. If we miss it then yeah, maybe a bit closer even. According to your map, it starts at a place called Maltahohe.'

'Never heard of it.'

'Me neither.'

The darkness became complete as we limped onwards, the road sweeping left and right as it crossed a gorge, while our headlights picked out walls of rock towering above the road. Occasional areas of corrugations on the gravel track caused a sharp intake of breath and a reduction of speed. I always thought the wheel was on the verge of coming off again, but somehow it stayed on. In the distance, silent flashes of lightning began to light up the undersides of the bulging clouds.

After about an hour, I turned to Laura: 'You know, I think we've cracked it. We can get back to the tarmac like this.'

I shouldn't have tempted fate. A few minutes later, the wheel fell off.

I got the inspection light and lay it on the ground to illuminate the wheel. As expected, the ball joint had come apart again. Despite hoping the first repair would hold, while we were driving along I'd been refining its finer points in my mind and had come up with a better way of doing it.

'Okay, we managed about half the distance to Solitare on the last bodge. Let's get it patched up and get the rest of the miles done before these storms reach us,' I said, trying to sound upbeat. 'Only this time, rather than holding the ball joint in place diagonally like before, I'm going to ratchet it right across onto the chassis beneath the engine. Should make it a bit more solid.'

'Fair enough,' was the general response.

'Same again to start with though. I'll get it jacked up and then Tom, if you can push down on the wishbone again, I'll pull it around a bit and Laura, tell us when it's in.'

We went through the same procedure again, more quickly this time. Forty-five minute's work had the wheel back on the Porsche ready to go, with the wheel hub prevented from moving outwards by a ratchet strap which ran horizontally beneath the front of the car to a hole in the chassis, beneath the engine. I was certain I'd cracked the problem and so we carried on into the night.

About ten minutes later, as we ground to a halt for the third time, I wasn't so sure. We jumped out and reattached the wheel again, in only twenty minutes this time; as we were all too tired to come up with a new and imaginative way to improve the repair, we just patched it up as before and pushed on. The sky was completely dark by the time we were moving again, but the lightning flashes were getting ever brighter. Pulling away, the first rumbles of thunder made themselves heard over the noise of the Porsche.

As I glanced across, a lightning bolt lashed into the hill to our right. It momentarily turned our surroundings into a ghostly image of white and shadow. We were limping across the middle of a wide plain, with not another object in sight. Prime targets for a lightning strike. The flashes were more frequent now, and it was hard to tell which rumble of thunder came from which bolt and thus work out how far away they were striking. I felt nervous and vulnerable. And then, shortly after midnight, the wheel fell off again, leaving us stranded for a fourth time.

'Well I'm not waving a scaffolding pole round above my head with these storms all around.'

'No, I don't blame you there,' Laura replied.

The Shogun pulled alongside.

'Off again?'

'Yep.'

'Fuck's sake,' said Tom.

'I'm not putting it back on in the middle of these storms either,' I added.

'So we're spending the night here then?'

'Yep. I'm going to sleep in the car; it's probably the safest place.'

'No roof tent tonight then?'

'No. If the car gets hit by lightning, I'd rather not to be lying on its roof at the time.'

Laura and I tried to get comfortable enough to sleep, but failed miserably. With everything behind the seats, it was impossible to recline them to anything less than bolt upright. I turned side on and tried to hunker down for the night.

'Are you sure it's safe in the car?' said Laura, through the darkness.

'Yeah, pretty sure. It's like a Faraday cage – a metal structure that transmits the electricity around its occupants, rather than through them,' I replied, hoping I remembered my school physics lessons correctly.

'You're not scared then?'

'Well, maybe just a little. I don't really want to be in the car if it does get hit and that storm cloud is coming straight for us.'

'It won't get hit. The Shogun is at least a foot taller,' Laura said. Despite the darkness, familiarly meant I could picture her face as she spoke, smiling her cheeky smile.

361

As we sat in the stricken car, awaiting either sleep or a direct hit – whichever came first – we watched the storm cells drift across the desert towards us. They were strangely beautiful, floating serenely in the darkness, lightning flaring from within their centres and revealing their swollen architecture. They looked like giant malevolent jellyfish, lashing out at everything in their path. Every bolt of lightning lit up the landscape around us and reminded us of how exposed we were – not that we could do anything about it of course. I watched as the most active storm cell drifted lethargically towards us and counted the seconds until the thunder came. Its lightning was striking less than half a mile away. I felt every roll of thunder in the pit of my stomach and was certain I could feel my body tingling with electricity. I kept touching my arms to see if the hairs were standing up, but couldn't be sure. *Don't be so irrational*, I thought to myself, annoyed by my nervous worry.

Luckily, the cloud just missed us, its lightning raking a conical mountain about four hundred metres to our left. As it passed, Laura and I took turns to blindly point my camera at it, hoping to be lucky with our timing and catch the lightning on camera. The next nearest threat to our position was to our right, a less active cell which seemed to linger above some hills on the edge of our wide plain. For a few hours, the danger of electrocution had passed. Dehydrated and exhausted, we passed into an uncomfortable and dreamless half-sleep, willing the morning to come.

I awoke when the first refracted rays of morning light began to silhouette the horizon ahead. It was three hours since I'd begun my attempts to sleep and I had been flitting in and out of consciousness ever since. My back and neck ached from a night curled up in a foetal position in the Porsche's unyielding driver's seat. I sat up and drowsily looked around in the half-light and remembered the wheel, and the storms. The only sound was the familiar rhythm of Laura's breathing. Her head hovered just behind the gear stick, balanced on a cushion.

I got out of the car and stretched my legs, movement coming more easily as I paced around. The storms had gone, replaced with a few pleasant cumulus, which the sunrise would soon turn red. I could see there was more grass here than where we were the previous day. A thick sea of yellow shoots carpeted the desert, rustling slightly in the cool, refreshing breeze. The air was wonderfully crisp and was saturated with the piquant aromas of the grasses and flowers all around. Wonderful smells of an exotic world, celebrating the gift of rain.

I looked at the Porsche. It stank of oil and petrol and sweat. The dim light hid its rough edges, presenting it as a white outline in the dawn. The damage to the back of the car was hidden in the shadows, but by its stance I could still see that the rear suspension was sagging nearly to the ground. As for the rest of its problems, my mind filled in what my eyes couldn't see. The clock couldn't be turned back to its younger, more innocent days.

'Good morning,' Laura said, as she made her first stiff steps of the morning. I snapped out of my daze.

'Hi there. How are you today?'

'Tired and sore.'

'That makes two of us then. Shall we get this wheel back on and push on to Solitaire?'

'Let's.'

While I was jacking up the car, Tom emerged from the Shogun. He looked exhausted and, like Laura and I, was covered in dust and sweat. The other residents of Hotel Shogun continued to sleep, Louise reclining spaciously behind the steering wheel, while Brummy appeared to be beached across the full width of the back seat.

We were well practiced at refitting the wheel by now and Laura and I had the car ready to go by sunrise. Louise moved into the Shogun's passenger seat, enabling Tom to get behind the steering wheel. On we went, into the rising sun.

It was one of those vivid mornings that etch themselves directly into the depths of your memory, to be relived at will in later life. The desert grasses shone silver and gold in the oblique light, their heady scents flooding in through the Porsche's open windows. Modest, chiselled hills rose from the carpeted plain, feeling intimately close in the rich light. The sky weighed down upon us, a thick, opaque blue in which patches of feathery cirrostratus lounged. Half a dozen gemsboks grazed in the distance, having survived the night despite their unfortunately lightning conductor-like horns.

The wheel fell off twice more before we got to Solitaire, the last occasion almost within sight of the settlement. Our repairs seemed to be getting less and less efficient with each attempt and increasingly, it was Laura and I who reattached it each time. Louise and Brummy continued to sleep, while the team's communal feeling of pulling together against a common problem had vanished overnight. During our fifth attempt to get the wheel to stay on, Tom's growing frustration had led to him suggesting they leave us in the desert and take the Shogun off to send a tow truck back to get us.

'Tell me you're not serious?' I had replied.

'Look, if we can't get this sorted soon we're going to be late getting to Cape Town. We'll take the Shogun to the first town out of the desert, find someone with a tow truck and send them back to get you.'

'We're not sitting in the middle of the desert with bugger all water, waiting for some tow truck which may or may not come,' Laura had said.

'They'd come. They could take you back to Swakopmund, where you could get the car repaired.'

'Tom, that's not going to happen. The only way to get this repaired is to get a replacement wishbone sent over from Europe. We're on our own here.'

The look on Tom's face suggested he was losing patience with the inflexible – and to his mind, irrational – determination of Team Porsche.

'Look, I just think we should start thinking about what we're going to do if we keep failing to fix this wheel,' he'd replied, in a matter-of-fact way.

Solitaire felt like some one-horse town that had been lifted from the American Wild West and dropped into the Namibian wilderness. A petrol station, a lodge and a few other buildings sat alone beneath the big sky. It looked a desperately lonely place, befitting of its name. At the tiny settlement's entrance, the lifeless carcasses of a couple of derelict 1950s American pick-up trucks sat half buried in the sand, surrounded by cacti and petrified trees. By the petrol station, a 1930s Morris Eight convertible had met the same fate. Sandstorms had eroded away much of its paint and a patina of rust clung to the exposed metal. Its delicate lines and slight frame looked like they would have stood no chance against the desert. A mottled lizard basked on the rocks beneath one of its front wheels.

'No way is our Porsche ending up stuck here like that,' I said to Laura. 'Whatever it takes, we're getting that car to Cape Town.'

Laura agreed.

The petrol station's chirpy proprietor told us there was a workshop in Solitaire, but it wasn't open yet. We grabbed a cold drink and waited, talking over the plans.

'So we're still heading to Sossusvlei?' Louise asked. She'd been looking forward to seeing the dunes.

'If we can get the Porsche fixed then we should. It's a stunning place,' Laura replied.

'And if we can't?' Brummy said.

'Then we're just going to have to keep strapping the wheel back on until we reach the tarmac. It's about another hundred miles,' I said.

'That could take forever,' Tom replied.

'Yes,' I replied, 'And?'

I had enough on my mind and Tom's building negativity was starting to wear thin on me, in just the same way that Team Porsche's inflexible attitude towards the problem was grating with him.

Eventually someone came along and opened the workshop up, but after taking a look at the Porsche's front suspension, they were adamant that they wouldn't be able to fix it. We were on our own. Disappointed, I topped up the Porsche's oil and we carried on our way. The wheel fell off for the sixth time a few minutes later. I jumped out and started to loosen the wheel nuts, while Laura got the jack ready. Tom walked purposefully over to us. His frustration had been growing throughout the morning, as we'd repeatedly failed to make any real progress.

'Ben,' he said, looking annoyed, 'We made four kilometres that time.'

'Yes Tom, we did,' I replied sternly, looking him straight in the eye. 'And if we have to, we're going to make another four kilometres next time, then another four kilometres, then another four kilometres, and keep doing so until we get to Cape Town. Okay?'

Tom said nothing, walking off back to the Shogun and sitting down in the shade behind it. Louise and Brummy had somehow managed to fall asleep again, while Laura and I continued with the repair.

'I don't get it,' I said as we worked. 'Why did the first repair get us forty kilometres, but since then they've all failed much sooner.'

'I think we're supporting the joint from too far away,' said Laura.

'Maybe, but we're only providing support in the same way as, say, the guy ropes on a tent do.'

'Yeah, but I just think it allows too much movement. Think of a shoulder joint. The muscles supporting the joint are right in close to the joint, where they can hold it most tightly. By running the strap under the car we're not holding the joint tightly enough.'

'Hmmm, sort of makes sense. But my way should still work better than this.'

'Let's try to move the ratchet closer to the ball joint.'

'Fair enough,' I agreed, before adding in a whisper, 'I don't think Tom's very happy.'

He was sat behind the Shogun, staring out into the desert.

'No, I'll go and have a word with him,' said Laura.

As I worked, I overheard Laura tell him that we were trying our best to get out of this difficult situation and she was sorry, but a negative attitude won't help us escape the desert. He replied by pointing out rather bluntly that there was a difference between being optimistic and realistic, and maybe it was about time we learnt what it was. It was a short conversation.

Once the car was jacked up with the wheel removed, we reassembled the ball joint and tried to come up with a more effective way of holding it together.

'What about ratcheting it from the back of the wishbone?' I suggested. 'We can run the ratchet underneath it, around the back of it, then onto the hub. The second ratchet can stay where it is.'

'Yeah, that should work.'

We did as planned and the repair looked good. Confidence inspiring. The wheel went back on and the car was lowered to the ground. Ten minutes and breakdown number seven later, the wheel was off and the car was back in the air again, with Laura and I lying beneath it.

'I don't get it,' said Laura in frustration, 'I thought we had it that time.'

'Maybe something just wasn't sitting right. We'll try again,' I replied.

'Get a fucking tow truck,' Tom shouted over.

'Fuck off,' was my considered reply.

We put it all back together and carried on, but to no avail. A mile later, the steering wheel's random meanderings told us all we needed to know. Close to despair, we coasted to a halt in the sand. In the rear view mirror, I could see Tom thumping the steering wheel and swearing at us with frustration.

We'd only managed about fifty miles in the previous eighteen hours and after seven unsuccessful attempts at a repair, we were running out of ideas. I hated that Tom's pessimistic attitude had more of a point every time we stopped and while there was no way I was going to admit it, I wasn't sure how we were going to pull through this one. We were thirsty and exhausted, and the desert was beating us. With every breakdown the suspension components were getting more twisted, and soon the spring would be so bent out of shape that any repair would become impossible. The prospect of abandoning our car in the Desert, seven hundred miles from Cape Town, was becoming reality and there seemed to be nothing we could do about it.

We were out of ideas.

Tom didn't get out of the car this time, preferring to stay in the driver's seat, stewing with frustration. Brummy appeared to be asleep, while Louise came over to see how we were doing.

'Any ideas?' she asked.

'No. I really don't understand it,' replied Laura. 'It should be working better than this.'

'Well all we can do is keep strapping it back together and plodding on until we're out of the desert,' I said.

'Yep, we've not driven the Porsche all this way only to abandon it here,' said Laura.

We jacked up the car and looked over the repair. The slings were becoming frayed and tattered from the continuous rubbing, while the suspension spring had bent so far backwards that it was banana shaped – a result of it being twisted every time the wheel came adrift. A few more failures and the spring would become so bent that that any repair would become impossible.

We were in real trouble.

'Any ideas?' I asked.

'Nope. I don't understand. This should be working.'

'So shall we just rebuild it the same way we did the last few times and hope we have better luck?'

'We don't really have any choice,' Laura said.

The desert sun beat down mercilessly as I began to untie the tangled mass of ratchet straps which had failed to hold the suspension together for even a single mile on our previous attempt. It felt futile. We'd been giving it everything to get the car out of the desert for eighteen hours, and had failed on eight occasions already. We were dehydrated, filthy, exhausted and out of ideas. *Why should it be any different this time?* I thought to myself.

I looked around as I worked, at what was beginning to seem like it might become the Porsche's final resting place. A dead landscape of sand and gravel, burning beneath a raging sun. What a sad ending it would be for the stout-hearted car, being abandoned in the desert a hundred miles from the nearest village.

Once the previous repair attempt had been dismantled, we began to reassemble the suspension.

'We've only got a few shots left at this, so let's make sure everything is as perfect as possible this time,' I said.

'Well we've had enough practice,' Laura replied.

And so we began to work. While I went to replace one of the worn out ratchets with a fresher one, Laura re-greased the ball part of the broken joint and put her finger in the socket to check it was clean.

'There's a tiny bit of grit in here!' she said.

'What, in the actual socket?'

'Yep.'

Laura cleaned the grit out of the socket and we slotted everything back together. The ratchets were replaced, the wheel refitted and soon we were on our way.

'Please let this be the last time we have to do that,' I exclaimed to nobody in particular, as we pulled away.

Almost immediately, I noticed that the steering felt a little more taunt, a sign that there was less movement in the ball joint than before. I accelerated away cautiously, and the wheel seemed much more dependably attached than it had at any point in the previous eighteen hours. The grit must have been preventing the broken components from slotting together as they should, and once removed, the fact that we'd gone through eight iterations of the repair meant we'd arrived at an efficient way to hold everything together. Driving at about twenty miles per hour, it would take us five hours to escape the desert, but at least escape now seemed like it might be possible. After about ten miles, the Shogun pulled alongside us and I grinned and gave them the thumbs up. Brummy and Louise looked overjoyed. Tom looked faintly embarrassed. They then slotted in close behind us, as the desert rolled past.

It took five hours for the limping, overheating Porsche to drag itself to the next settlement, the village of Maltahohe, on the Namib Desert's eastern edge. The landscape became more precipitous, jutting domes and towers of sandy rock crowding in around the road, forcing it to swing left and right along the path of least resistance. The grasses became greener and shrubs appeared more often, sometimes crowding into dense thickets that hinted we were leaving the Namib Desert and climbing gently up onto the Nanania Plateau. Above, the cumulus clouds were growing upwards, hinting at another night of storms.

Reaching Maltahohe felt like an enormous achievement. Symbolically, in the middle of the town, a well-defined step a few inches high stretched across the road. To our side of the ridge, all was gravel, stretching hundreds of miles back through the desert to the Atlantic Coast. But on the far side of the ridge there was tarmac. Silky smooth tarmac, all the way to Cape Town.

'We did it!' Laura said, 'we made it to the road.'

'Not yet we haven't,' I replied. 'It would be just our luck if I knocked the wheel off again on that step.'

'Please don't.'

'I'll try not to.'

'I can't believe we got through that though. We work so well together, don't we Ben?'

We held hands.

'Yes Laura. We really do.'

The residents of Maltahohe must have anticipated our celebratory mood, as there was a bar just where the gravel ended. We parked the cars a few feet from the start of the tarmac and headed in for a cold beer to toast our escape from the desert.

'I'm almost disappointed we didn't need plan B,' I joked as we waited for our drinks.

'What was plan B?'

'We take the dodgy wheel off completely and wedge the scaffolding pole in the boot so it hangs out over the opposite, back corner of the car. Then, we get Brummy to perch all his ample kilos on the pole, providing a counterweight which would keep the three-wheeled car's front corner off the ground until we made it out of the desert.'

I checked the repair over, before cautiously bouncing the Porsche up onto the sealed section of road and accelerating gently out of town. The repair had survived the rough desert, so I knew it would allow us to drive safely on the smooth tarmac, but even so, forty miles per hour was our maximum speed. Any more and the vibrations would start, violent shimmies which transmitted right through the car as the wheel tried to break free from its strapping. There were a few hours of daylight left, so we continued our climb up onto the central plateau, just over a kilometre above sea level. As on the previous night, storm clouds were brewing, preparing for the night's entertainment. Just before sunset, we reached the B1, Namibia's main north-south artery, and pulled over into a lay-by sandwiched between the road and a railway line.

'So, what are we doing tonight?' Brummy said.

'Sleep would be a good start,' I replied.

'And where do you suggest we do that?'

'Well there's a service road for the railway just there. We could carry on along it for a bit, until we're out of sight of the road, then camp.'

'Or we could head back up the road to that town a few miles back?' suggested Tom.

'But that will involve spending money,' said Louise.

'Well I'm not sleeping here.'

'Why not?'

'It's not safe,' said Tom. 'It's too close to the road and someone will see us. And I don't want to sleep next to the railway line.'

'It'll be fine,' I replied.

'I'm not sleeping here.'

'Tom, we've been sleeping in places like this all trip,' Laura pointed out bluntly. 'They've always been fine.'

'Come on, let's head back to Mariental and find a hotel. I want a shower.'

'No.'

'Well I'm not sleeping here.'

'Fine,' said Laura, 'If you want to take the Shogun back to the town you're welcome to, provided you're back here by the time we want to leave.'

He chose not to.

We all drove a short way up the sandy track by the railway and set up our tents. All around us, storms were reaching critical mass and releasing their energy. Sheets of rain and blinding flashes swept away the fiery sunset.

It was a fitting backdrop to our camp. Louise and Laura were noticeably tense as they set about cooking the dinner, as both were still fired up from their recent confrontations with Tom. I was tense for similar reasons, and so took some time alone, wandering off to photograph the stormy sunset, while Brummy disappeared into town to get us some beers. Tom sat quietly, keeping himself to himself. He wasn't happy. That morning, he had forcefully declared that Laura and I were wasting our time trying to get the Porsche out of the desert. We had shunned his opinion rather bluntly then, by the skin of our teeth, had proceeded to prove him wrong and in doing so had dealt his pride quite a blow. For most of the day, he had been forced to follow the limping Porsche at a painfully slow speed, a deeply frustrating way to lose an argument.

I wasn't surprised he was feeling a bit cross.

In times of stress, Tom's relationship with the rest of the group had been slowly becoming more embattled over the course of the trip. Unfortunately, our collision in Botswana, followed by the eight breakdowns in the desert heat, had fanned the flames and strained relationships way beyond breaking point.

Brummy returned in the Shogun, the front passenger seat piled high with beers. A few minutes later, dinner was ready – a delightful dish of chilli pasta, brightened up by some vegetables we'd brought in Swakopmund. We laid everything out on the table and sat down. Behind us was the Porsche; in front of us our plates were framed in the beams of our head torches. And beyond our little pool of light, a thrilling panorama of strobing lightning and raging storms spanned the dark horizon, providing a stunning backdrop. I smiled to myself and cracked open a beer. There are few more memorable ways to dine.

'This is great, thanks guys,' said Brummy. He was right and I would have been impressed by the meal were it prepared in a well-stocked kitchen back home, let alone a Namibian lay-by.

'I'll second that,' I added.

'Yeah, I think it's one of my best efforts yet,' said Laura, pausing for another swig of beer.

'You could have wiped the dust out of the plates,' commented Tom coldly.

The conversation ended for a few minutes, replaced by the far off rumble of thunder.

After dinner Brummy went to sleep in the Shogun and Tom retired to his tent not long afterwards. Laura, Louise and I stayed up a bit longer, working through the beers and playing with my camera, before the storms finally reached us. Big raindrops thudded heavily into the dry ground as we scrambled to get everything under cover and made a dash for our tents.

'Ben.'

'Yes Laura.'

'There's water coming in again.'

'I know. I'm trying to ignore it.'

'Well don't.'

A coarse light erupted from Laura's side of the tent. After a few seconds, my eyes adjusted to the glow of her head torch and I looked around. Just as in Windhoek, water had seeped into the tent, turning our camping mattresses into the only havens of dryness. Through the tent's flysheet, I could see the porch had become a lake, filled ankle-deep with standing water. I looked at my watch. It was half past one.

'Oh, not again,' I said.

'Let's gaffa tape our mattresses together and try to stay dry until daybreak.'

'Okay, it's worth a shot.'

We ran the tape down between the mattresses, sealing them together and huddled close together, grabbing another few hours' sleep before our five o'clock alarm call. It was going to be another long, slow day on the road.

Daylight revealed that the tents had all been flooded when the slight depression in which we'd pitched them – while attempting to keep a low profile – had flooded. Tom had cut his losses by joining Brummy in the Shogun, while

Louise had managed to stay dry by curling up on my thick foam bouldering mat. We packed our wet gear away and set off. The Shogun did a U-turn, rejoining the tarmac at the lay-by where we had originally pulled off the night before. I was somewhat intimidated by the thought of doing U-turns, so carried on down the service road, intent on finding a way regain tarmac further down. After a mile, the way was blocked by a sizable wadi, full of water and impassable. So it was to be a U-turn after all. Halfway through the manoeuvre, the thick mud wrenched off the wheel for the ninth time. On closer investigation, the dampness had caused the slings to stretch, allowing the wheel freedom to move around. We were well-practiced and a repair soon had us on our way south.

It was the ultimate backdrop for a road-trip movie. Endless sweeps of empty plains dotted with protrusions of bubbling granite and jewelled with exotic trees and bushes. We dripped south through the landscape, the red needle of the Porsche's speedometer quivering on the forty miles per hour mark. We'd looked at the map the previous night and still had six hundred and twenty miles to cover before we reached Cape Town. Sixteen hours of driving at the speed we were going. Our first goal for the day was the town of Keetmanshoop, a hundred miles south of our flooded campsite. We were half way there when we were flagged down at a police checkpoint.

'Good morning, documents please.'

He was a young policeman and his smart, spotless uniform contrasted greatly with our filthy appearance. None of us had showered in days and the cars didn't look much better. I handed him the ownership documents and insurance certificate. He took them from me, but didn't look at them, instead holding them in his hand as he paced around the Porsche.

'Where are you going?' he asked.

'Cape Town.'

'Where have you come from?'

'England.'

'You have driven?' he said, first looking at the car, then at me, before raising a sceptical eyebrow, 'In this car?'

'Of course. We came through Europe, the Middle East, then down from Cairo...'

'Impossible!' he laughed, turning to his female colleague with a look of disbelief.

'Seriously, we have. It's a good car. It's German.'

The policeman paced around, taking in the Porsche from all its battered angles. I felt slightly embarrassed by the terrible state it was in. When he reached the car's mangled rear end, he frowned.

'Is this car in a roadworthy condition?'

'Yes, of course. Our friends crashed into the back of it the other day, but don't worry about that, its fine.'

'You are sure it is safe to drive on the highway?'

'Of course. I wouldn't be driving it on the road if I wasn't.'

'Very well,' he replied, handing me back the paperwork. 'You are free to go.'

I climbed back in and restarted the engine. Laura was still in the passenger seat, looking nervous. I glanced ahead and immediately saw why. The sand at the edge of the road had been washed away, leaving a jagged, kerb-like rise to negotiate before we would be back on the tarmac. From our position, we had no choice but to hit it at an acute angle, which would unload the dodgy ball joint and force it apart. I had just convinced the Namibian Police Force that the car was roadworthy and now its front wheel was about to fall off, right under their noses.

I pulled off gingerly, turning the wheel towards the kerb as hard as I dared, all the time muttering, 'shit shit shit' under my breath. Next to me Laura was being slightly more polite, whispering repeatedly 'don't fall off, don't fall off.' The policeman and his colleague watched our departure apathetically.

I felt the wheel touch, and let the steering wheel deflect away slightly as it climbed the rise. I could feel it straining against the slings holding it in position. No way could our repair survive such a lateral force. I held my breath. And then somehow, we were up. The rear wheels bounced onto the road easily, and we carried on our way.

'Thank goodness for that,' summed up Laura. 'We'd be in so much trouble if the bodge didn't hold.'

'Yep, they probably would have impounded the car as unroadworthy at the very least.'

'Maybe locked you up for being economical with the truth too.'

'Yeah, probably. That would have been interesting.'

I gave the policeman a relieved wave out of the window and carried on south, thanking the stars.

* * *

The Fish River Canyon is the second largest canyon in the world, beaten only by the Grand Canyon in Arizona. Serendipitously, it is also located just to the west of the road that was taking us to Cape Town. We parked the Porsche in the settlement of Grunau and all climbed into the Shogun to head over and take a look.

Gravel tracks led us through a Martian landscape of crag and sand, towards the rim of the gorge. Herds of gawky ostriches ran from our path as we drove. Squally showers and the omnipresent lightning dramatised our approach and ensured we didn't want to linger too long once we arrived.

The exposed viewpoint perched on the edge of a five hundred metre high cliff, which plunged straight down to the improbably small river trickling along the canyon floor. The gusts of wind unsettled us as we stood at the edge of the abyss and a blustery shower soon sent us retreating back into the Shogun's warm cabin.

Back on the road south, the weather abated and the sun began to set on our time in Namibia, over a landscape befitting of such a beautiful country. Flat-topped mountains rose from the barren desert, their modest elevations contrasting with the spirit-level flatness of the plain from which they rose. Whenever we thought Namibia might run out of beautiful landscapes to cross, it always seemed to conjure up something our minds couldn't begin to conceive.

'It's a good job the wheel fell off in Namibia,' I said jokingly. 'I don't think I could have put up with crawling along at this speed in most of the other countries we've crossed.'

'It is amazing, isn't it,' Laura replied. 'It's a shame for you guys that we didn't get to Sossusvlei though. First thing in the morning it's just the most amazing place.'

'Yeah, next time maybe.'

'You think you'll be back?'

'I know I will. It's my favourite country of the trip so far.'

Laura looked at me thoughtfully, with a relaxed smile on her face. I returned her gaze and she looked away when I caught her eye.

'If we ever did get married, we should come here for our honeymoon,' she said unexpectedly. 'Go to the Etosha salt pans and the northern Skeleton Coast where elephants roam on the beach, and visit Sossusvlei and do all the other things we've missed.'

'That's some bold assumptions you're making about us!'

'Well obviously, I'm not seriously planning anything. But if it did come to it...' Her voice tailed off, slightly nervously.

'It's a nice idea, though. Provided we didn't take a Porsche,' I said.

'Yeah, we could get one of those kitted out Land Rovers and stay in nice lodges. Do it properly.'

'That's a bit unadventurous, isn't it?'

'Honeymoons aren't about adventure,' she replied.

The sun was now nearing the end of its descent to the horizon, passing behind some delicate clouds, bleaching their outlines silver and sending shafts of hazy light soaring into the sky. Beneath the clouds, the first vestiges of red were reaching our eyes. I broke the heavy silence: 'Don't you have to get married before you have a honeymoon?'

'It's the usual way of doing things, yes.'

'My god, could you imagine it if we got married!'

'That would be scary! Imagine Brummy as best man!'

'And you'd have Gina and crazy Jenny as bridesmaids,' I suggested, referring to Laura's best friends from university. 'It would be carnage!'

'Would you want an old-fashioned church wedding or something a bit more random and, well, us?' Laura asked.

'I thought it was already planned?'

'What?'

'I thought you were going to get married at that church on the lake in Bled, Slovenia?'

'Oh yes. That would be such a funny wedding!'

'We'd have to have a nice Porsche as our wedding wheels. An old air cooled 911, or maybe a 356,' I said.

'Or Daisy?' Laura suggested, referring to my brown Mini we'd driven around Europe eleven months previously. 'We could turn getting to Bled into a fun road trip?'

'What we could do is have two road trips. One for the stag do and one for the hen night. Both finishing in Bled the day before the wedding.'

'I like it.'

And so the banal chatter continued as the sun's rich rays became ever more horizontal and fleeting. We talked of Brummy hitting on bridesmaids, of Porsches and Minis, and of whether we could get Patrice, our favourite French bar owner, to serve the drinks. Obviously, the conversation wasn't exactly serious, but beneath the banter lay a powerful fact. We had become closer than either of us could possibly imagine during our time together in the cramped, broken Porsche, struggling our way down through Africa.

As the last of the sun's rays floundered in the blackness, we found ourselves at a cluster of buildings, glowing coldly in pools of artificial light, which stung our relaxed eyes. It was the last border. South Africa was a few stamps away.

SIXTEEN

TEARS

2nd December 2008
Noordoewer, South African Border

The border post hovered lazily in its own pool of soft light, the world beyond being lost to the African night. A cluster of utilitarian buildings was all the eye could see. After crossing the bridge over the Orange River, we parked in the covered customs area, where the cars would be checked over before being allowed into South Africa. An overnight bus was travelling in the opposite direction, probably bound for Windhoek. Its occupants filed out to have their passports checked. Looking like the living dead, they moved lethargically towards the requisite office with heads bowed beneath the cold lighting, resigned to this interruption to their sleep. Their pasty skin, drawn faces and aura of tiredness were straight out of some old zombie film.

We brought a little more motivation with us to the border, purely because we had to if we were going to get the vehicles across. We did also bring a worryingly zombie-like smell with us, however. The speed with which we crossed into South Africa was refreshing, but not unexpected. Ever since we'd left Zambia, efficiency had been on the up. I felt like we were gradually returning to a place similar to the one which we had left months previously, a place which just... worked. Fortunately it didn't work too well however, as no fault was found with the Porsche and we were soon free to go onwards into South Africa, our last border behind us.

We were all ravenously hungry and so pulled into the first town we came to in the hope that somewhere would still be open at eleven PM. Steinkopf was poorly lit and the only fast food place had just shut. Some bored youths, lingering in the street, shouted something at us as we turned to leave. They were quite drunk, but even so, it didn't feel friendly.

Another slow hour on the road brought us to Springbok, where we pulled into a truck stop which still had a light on. There was a motel, an unmanned petrol pump and a shop. The light was coming from the shop, so we knocked on the door. It swung open and a rather matronly-looking woman spoke to us from behind a locked portcullis of wrought iron. We must have made for an odd sight, materialising out of the night with our battered vehicles, in this unfrequented corner of the country, but despite this she did all she could to help us. Soggy chips and pies fresh from the microwave were served through a gap in her defences and when a drunken truck driver started insulting us in Afrikaans, she chastised him rather sharply, before offering a profuse apology.

People like her had accompanied us all the way across Africa and often seemed to be a ray of light when our trip most needed one.

We didn't feel like camping given the hostile vibe nocturnal South Africa was presenting to us and luckily our hostess had two rooms available. Brummy and Tom took one twin room, while the girls and I took the other. I lay my camping mattress on the floor, ready for the night, then we locked the door and sat on the beds, finishing the chips and taking it in turns to go to the bathroom and clean ourselves up.

I went into the shower room, stood at the sink and ran the tap. I was too tired and uncaring to use the cold, dribbling shower but could just about summon up the energy for a quick clean up. As I stood there, an unexpected face stared back at me from the small mirror hanging above the sink. I recognised him from years before. His skin was stained brown with dust, sweat and oil, while his creases and pores were filled with black grime. Five weeks of beard clung to his chin, mousy with dust. I knew it would turn ginger when washed. His grandfather was ginger. I thought back to when I had first seen the face, on that fateful day in Mongolia when it had all begun.

The dirt ran anticlockwise down the plughole as I brushed my teeth. Slightly refreshed, I returned to the bedroom and turned off the lights. A strobing electrical storm rolled in shortly afterwards and torrential rain drummed on the corrugated iron roof as we drifted off.

'At least we won't be flooded in here,' Louise said into the darkness.

We were all awoken before the alarm by an almighty crash and a deep rumble that seemed to roll on for an eternity. I tried to turn on the light, but the electricity supply had failed, one of the pylons taken out by the nearby lightening strike. None of us felt like making coffee on our stove at such an early hour, so we just folded ourselves straight back into the cars and set off. By six in the morning we were back on the road to Cape Town.

Laura drove and I dozed for a bit in the passenger seat, until the heat and light became uncomfortable. It was our third day of limping along and already it felt like forever since the wheel had fallen off in the desert. Drifting back into consciousness, it felt like this was our Groundhog Day, condemned to drive across vast landscapes at forty miles per hour until the end of time. I knew that Cape Town was only nine hours away at the speed we were going, but even another nine hours seemed difficult to comprehend. We stopped at Bitterfontein for breakfast then drove on some more.

Seven hours to go.

The monotony of the crawl was not because of boredom. Laura and I chatted away continuously, about home and Porsches and mutual friends and climbing and travelling and how on earth we had made it through northern Kenya. We talked about weddings and ducks and relationships and careers and future plans. About politics and foreign aid and wars and everything else under the sun. And when the conversations were over, we sat contentedly in each other's company, comfortable in silence like only true friends can ever be.

But it was still monotonous. All we wanted was to get to Cape Town and the continuous lack of progress was torture. It must have been even worse for the folks in the Shogun, forced to drive exactly eighteen miles per hour slower than they otherwise would have been. There were few other road users around at that time in the morning, but occasionally a car or bakkie would whip disdainfully past. Even trucks and coaches caught us from behind, barging impatiently past when the opportunity arose.

Six hours to go.

We swept through yet another barren world of semi-desert; hillsides carpeted with dust and boulders. Then the amount of greenery slowly began to increase. I didn't care anymore. I just wanted to get to Cape Town.

Five more hours.

The road rose as it crossed the western reaches of the Cederberg Mountains. Waves of greenery washed over the landscape. We cruised past pretty lakes nestling beneath the rocky summits, the lower slopes yielding farmland and the occasional vineyard. The towns of Clanwilliam and Citrusdal were passed without stopping. And then we crested the Piekenierskloof pass and a view of the Western Cape opened up beneath us. The road, a dual carriageway now, swept down the side of the mountain into a wide flat valley below, framed by the Cederberg to the left and some more modest hills to the right. Ahead, a grey smudge rose suggestively from the horizon.

'Is that it?' I asked Laura.

'Not sure.'

I looked at the map.

'Two and a half hours to go.'

The landscape was more populated now, houses and towns and factories and farms all around. And as the road wound its way south, the smudge on the horizon morphed into a beautiful, familiar form. Table Mountain's distinctive outline was now ahead, its summit snuggling beneath the thinnest blanket of cloud.

I knew without a doubt that we would reach the mountain on the horizon. *We're actually going to do this*, I thought. *Nothing can stop us now.*

Two hours to go.

An expensive BMW overtook us, its driver taking photos on his mobile phone in disbelief. He pulled into a lay-by ahead and snapped away hungrily as we crawled past.

Then the warning light for low fuel came on. Half an hour later, when we still hadn't seen anywhere to get petrol, it began to become a worry.

'How long have we got from when the light comes on?'

'I don't know,' I replied, 'about thirty or forty miles maybe.'

'Well we've already done nearly thirty.'

'Not good.'

The prospect of running out of fuel a few miles before getting to Cape Town really didn't appeal.

'We can't finish the trip being towed into Cape Town by Tom because we've run out of fuel with Table Mountain in sight,' mused Laura. 'That would be too much.'

'I don't think we'd ever live it down. For goodness' sake, there's got to be a petrol station around here somewhere!'

A few miles down the road, a sight just as beautiful and welcome as Table Mountain came into view. Running on fumes, we pulled into the petrol station and pumped a hundred rand's worth of fuel into the Porsche. Enough to complete the trip. The Shogun also filled up and we parked in the rest area for a break before the final run into the city. Nothing could stop us now and emotions were building as a result – and not just in the Porsche. As I walked into the shop to find a cold drink, the dulcet tones of Brummy rang out across the forecourt behind me.

'I'll shove a can of Fanta up your arse!' he yelled.

I didn't need two guesses to figure out who he was shouting at – evidently, the tension of going so slow for so long was showing in Team Shogun!

Table Mountain had been lingering in our windscreen for hours, but now it began to dominate our view. We swung right off the main road and chased the sun out west, down pleasant tree-lined avenues to the coast. The Atlantic shimmered intricately beneath the retreating sun. We were so close. After reaching the ocean at Melkbosstrand, we swung south for the last time. Ahead, the bay curved gracefully around, its sandy beach cradling the Atlantic and leading the eye onwards to Table Mountain's dominating mass. We could see Cape Town now, glittering silently beneath its mother mountain. We drove slowly, for we felt we had already arrived and suddenly all of the impatience of the previous few days evaporated as we enjoyed the moment we'd been struggling towards for months.

Laura picked up her iPod and selected a cringingly slushy song by Shania Twain, singing along quietly to herself as the song filled the Porsche.

'Looks like we made it, look how far we've come now baby,' she hummed self-consciously.

'We mighta took the long way; we knew that we'd get there some day.'

Our fingers intertwined as we coasted dreamily down to Table View.

She began to sing along louder as we held hands.

'They said 'I bet they'll never make it', but just look at us holding on.'

'We're still together, still going strong.'

The irony of completing the gutsiest achievement of my life while being subjected to the feminist whining of Shania Twain was lost on me at the time.

Laura tired of singing along and we said nothing, listening to the music as the moment we'd been dreaming about for months washed through us. I thought back to the engine breaking in England and to Laura and I falling out the previous summer. It was unbelievable that we were here. I began to well up and the smallest of tears trickled down my cheek, the first since that crushing grey day in Plymouth when I'd reversed the Porsche off the drive and set out into the unknown. This time, the tears were very different.

We parked at Table View, still a few miles outside Cape Town proper, but close enough that it didn't matter. Beneath the mountain, the city lights were just coming alive in the perfect dusk. The Shogun pulled in behind us. Laura and I embraced each other urgently and kissed, partly in celebration and partly in relief that we'd made it through. Table Mountain's angular reflection fell upon the Porsche's chunky, tired bodywork. We all climbed out of the cars and headed over to a bar, where we popped open a bottle of champagne.

All friends now, our bubbling glasses chinked as the five of us toasted our achievement, while the sun dissolved in a golden sea.

POSTSCRIPT

12ᵗʰ December 2008
Cape Town, South Africa

The knife floated in my peripheral vision, a few inches from my throat. The dim street lighting painted its polished blade a burning amber colour. Time stopped as my startled mind passively considered what was coming next. It had all happened too suddenly for me to be scared.

My accoster was tall and thin, and possessed an air of flighty nervousness. He smiled weakly as he caught my eye, almost in apology. We both understood the situation. I was about to become another statistic in South Africa's 'informal redistribution of wealth.'

'Your phone and money.'

I didn't react. We both knew the script and it was still his move. After what seemed like another eternity he reached into my pocket, deftly lifted my wallet from it and melted into the night.

We had been in Cape Town for just over a week. Brummy and Tom had both flown back a few days after our arrival, while Louise had left a few hours before I was mugged. Fortunately, Laura's replacement bank cards had arrived that day, so at least we still had access to money.

Except for the robbery, the two weeks Laura and I spent in the Cape was a much needed holiday. We went wine tasting at Franschoek, watched whales breaching at Hamanas and spent many relaxing evenings on Long Street and the waterfront. Laura and I headed back up to the Cedarberg Mountains, where we climbed at the appropriately named 'Rocklands', a stunning sea of perfect golden sandstone. Robbin Island was visited and Table Mountain was walked up. And both the Porsche and the Shogun were pampered while we relaxed, the Shogun

389

receiving a full service and the Porsche having its suspension expertly welded back together. This was very necessary, as both cars still had to cover a few thousand miles more. With everyone else having left, it was down to me and Laura to drive them up to Mozambique, where we planned to sell the Porsche and donate the Shogun to a representative of the Kenyan Orphan Project, the charity we had visited in Kisumu.

We went out for a meal on our last night in Cape Town and during the meal I received a message telling me that my granddad's health had taken a turn for the worse. He'd already been living in a care home for a few years, as Alzheimer's disease slowly eroded away his quality of life until nothing was left. I went to sleep morosely that evening and awoke to a message telling me he had passed away during the night. His funeral had already been arranged for Christmas Eve.

I phoned my father. He was downbeat, but urged me not to fly back to the UK for the funeral, insisting that I had to stay in Africa and finish what I'd started. A few hours later I climbed into the Porsche and set off on its last journey, following the coast up to Mozambique.

Following the highway through the Cape Flats that morning, we passed a horrific accident. Some poor soul had fallen from the back of a pickup truck into the path of another car. A red stain led to a forearm, then on to other recognisable shapes. Everyone on the scene was in a terrible state of shock, even the police.

I drove past without looking, not wanting to etch the sight permanently into my mind.

For the rest of the day's drive I wished Laura and I were in the same car, as I knew the sight would have shaken her and she would appreciate someone to talk to. We had grown even closer during our time in the Cape and it was strange to be travelling in separate vehicles for the first time in months.

That night, after a quiet dinner together, we each raised a glass of whisky and toasted the memory of my grandfather, and the unfortunate guy on the N2.

We drove along the Garden Route, past the beaches and pretty towns which line Africa's southernmost coast, then on through the unwelcoming towns of Port Elizabeth and East London. We looped over the Transvaal, a region of rolling green grasslands, dotted with hard-up villages. Swinging back towards the coast, we entered KwaZulu-Natal where dolphins played for us in the surf outside Durban, before heading up into the Drakensberg Mountains for Christmas.

Christmas Day was baking, surreal forty degrees. We cooked a braai for dinner and thought about our families back home. Having reached Cape Town weeks before, our momentum seemed to have left us. We wished we were already home.

Two days after Christmas we left for Mozambique and, following a Shogun safari in Kruger National Park, we crossed the border into our twenty-sixth and final country.

Mozambique was to be our home for eleven days. We headed up to the beautiful Inhambane peninsula, where we went scuba-diving and saw in the New Year at a beach party in Tofo. The Porsche was sold to a bus driver in Maputo for ten thousand meticas (£300) and I watched solemnly as it accelerated away down Avenue Mao Tse Tung, and then turned right into a side street – out of my life.

It had been incredible. And now it was gone.

The Shogun was handed over to a representative of the Kenyan Orphan Project, who drove it back to Kenya and we boarded an overnight bus to catch our flight in Johannesburg.

* * *

England was freezing. Rain sheeted through the darkness into the side of the bus as it plodded along the motorway towards my home. As I arrived and saw my family for the first time in months, I received a message from Laura, saying 'Where are you? It's so weird not being around you anymore.' We'd barely left each other's company for three months and it was surreal to suddenly be apart.

Laura's emotions were torn as she returned to her life in the UK. She attempted to salvage the relationship she'd put on hold before leaving for Africa, but it was impossible. The doubts she'd had about it three months earlier had been exaggerated by a lifetime of experiences on the road. Six rocky weeks after getting back, she called me to tell me they'd split up. Soon afterwards, we returned to our African closeness and officially became a couple.

Other aspects of returning to my former life didn't go so well however. The recession was raging and people were talking like it was the end of the world. Business was down. I contacted the people who'd been babysitting my marine surveying business for the previous three months and started work once again, but even this wasn't plain sailing.

I sat in the office of my biggest client on a freezing Monday morning. Outside, I could hear the familiar beeping of the gantry crane as it traversed the muddy yard. In front of me was the manager. We'd known each other for five years. We chatted briefly about Africa and I listened as he promised me that everything would be fine. Yes, there was a recession on, but he still had full faith in my abilities and assured me there would be plenty of work for me in the coming year. I left the meeting feeling reassured. That Friday, I phoned the same manager and got a slightly different story. Meetings had been held, arms had been twisted and my work would now be covered by the person I'd trusted to cover it for me while I was away.

In an instant, my business ceased to be viable.

At the first opportunity, I drove the two hours up to the site office. An hour of conversation went nowhere. Yes, I'd been assured the previous week that I had nothing to worry about and yes, meetings had been held behind my back. But the other guy had taken my work off me. And that was that.

Such was my reward for five years of loyalty and good service.

I drove home through a stormy night, while my mind surged with rage and anger. I felt like I'd been stabbed in the back. I'd just come back from a continent where people have nothing, to a place where people who have everything are willing to destroy other's livelihoods to get even more. A place where going back on your word is okay and trust and principles are an irrelevance.

When I was nearly home, my anger died down a little and I thought about the future. I wondered how I could cover the mortgage and my African debts now, as the world around me slid into recession.

Maybe I could drive those overland trucks in Africa? They'd have me.

I swung the car off the dual carriageway into Plymouth.

What about becoming a rock climbing instructor?

My mind continued to race as I drove towards the city centre. I still wasn't sure what I was going to do as I parked the car and went inside. However after pouring a dram of Ardbeg whisky, everything suddenly became clear. I turned on my computer and opened the word processor. The cursor blinked at me intimidatingly from the blank screen. Thinking back to that day in Mongolia, I took a sip of whisky and began to write.

14814707R00231

Printed in Great Britain
by Amazon.co.uk, Ltd.,
Marston Gate.